THE TIME TRAVELLER'S
TRAVELLER'S
GUIDE TO
BRITISH
THEATRE
THE FIRST FOUR
HUNDRED YEARS

ALEKS SIERZ AND LIA GHILARDI

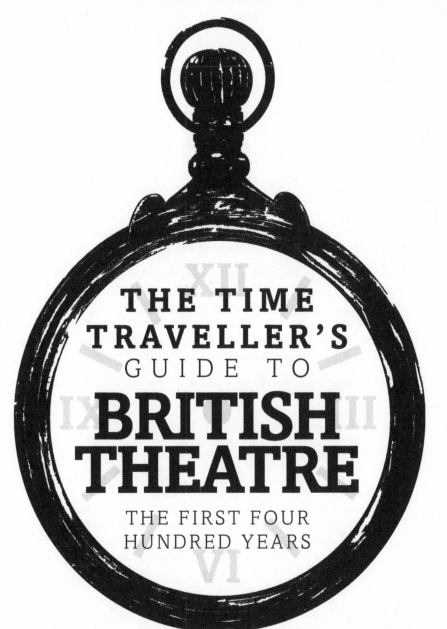

THE TIME TRAVELLER'S
GUIDE TO
BRITISH THEATRE

THE FIRST FOUR
HUNDRED YEARS

WITH ILLUSTRATIONS BY JAMES ILLMAN

First published in 2015 by Oberon Books Ltd
521 Caledonian Road, London N7 9RH
Tel: +44 (0) 20 7607 3637 / Fax: +44 (0) 20 7607 3629
e-mail: info@oberonbooks.com
www.oberonbooks.com

A catalogue record for this book is available from the British Library.

PB ISBN: 978-1-78319-208-3
E ISBN: 978-1-78319-707-1

Cover design and book illustrations © James Illman

Printed, bound and converted in the United Kingdom

Visit www.oberonbooks.com to read more about all our books and to buy them. You will also find features, author interviews and news of any author events, and you can sign up for e-newsletters so that you're always first to hear about our new releases.

Contents

Introduction   vii

Timeline   x

1. Elizabethan Theatre (1550-1603)   1
....

2. Jacobean Theatre (1603-1642)   37
....

3. Restoration Theatre (1660-1714)   63
....

4. Georgian Theatre (1714-1780)   101
....

5. Regency Theatre (1780-1837)   139
....

6. Victorian Theatre (1837-1901)   171
....

7. Edwardian Theatre (1901-1918)   215
....

8. Modern Theatre (1918-1955)   257
....

Book List   296

Acknowledgements   299

Index   300

Introduction

B ritish theatre is booming. In 2014, the Society of London Theatre — which represents the commercial producers of the West End — announced record box office figures for 2013: 14.5 million people went to the theatre and they spent a total of almost £600 million, a rise of 11 per cent, on tickets. These figures are not unique. Year on year, the West End of London enjoys enormous popular success, with its long-running musicals making more profits than even the most successful films. A 2014 report by *The Stage* newspaper — the industry bible — counted a grand total of some 240 professional theatre spaces in the capital, with more than 110,000 seats available at any one time. On any night, London's theatres employ more than 3000 performers, with more than 6000 people working in backstage roles. The longest running show in history is Agatha Christie's *The Mousetrap*, a country-house murder mystery, which opened in 1952 and is still going strong. Outside the metropolis there are some 260 other theatres across the country, and theatre contributes more than £2.5 billion a year to the economy.

So many theatres and so many shows! Each of these tells a story, but what about the story of British theatre? Where do these beautiful buildings and exciting plays come from? And when did the story start? To find out we decided to time travel back to the age of the first Queen Elizabeth in the sixteenth century, four hundred years ago when there was not a single theatre in the land. This is where the story of British theatre starts, not with the religious dramas of the medieval mystery plays, but with the invention of new secular plays performed before large audiences in public spaces in an urban setting. So we go back to the 1550s, when magnificent nobles put on shows to amaze and delight their queen. Within a decade, a couple of statesmen had penned *Gorboduc*, the first English tragedy to be written in blank verse, and by doing so they kicked off the whole history of British drama. Who were these people? Read on, and find out.

As we set out on our trip to the foreign country that is the past, we get a helping hand from several guides, characters who live in the past and know all about its customs, rituals, food, politics, personalities — and, of course, its theatre. Our guides have their own idiosyncracies, personal prejudices and memory lapses, and we make no apology for them. Instead, we salute our guides for the trouble they took to inform and entertain us. They have helped us not merely to understand what the historical past is like, but also to experience it as if we were there. For us, time travelling has been an immersive adventure.

So in the first chapter, which covers the age of Queen Elizabeth and its star William Shakespeare, our guide is Walter Wickson, a fussy clerk who knows all about the Globe and the other theatres of this age. In 1603, when Queen Elizabeth, the last of the Tudors, dies, he hands us over to his son, Wilt, a young student of law who prefers to see plays rather than studying, and who knows all the theatre gossip at the time of James I and Charles I, the first two Stuart kings. In the 1640s, the Puritans — who are enemies of the theatre — come to power and shut all the theatres for eighteen years so our next stop is 1660, when the monarchy is restored. For the Restoration era our guide is Moll Farthingale, who, having been an actress herself, is perfectly well informed about the thespian highs and lows of the time. For the next century, after Britain was united in the Act of Union of 1707 (bringing England and Scotland together) and ruled by four kings called George, our guide is the formidable Henry Holme Lord Edgcott, a real-life lord. He will show us around British theatre in the age of the super-star actor-manager David Garrick. By the 1790s, with news of the French Revolution crossing the English Channel, followed by war with Napoleon Bonaparte's France, we need a new guide. Step forward Gabriel Freeman, a young black gentleman who both campaigns for the abolition of slavery in these revolutionary times and is able to show us around the theatres of the age. By 1837, when Queen Victoria comes to the throne, the fires of revolution have died down and it's time for another guide, Jack Goodheart, a teenager who is as familiar with the slums as with the salons of Victorian London. Victoria dies in 1901 and then we meet Constance Wright, a New Woman of the Edwardian age who takes us around all the venues where some of the most radical experiments in early twentieth century drama are taking place.

After the end of the First World War in 1918, a new era dawns and with it comes our last guide, the redoubtable Sidney Roberts, a gentleman's valet with perfect manners and great theatrical knowledge. He will introduce us to the shows of entertainer Noël Coward in the Roaring Twenties, survey the grim wartime years of 1939—45, and end with the postwar plays of modern greats such as Terence Rattigan. By the mid 1950s, traditional plays such as his come under attack from the most recent innovations in theatre style and that's where our story comes to an end. For now, the tale that began with the coronation of Elizabeth I finishes with the coronation of Elizabeth II.

So welcome to *The Time Traveller's Guide to British Theatre*. We hope that you will enjoy the trip as much as we did!

Timeline

1558	Elizabeth becomes queen.
1561	Thomas Norton and Thomas Sackville's *Gorboduc*.
1567	The Red Lion theatre opens.
1572	'Vagrancy Act'.
1576	The Theatre opens.
1583	Queen's Men formed.
1587	The Rose opens; Thomas Kyd's *The Spanish Tragedy*.
1588	Christopher Marlowe's *Tamburlaine the Great*.
1589	Christopher Marlowe's *Doctor Faustus*.
1593	William Shakespeare's *Titus Andronicus*.
1594	Duopoly of Chamberlain's Men and Admiral's Men.
1595	William Shakespeare's *Richard II*.
1599	The Globe opens.
1600	The Fortune opens.
1601	William Shakespeare's *Hamlet*.
1603	James I becomes king of England and Scotland.
1604	Red Bull opens; William Shakespeare's *Othello*.
1605	The Hope Theatre opens; Ben Jonson's *Volpone*.
1606	William Shakespeare's *Macbeth*.
1607	William Shakespeare's *King Lear*.
1608	Blackfriars Theatre opens for the King's Men.
1610	Ben Jonson's *The Alchemist*.
1612	John Webster's *The White Devil*.
1613	Globe Theatre burns down; John Webster's *The Duchess of Malfi*.
1616	Cockpit Theatre opens.
1635	William Davenant's *The Temple of Love*.
1642	Theatres closed by the Puritans.
1642-51	English Civil War.
1660	Restoration of Charles II.

1662	Royal Letters Patent issued to Thomas Killigrew and Sir William Davenant.
1663	Theatre Royal, Bridges Street, Drury Lane, opens.
1671	Dorset Garden opens.
1675	William Wycherley's *The Country Wife*.
1676	George Etherege's *The Man of Mode*.
1677	John Dryden's *All for Love*; Aphra Behn's *The Rover*.
1678-81	Popish Plot.
1679	Theatre Royal Drury Lane opens.
1682	United Company formed; Thomas Otway's *Venice Preserved*.
1688	Glorious Revolution; William and Mary become joint monarchs.
1695	Actors Company formed.
1696	Colley Cibber's *Love's Last Shift*; John Vanbrugh's *The Relapse*.
1698	Jeremy Collier's *Short View of the Immorality and Profaneness of the English Stage* published.
1700	William Congreve's *The Way of the World*.
1706	George Farquhar's *The Recruiting Officer*.
1714	George I becomes king.
1715	John Rich at Lincoln's Inn Fields.
1722	Richard Steele's *The Conscious Lovers*.
1728	John Gay's *The Beggar's Opera*.
1731	George Lillo's *The London Merchant*.
1732	Covent Garden opens.
1737	Henry Fielding's *The Historical Register for the Year 1736*; 'Licensing Act'.
1741	David Garrick's debut in *Richard III*.
1747	David Garrick becomes manager of Drury Lane.
1763	Riots at Drury Lane and Covent Garden against abolition of half-price entrance.
1765	Sadler's Wells theatre opens.

1766	George Colman and David Garrick's *The Clandestine Marriage*.
1769	David Garrick's Shakespeare Jubilee.
1773	Oliver Goldsmith's *She Stoops To Conquer*.
1775	Richard Brinsley Sheridan's *The Rivals*.
1776	David Garrick retires.
1777	Richard Brinsley Sheridan's *The School for Scandal*.
1789-99	French Revolution.
1798	Elizabeth Inchbald's *Lover's Vows*.
1799	Richard Brinsley Sheridan's *Pizarro*.
1802	Thomas Holcroft's *A Tale of Mystery*.
1803-15	Napoleonic Wars.
1804	Infant prodigy Master Betty tours Britain.
1818	Thomas Bowdler publishes *The Family Shakespeare*.
1822	William Thomas Moncrieff's *Tom and Jerry*.
1829	Douglas Jerrold's *Black-Eyed Susan*.
1833	Ira Aldridge in *Othello*.
1840	Edward Bulwer-Lytton's *Money*.
1841	Dion Boucicault's *London Assurance*.
1843	'Theatres Act'.
1849	Astor Place Riot in New York.
1852	Dion Boucicault's *The Corsican Brothers*; Canterbury Hall music hall opens.
1860	Dion Boucicault's *The Colleen Bawn*.
1861	T A Palmer's *East Lynne*.
1863	Colin Henry Hazelwood's *Lady Audley's Secret*.
1867	Tom Robertson's *Caste*.
1871	Leopold Lewis's *The Bells*.
1874	Dion Boucicault's *The Shaughraun*.
1875	Henry James Byron's *Our Boys*; William Schwenck Gilbert and Arthur Sullivan's *Trial by Jury*.
1879	Shakespeare Memorial Theatre opens.

1881	Savoy Theatre opens.
1889	Henrik Ibsen's *A Doll's House*.
1891	Independent Theatre Society set up.
1892	Brandon Thomas's *Charley's Aunt*.
1893	Arthur Wing Pinero's *The Second Mrs Tanqueray*.
1895	Henry Irving knighted; Oscar Wilde's *The Importance of Being Earnest*.
1896	First film shows in London.
1899	Stage Society set up.
1900	George Bernard Shaw's *Candida*.
1902	George Bernard Shaw's *Mrs Warren's Profession*; James Matthew Barrie's *The Admirable Crichton*.
1904	James Matthew Barrie's *Peter Pan*; Abbey Theatre opens.
1904-07	The Barker—Vedrenne seasons at the Court.
1905	Harley Granville Barker's *The Voysey Inheritance*; George Bernard Shaw's *Man and Superman*; Edward Gordon Craig publishes *The Art of the Theatre*.
1907	Harley Granville Barker's *Waste*; Elizabeth Robins's *Votes for Women!*; music hall strike; John Millington Synge's *The Playboy of the Western World*; William Archer and Harley Granville Barker publish *A National Theatre: Scheme and Estimates*.
1909	John Galsworthy's *Strife*.
1910	Harley Granville Barker's *The Madras House*.
1912	Githa Sowerby's *Rutherford and Son*; Stanley Houghton's *Hindle Wakes*.
1914-18	First World War.
1914	George Bernard Shaw's *Pygmalion*.
1916	Harold Brighouse's *Hobson's Choice*; Oscar Asche's *Chu Chin Chow*.
1921	Gerald du Maurier's *Bulldog Drummond*.
1924	Noël Coward's *The Vortex*; George Bernard Shaw's *Saint Joan*; Sean O'Casey's *Juno and the Paycock*.

1925	Noël Coward's *Hay Fever*.
1926	Ben Travers's *Rookery Nook*; Workers Theatre Movement formed.
1928	Robert Cedric Sherriff's *Journey's End*.
1929	Patrick Hamiliton's *Rope*; John Gielgud in *Romeo and Juliet*.
1930	Noël Coward's *Private Lives*; Paul Robeson in *Othello*.
1931	Lilian Baylis runs both the Old Vic and Sadler's Wells.
1932	New Shakespeare Memorial Theatre opens.
1933	Noël Coward's *Design for Living*.
1936	Terence Rattigan's *French Without Tears*; Unity Theatre opens.
1937	Laurence Olivier in *Hamlet*.
1939-45	Second World War.
1945	John Boynton Priestley's *An Inspector Calls*.
1952	Terence Rattigan's *The Deep Blue Sea*.
1953	Coronation of Elizabeth II broadcast on television.
1954	Terence Rattigan's *Separate Tables*.

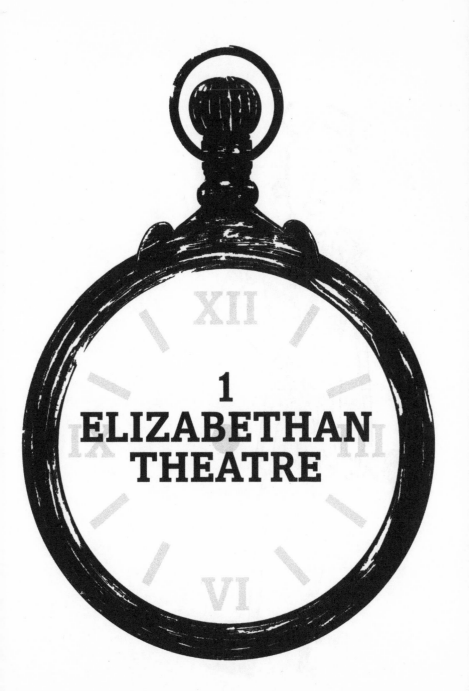

1
ELIZABETHAN THEATRE

1
Elizabethan Theatre

Meet our guide: Walter

Our guide, Walter Wickson, is enjoying a hearty breakfast of oat pottage and ale at the Boar's Head tavern in Eastcheap, a bustling noisy road in the old City of London. As we arrive, he hurriedly finishes eating, wiping his mouth briskly on his sleeve. Walter is in his late forties, has longish, salt-and-pepper hair and proudly sports a neat moustache and a short, trimmed and pointed beard. He is a clerk, but also owns a scrivener's shop, and has, in the past, been a copyist of play scripts, writing out the parts for actors to learn. As he sketches out the story of his life, we learn that he's gone up in the world, his father having been a humble carpenter who worked on staging plays at court. Walter is wearing the clothes of a successful middle-class professional: white linen shirt, dark doublet and hose, with a fur-edged gown for bad weather. He likes to show off, and tells us that he's the proud owner of well-dyed velvet clothes, but only wears them on special occasions. On the oak-wood table in front of him is his flat wool cap. His hands are sturdy and one of his fingers boasts a large silver ring engraved with a skull, a *memento mori*. He's a fastidious character, tending to get lost in detail, but we're immediately impressed by his compendious knowledge. We're less keen on him picking his teeth, though, but then again table manners are a recent invention. Anyway, he explains that on this trip we will be looking at London theatre from the 1550s to 1603, the reign of Queen Elizabeth I.

Tour Guide Badge

Enter Gloriana

Walter is a Londoner through and through so he is ideally placed to introduce us to the capital of Tudor England. In the 1550s, he says, 'It is a city of some 50,000 souls', although he's not really sure about the exact figure. At this time, London covers three main areas: the old square mile of the City of London, enclosed by a stone wall with massive gates and guarded by the grim Tower of London, a place where traitors are beheaded. This prosperous yet densely populated area is the historic heart of the capital. To the west, new buildings are expanding along the Strand towards Westminster. Here growing numbers of landed aristocrats, government officials and busy lawyers make their homes. This area is an upper-middle-class suburb. By contrast, to the north, east and south of the City dwell large numbers of craftsmen — like Walter's father — and semi-skilled workers, their number swelled by migrants from the countryside and abroad. Near the river Thames, which only has one ancient mildew-covered medieval bridge, sailors and dockers settle. Walter warns us against wandering around these poor areas at night.

A keen royalist, Walter gives us our first taste of theatre by taking us to witness Queen Elizabeth's triumphal progress through the City of London. It is Saturday 14 January 1559, the eve of her coronation. As we make our way through the narrow twisting backstreets, we have to tread carefully: the lanes are littered with rotting vegetables, horse shit and puddles of piss. 'In the summer the stench is unbearable,' says Walter, but now — thankfully — it's winter and we notice the cold on our cheeks more than the smell of the streets. As we come into broader avenues, we see that the skyline is dominated by the old medieval cathedral of St Paul's. Sir Christopher Wren's familiar dome hasn't been built yet and this cathedral is an old gothic building, with flying buttresses and a stubby tower whose 160-metre spire stabs at the sky. It is surrounded by gabled roofs, walled gardens, parish churches, law courts and royal palaces. Everywhere, just a short walk away from the cramped and stinky alleys, there are frost-covered fields and spiky trees.

Suddenly we step into a crowded avenue and see something truly amazing: over the heads of the multitude, their breath steaming in the cold, we see the twenty-five-year-old Queen Elizabeth.

She is bare-headed, as tradition demands, so that her subjects can see their new monarch clearly. What strikes us is the whiteness of her complexion and the ginger colour of her hair. But what is most impressive is the magnificence of her apparel: she wears a mantle of gold and silver cloth, furred with ermine, and her dress is of tasseled silk and gold. On this richest of materials is stitched the red-and-white rose symbol of the Tudor dynasty. Queen Elizabeth sits on a cushioned seat in a litter decorated with yellow cloth of gold lined with white satin, and borne by two strong mules, also draped in gold. From the sky, a flurry of snow. It's

Queen Elizabeth I

a cold afternoon so she has a white damask quilt for warmth. All around her are nobles, courtiers, attendants, gentlemen pensioners and sturdy footmen. A thousand people on horseback; a thousand more on foot. It is a carnival of regal crimsons, starched ruffs and flashing jewels. The crowd loves the spectacle; one man weeps for joy; one poor woman hands Queen Elizabeth a sprig of rosemary, a symbol of remembrance. Everyone is cheering, with several cockney voices praising her father: 'Good old King Henry VIII!'

As we follow the procession Walter, who warms his hands by blowing on them, calls our attention to the pageants with which the City welcomes its new sovereign. They are little mimed playlets with speeches declaimed in Latin. Crossing London from East to West, Queen Elizabeth watches five of these pageants, each introduced by trumpet blasts: the first, in Gracechurch Street, celebrates her ancestry, harking back to her namesake Elizabeth of York, whose marriage to her grandfather, Henry Tudor, ended the bloody Wars of the Roses. The second pageant, at Cornhill, shows four virtues: Religion, Love, Wisdom and Justice. The third illustrates the Beatitudes from the New Testament: 'Blessed are the poor; blessed are the meek.' The fourth features the figure of Time, with one tableau showing a decayed nation under Queen Mary, Elizabeth's Catholic older half-sister and the previous monarch, and another featuring a flourishing nation under the new queen. The final pageant, at Fleet Street, depicts the new queen as Deborah, the Hebrew prophetess of the Bible, and predicts that, like Deborah, Queen Elizabeth will rule in harmony for forty years. In fact, Walter whispers, she will rule for forty-five years. Yes, this is Gloriana, the shining star of the Elizabethan world.

Our next stop is the Inner Temple, one of the four inns of court. Walter knows it well because his son, Wilt, is a student here. We can't see much, but in the light of flickering torches Walter hurries us through gothic oak-panelled passages in an old building that functions both as a training ground for lawyers and as a third university (the other two are Oxford and Cambridge). We can hear music and see people dancing, and Walter says that revels are being held to celebrate Robert Dudley, one of Queen Elizabeth's favourites and the future Earl of Leicester. It's a glittering occasion. The word that comes to mind when describing Leicester is 'magnifico'. The man loves his clothes, which drip with jewels; he entertains his sovereign at vast expense, perhaps because he has designs on the Virgin Queen. With his carefully trimmed moustache and beard, and his severe look, he is every inch the noble courtier. And he's a patron of the arts. We see jesters and musicians, as well as actors preparing their interludes, the short playlets that, Walter says, 'are all the rage.' There are shouts, cheers and the sound of drums. But what's that funny smell? 'Tallow candles,' says our guide, 'made from animal fat.'

In the great hall of the Inner Temple a group of lawyers, not content with mere interludes, perform a full-length play. It's called *Gorboduc*. In the flickering candlelight, watching from the back of the room, we struggle to follow what is happening but later Walter fills us in. *Gorboduc* has been penned by Thomas Norton and Thomas Sackville, two high-profile statesmen, and its plot is set in ancient times. Gorboduc is a mythical king of Britain, who divides his kingdom between his sons, Ferrex and Porrex. They argue, and Porrex kills his older brother. In revenge, their mother Videna kills Porrex. The result is a civil war that lays waste the kingdom.

So this is a cautionary tale about the dangers of a disputed royal succession. What Norton and Sackville are doing is using the play to lobby Queen Elizabeth, indirectly suggesting that she should get married and produce an heir to the throne, as soon as possible. A month or so later, on 18 January 1562, the play is performed in front of her. She understands the allegory, but ignores the advice to get married, and so the issue of the royal succession rumbles on for the rest of her reign. As Walter takes us away from the Inner Temple, he explains that the play is highly innovative because it is the first English tragedy to be written in blank verse, which means that the

THEATRE THEORY: CLASSICAL MODELS

Every intellectual and artist in Elizabethan England is steeped in humanist learning, and influenced by the culture of ancient Greece and Rome. This is cultural cringe big time: Elizabethans believe that the ancient world is cleverer, more cultured and more intellectual than their own. So they take their ideas of what makes a good play from the ancient Greek philosopher Aristotle and his *Poetics*, the first work of drama theory (dating from about 350 BC). They also read the plays of Roman playwrights such as Lucius Annaeus Seneca (4 BC—AD 65), a stoic philosopher whose work includes the blood-soaked tragedies of Medea, Phaedra and Oedipus, all in five acts. From these sources, Elizabethan scholars come up with a model called The Unities. This theory is that the best drama has to be convincing and for that to happen it should have one main plot, take place in one location, and over one time span (the play should run for the same length of time as the events it portrays). Also, sex and violence can be talked about by a play's characters but never shown on stage. A case of tell, don't show. The trouble with this model is that if you follow it for every play you get boring drama. One reason for the energy of English playwrights is that they know these rules, but have no problem with breaking them: using subplots, multiple locations and jumps in time. So from the start our drama is a hybrid, partly an imitation of classical models, partly the invention of new ideas.

ends of the lines don't rhyme. Rhyme makes lines sound clunky, while blank verse gives the speech of noble characters both dignity and resonance. *Gorboduc* is a game changer — it heralds the age of Elizabethan tragedy.

Fast forward a couple of years and Walter is showing us around one of the many inns of the City, stroking his beard as he concentrates on giving us the big picture. Basically, British theatre is in 'a mess', he tells us. There are no theatres, only pop-up venues. Most plays last less than an hour, with the typical entertainment being a comedy with fart and burp jokes; a typical title being *Ralph Roister Doister*. All around the country, such comedies are performed in the courtyards of inns, in the halls of great mansions, in the guildhalls of towns, even in churches. Some actors are amateurs, some are students and some the servants of a rich lord. There are many strolling players, grouped into companies of some six men, who perform on the back of wagons parked in town squares. In London, plays are put on using makeshift stages at those inns which have an open yard surrounded by galleries. Walter takes us out into the yard and shows us where the audience stands, and points out the upper galleries where there are benches. The common people stand below while the richer folk sit above. The four City inns that put on plays are the Bel Savage, the Bull, the Bell and the Cross Keys. But change is afoot. Over the next twenty years, the mess that is British theatre will be transformed into a cultural treasure.

By Royal Command

Walter now takes us on a tour of Richmond Palace, one of Queen Elizabeth's most sumptuous residences. Built of white stone, with tall decorated chimneys in brick, it is an imposing and impressive edifice. He moves easily around the building, and we can see that he is familiar with the place and all its rituals. As we stride down corridors and cross courtyards, he says, 'The great thing about Queen Elizabeth and her court is that they love the theatre. But her majesty would not be seen dead watching a play at a common inn. No, when she wants to see a show she summons a theatre company to come and perform it at one of her palaces.' It's called a command performance. The best companies, which attract the best actors, are those sponsored by her favourites. So Lord Leicester's Men have as their patron *il magnifico*, Robert Dudley, and consist of actor James Burbage — a joiner from Bromley who leads the troupe — and a handful of other thespians.

As we perch nervously on richly upholstered seats in one of the palace's long galleries, Walter explains how the system works: under 'The Act for the Punishment of Vagabonds' of 1572 all actors are classed as 'masterless men' and such 'rogues, vagabonds and sturdy beggars' are liable to be whipped out of town. However, when a nobleman sets up a company, the actors come under his protection. They wear his livery; they are safe. If anyone questions their right to put on a play in public, they can always say that they are just rehearsing for a royal command performance. And who would dare question their right to do their best for the queen? From the point of view of the patron, having a company is a demonstration of status: when Leicester's Men play in front of Queen Elizabeth or tour the country they spread the word about his importance — a form of celebrity branding. Other nobles are also in on the act. As well as Leicester's Men, there are Lord Sussex's Men, Lord Pembroke's Men, Lord Worcester's Men and Lord Strange's Men.

'But theatre is a tricky business in uncertain times,' says Walter, rubbing his beard as he usually does when he makes a serious point. For example, whenever the bubonic plague hits London, the Lord Mayor and City Aldermen (the local government) close down all public performances because they fear that large gatherings will spread the contagion. During a couple of dreadful summer months, the plague kills anything between 10,000 and 20,000 people, up to a tenth of the entire population of London. Bodies lie unburied in the streets as fear sets in. With venues closed down, and no work in the capital, the theatre companies leave town and go on tour. So Leicester's Men travel up north to Newcastle and west to Bristol. Usually, they stop to perform one free show for local bigwigs, and then one for the general paying public at an inn or other pop-up venue. On tour, life is tough. Using a wagon to transport their costumes and props, while the actors ride on horseback, the company spends days and days on rough and dusty roads that any old storm can turn into a quagmire. In the winter, travel is a nightmare of mud, rain and illness. On tours money is also a problem: it's hard to drum up a good crowd and, when the hat is passed around after the show, some people simply don't pay.

The first Theatre

While Queen Elizabeth is being royally entertained at court, especially during the Christmas festivities, by Leicester's Men and other troupes, the face of London theatre is being changed not by noble lords, but by commoners. Movers and shakers are emerging who have a passion for acting — coupled with a buccaneering entrepreneurial spirit. The task these ordinary men take on is to clean up the messy system of temporary venues and create special theatre buildings which can attract large audiences. London's population is booming, doubling every decade, and this mass of people is aching to be entertained. It is a great potential market; there's money to be made. But the first attempts at creating theatres run into problems.

In 1567, when Shakespeare is still a three-year-old infant, a Londoner called John Brayne builds the first open air theatre in the garden of a farmhouse at Mile End, east of the City. It is called the Red Lion, and has a platform stage surrounded by gallery seats held up by scaffolding. He is a former grocer and an entrepreneur, but his investment is small and the structure is temporary. It proves to be too far away from the City for audiences to get to easily so the place only lasts for one summer. But Brayne's can-do attitude suffers a setback when he is sued for having raised a mortgage on the land by trickery. Then he disappears from view until, almost ten years later, he has another go. This time he teams up with the theatre pro James Burbage, and together they strike gold. Burbage is by now the bustling actor-manager of Leicester's Men, and also Brayne's brother-in-law, which means that both men can keep the business in the family. Together they invent something wholly new: a building whose sole purpose is to put on plays. For the first time in England since Roman times, a proper theatre opens its doors in 1576.

To show us this wonderful achievement, our guide Walter takes us north out of the City through Bishopsgate to the nearby parish of Shoreditch, a place of open fields and country lanes. On our way, we catch the acrid smell from tanning works and other small factories. 'It's important to remember,' says Walter, 'that Shoreditch lies outside the City walls, beyond the reach of the Mayor and Aldermen, killjoys who disapprove of theatre.' From a distance, we soon see Burbage and Brayne's new construction, a polygonal three-storey building which towers above the ramshackle village

ENEMIES OF THEATRE: PURITAN KILLJOYS

Theatre is under threat from killjoys. The Lord Mayor of London and City Aldermen think that any large crowd of people is a threat to law and order. Like taverns, bowling alleys and brothels, the theatre is a magnet for thieves, prostitutes and criminals. What happens if they riot? In 1597, for example, the Mayor writes to the Privy Council, the ministers of Queen Elizabeth, complaining that theatres are meeting places for 'thieves, horse-stealers and plotters of treason'. Many aldermen are Puritans, who think that the theatre is ungodly and that watching plays will corrupt ordinary folk. They take a fundamentalist attitude to the arts. Puritans believe that people should pray and work, instead of having fun. They disapprove of actors, who pretend to be other than they are, impersonate their betters and cross dress. In 1585 the Puritan pamphleteer Philip Stubbes says that boys playing women encourages men in the audience to 'play the sodomites or worse' (homosexuality is illegal). So the authorities frequently try to close down playhouses within the City walls.

houses. As we get closer we note its typical Tudor style, with white walls and a dark timber frame.

Walter takes us nearer. He points out that in the 1570s purpose-built venues dedicated to putting on shows are such a new thing that the first one is simply called The Theatre (after the Latin *theatrum*, meaning 'seeing place'). This is also a piece of clever marketing: the message is that Elizabethans are the new Romans. Burbage and Brayne's financial investment in this new building is considerable: £700 (a nobleman gets about £2000 a year and a successful merchant £100). It's a risky venture, but it turns out to be a success. The reason for this is location. The venue is easy to get to from the north of the City so there is a big potential audience.

It's noon on a weekday, and as we get closer to The Theatre a noisy crowd is gathering, enjoying the spring air. There are play bills fixed to buildings announcing a show, and a musician is literally drumming up interest in the nearby streets. There's a press of people, all moving towards the theatre, all talking and gesticulating. The smell of sweat is strong, but even worse is the stench of sewage and horse manure. We see a noblewoman, escorted by a gallant, a man of fashion. To sweeten the air, she holds a jewelled pomander while he smokes a pipe — tobacco smells better than shit! During this time, all classes of people go to the theatre: one in ten Londoners regularly see a show.

We enter the Theatre. As we do so, we put one penny in a box held by collectors, guarded by a pair of heavies. 'The room where these boxes are kept,' says Walter, 'is called the box office.' Once inside we realize that there is no roof, but a large yard in the middle that is open to the elements (luckily it's not raining), and a platform stage jutting out. In the yard, standing room is cheap, and the groundlings (poorer audience members) are referred to as 'penny stinkards'. They are craftsmen, artisans and their wives, plus some apprentices and servants. If we don't want to stand in the yard in front of the stage, we can go upstairs to the galleries. Here, for an extra penny, we can sit on a bench, or for six pence get a private box. This is where the nobles, merchants and richer folk sit, while students often stand in the yard. There are no seats in the open yard, where the audience stand or squat on the ground. No toilet facilities either. So, if needed, we have to find a quiet corner in the nearby fields. The Theatre can hold anything up to about 2500 people, but normally the audience numbers anything from six hundred to a thousand.

It's now past two o'clock in the afternoon. A fanfare from a trumpet announces the start of the play. The actors enter the stage and the story begins. There are few props and no scenery so we have to use our imaginations. There is no interval and the play is acted straight through, lasting between two and three hours. The acting is rough and ready, but nobody minds. In the glare of daylight, the actors use broad gestures as if they were at a great public meeting. But what really takes our breath away is the dazzle of their costumes: they are made from the richest silks, linens and damasks, with jewels gleaming in the sun. There's a massive contrast between the ordinary spectators, in their browns and greys, and the splendidly colourful actors. We also notice that all the female roles are played by boys, whose voices have a higher pitch. 'Women are not allowed on stage,' explains Walter — acting is a men-only job.

Looking around at the audience, we see that they are noisy: they call out, they cheer, they boo, they chat among themselves. Even the staid Walter sometimes joins in, carried away by the excitement. The atmosphere is boisterous, a bit like a football match today. During their soliloquies, the actors talk directly to the audience, and sometimes spectators answer back. Working their way through the crowd we might spot pickpockets, known as cut-purses. 'If a thief is caught,' says Walter, 'they are shamed by being tied to a pillar in full view.' Prostitutes are also at work in the crowd. A couple of other women are selling beer, and fruit. Walter explains that if actors forget their lines they are pelted with fruit. In various corners, bored audience members are munching apples, cracking nuts, drinking ale and flirting. Someone spits on the ground; a small group starts playing cards. At the end of the show, there's a jig, which is the name given to a short show with bawdy jokes and dance music; people clap along; they dance. It's full-on jollity.

Here come the Queen's Men

The Theatre is an amazing success. The audience now knows they have a permanent place that stages plays regularly six days a week (closed on Sundays for religious reasons). The play changes every day and there is a lot of variety. So successful and so profitable is this venture that a rival theatre, the Curtain, is built about two hundred yards away a year after Burbage and Brayne's prototype. London is gradually creating a theatreland.

But Queen Elizabeth, by now an established patron of theatre, has a problem. Her lords are busy competing with each other with shows, especially during the Christmas festivities, and she cannot control what their companies are doing or saying. So in 1583 she asks Edmund Tilney, her Master of the Revels and distant kinsman, to set up a new company, with the awesome title of the Queen's Men. As the queen's minister of fun, the forty-seven-year-old courtier is one of two officials who control the theatre, licensing plays and if necessary censoring them. The other official is the Lord Chamberlain, who organizes the royal household and court entertainments. Tilney cherry-picks twelve of the best actors from different companies and creates the Queen's Men, a company twice the size of all its rivals. It has a monopoly on playing at court for five years, and charges twice as much as other companies when performing to the public. It's a royal winner.

Walter tells us that the Queen's Men have a repertory of history plays that exalt the Tudor dynasty. Londoners love patriotic plays and public spectacle, especially when royal events are depicted in all their pomp: the theatre is as well attended as executions and blood sports. During the winter, the Queen's Men entertain at court; during the summer months they tour, taking the monarch's good will to her people. One of the towns they visit is Stratford-upon-Avon, in Warwickshire, where an unknown eighteen-year-old lad called William Shakespeare has just married the twenty-six-year-old Anne Hathaway, who is already pregnant with their first child. He watches the actors in action and dreams of joining a theatre company, of going to London. During such tours the actors live in each other's pockets and disputes flare up. On one occasion, on a visit to Thame in Oxfordshire, the main actor of the Queen's

Men, William Knell, is stabbed in the neck during a fight with John Towne, another thesp. He dies, and, about a year later, his young widow Rebecca remarries. Her new husband is actor John Heminges, who later becomes Shakespeare's friend and, after the bard's death, co-publisher of his collected plays. Theatre is one big family!

But the greatest celebrity actor of the Queen's Men is Richard Tarlton, a comedian who rises to become the first big star of British theatre. Walter tells us that he is the son of a pig farmer, and there's more than a whiff of the farmyard about him. Stocky, squint-eyed and flat-nosed, he makes his appearance work for him. Even his pig-face is funny — all he has to do is jump on stage for people to start cheering. He joins the Queen's Men and is Queen Elizabeth's favourite court jester. And he deserves his success because he's come a long way, having started out as a humble pub landlord doing stand-up comedy, with a talent for doggerel verse, and for provoking and then putting down hecklers. He specializes in jigs, which are the satirical and naughty verse playlets performed after a main play, along with lively dances and silly songs. Tarlton's brand image is that of a man smoking a pipe and banging a small drum, and it appears in pamphlets, on inn signs and even on the doors of toilets. This master of buffoonery is popular with every class in society. He is even honoured by the rich and powerful: Sir Philip Sidney, the poet and courtier, agrees to be godfather to his offspring. Not a bad result for the son of a pig farmer. However, after his death in 1588, the Queen's Men lose their sparkle.

But even before then the company has to reckon with a powerful rival. In 1585, Charles Lord Howard — Queen Elizabeth's cousin — becomes Lord High Admiral, and he names his company of actors the Lord Admiral's Men. Howard is a big cheese: not only is he a major political player — having an important role in the trial and execution of Mary Queen of Scots — but he also leads the navy which defeats the Spanish Armada in 1588. He's a national hero. For him, a theatre company is a status symbol, but he doesn't have time to supervise its day-to-day activities. That job goes to Edward Alleyn, an actor of enormous calibre who becomes the greatest tragedian of his generation. Born in 1566, he is the son of an inn-keeper who was once the queen's porter. Very tall, with a russet-brown beard, he is famed for his roaring voice and strutting style: audiences love his majestic delivery, which seems to shake the walls of both the Theatre and the Curtain. His style is crude, but it works. But what kind of plays does he act in?

Kyd and Marlowe

The London theatre is flooded with plays, but they're not very good; clunky verse and clunky stagings. By the mid-1580s, however, the playwriting scene is dominated by a group known as the University Wits (most of them went to Oxbridge). As Walter tells us about them, our eyes glaze over — there is too much detail about people we've never heard of. We are sitting in the upstairs room of his scrivener's shop, with printed copies of various plays on the table in front of us, and the warmth of the day is sending us to sleep. But then, as he mentions two names, we soon perk up: Thomas Kyd and Christopher Marlowe.

A grammar-school boy, Kyd is the son of a London scrivener, and Walter knows his father well. Kyd the son does his father proud — he invents a whole new genre — the revenge tragedy, stories in which an unlawful killing demands violent vengeance. His smash hit is *The Spanish Tragedy*, first staged in 1587. Set in the Spanish court, it starts with two characters coming on stage: one is called Revenge, dressed in black, and the other is the Ghost of Don Andrea (made up to look as pale as death). Don Andrea is a courtier who has fallen in love with the noble Bel-Imperia and has been killed in battle by Balthazar of Portugal. He has now returned as a ghost to seek revenge. The story is complicated, but after Don Andrea's friend Horatio captures Balthazar in battle, Horatio ends up getting killed. Then Hieronimo, Horatio's elderly father, demands revenge. In

Edward Alleyn

a key scene, Hieronimo presents a play to the court, using Bel-Imperia and his enemies as actors. During this play within the play, there's a flurry of stabbings and the stage is left littered with bodies. At one point, Hieronimo bites off his own tongue rather than explain his actions. It's the kind of play that uses a lot of stage blood, which, explains Walter, is sourced from pigs or sheep, and kept in a pig's bladder until used.

What Kyd does is take the blank verse introduced in *Gorboduc* and give it a new vigour and rhetorical style: the rhythm of his lines is almost hypnotic.

Thomas Kyd's *The Spanish Tragedy* (1587)
Hieronimo's soliloquy on discovering his son's dead body:
Oh eyes, no eyes, but fountains fraught with tears;
Oh life, no life, but lively form of death;
Oh world, no world, but mass of public wrongs,
Confused and filled with murder and misdeeds!
Oh sacred heavens! If this unhallowed deed,
If this inhuman and barbarous attempt,
If this incomparable murder thus
Of mine, but now no more my son,
Shall unrevealed and unavenged pass,
How should we term your dealings to be just,
If you unjustly deal with those that in your justice trust?

This time, in a big break from classical tradition, the sex and violence is put on stage: a case of show, don't tell. The result is hugely popular, the first British blockbuster, being constantly staged at the Theatre and other venues, and ten editions published in book form. A couple of Hieronimo's lines — 'What outcry calls me from my naked bed!' (as he is woken to hear of his son's death) and 'Beware Hieronimo, go by, go by' (whispered to himself when he thinks he has offended the king) — become catchphrases, and the play is often parodied. The play is also popular because it gives an image of the Catholic Spanish court as corrupt and bloodthirsty, and this goes down well in an age when the Spanish Armada threatens the country, and when most true Englishmen are proudly Protestant. *The Spanish Tragedy* creates a taste for gory stories that lasts for

CHRISTOPHER MARLOWE

Baptised: 26 February 1564.

Family: Son of a Canterbury shoemaker.

Education: King's School, Canterbury. At sixteen goes to Corpus Christi College, Cambridge, on a scholarship. However, university withholds his MA in 1587 because he is suspected of being a Catholic convert.

Private life: Never married.

Career: Iconoclastic dramatist, talk of the town and game changer, the bad boy of Elizabethan literature; starts young and writes a string of successes.

Greatest hits: Two-part *Tamburlaine the Great* (1587-88), *Doctor Faustus* (1589), *The Jew of Malta* (1590) and *Edward II* (1592).

Influence: Inspires Shakespeare.

Scandal: Probably recruited as government spy while at Cambridge. Imprisoned in 1589 after being involved in a stabbing and in 1592 is sent home from army service in the Netherlands for counterfeiting money. The following year accused of heresy. Killed in mysterious circumstances at a lodging house in Deptford.

Death: 30 May 1593.

Epitaph: In his own words: 'All they that love not tobacco and boys are fools.'

Afterlife: His early death cuts short his chances of becoming an even greater playwright than Shakespeare.

decades. The genre of the blood-soaked revenge tragedy proves to have a great future: the royal road that leads to Shakespeare's glorious verse starts here.

The most notorious playwright of the 1580s is Christopher Marlowe, who also happens to know Kyd (at one point sharing lodgings with him). A Cambridge university scholar, Marlowe is a handsome young man who is reputed to be three things guaranteed to appall any respectable citizen: an atheist, a homosexual and a spy — the playwright as romantic scoundrel. He gets involved in street brawls. He forges coins. But he writes like a dream. And for about six years his star shines bright. Dazzling. Already, at the age of twenty-three he makes his mark. He writes *Tamburlaine the Great*, a dramatization of the rise and fall of a barbarian Scythian shepherd, who goes on to conquer the world. And so successful is the play that he writes a follow up, thus we now have Tamburlaine parts one and two.

What is the secret of Marlowe's success? In four words: great stories; great language. Marlowe grabs the crude blank verse of previous playwrights, gives it a shake and a stir, turning it into a majestic vehicle for evoking thrilling visions of wonder. Full of sonorous place names and imagery from classical mythology, *Tamburlaine the Great* is written in a grandiloquent yet rhythmic language of an enormous power and resonance. It is polysyllabic heaven. As another playwright, Ben Jonson, is later to say, it's his 'mighty line' that carries the drama. Audiences are transfixed by the exhortations and orations of the play, especially when they watch the imposing figure of Edward Alleyn, star actor of the Admiral's Men, perform the role. As he paces the stage, declaiming his lines, he has an electrifying effect. The play also has its share of memorable stage images: at one point, the hero enters with two of his vanquished adversaries, the kings of Trebizond and Soria, pulling his triumphant chariot with bits in their teeth like dray horses: in this scene, one line —

'Holla, ye pampered jades of Asia' (Tamburlaine urging on the kings) — becomes a popular catchphrase. At another point, the imprisoned Emperor of Turkey commits suicide by smashing his head against the bars of his cage — heady stuff!

Christopher Marlowe

The full title of Marlowe's greatest hit is *The Tragical History of the Life and Death of Doctor Faustus*. Its plot is a legendary cautionary tale: Faustus, a German scholar dissatisfied with the limits of knowledge, sells his soul to Lucifer in exchange for twenty-four years of immense power, but as this term expires the fear of Hell grows in him. The key figures in a drama that takes the audience to the ends of the Earth include Mephistophilis, a demon, and Wagner, Faustus's clowning servant. Scene after amazing scene follow in quick succession: on a visit to the Pope, an invisible Faustus plays childish tricks on the pontiff; Faustus conjures up an image of Alexander the Great; the Seven Deadly Sins appear in a parade; Faustus has Mephistophilis summon up Helen of Troy, and exclaims rapturously about her beauty: 'Was this the face that launch'd a thousand ships,/ And burnt the topless towers of Ilium?' Another evocative exchange comes after Faustus asks Mephistophilis how he managed to get out of Hell, and Mephistophilis replies: 'Why this is hell, nor am I out of it.' At midnight of the final day, a host of devils appear and carry Faustus's soul to Hell.

Christopher Marlowe's *Doctor Faustus* (1589)

Faustus faces the prospect of eternal damnation:

Ah, Faustus,
Now hast thou but one bare hour to live,
And then thou must be damned perpetually!
Stand still, you ever-moving spheres of Heaven,
That time may cease, and midnight never come;
Fair Nature's eye, rise, rise again and make
Perpetual day; or let this hour be but
A year, a month, a week, a natural day,
That Faustus may repent and save his soul!
Oh lente, lente, currite noctis equi!
The stars move still, time runs, the clock will strike,
The Devil will come, and Faustus must be damned.
Oh, I'll leap up to my God! Who pulls me down?
See, see where Christ's blood streams in the firmament!
One drop would save my soul — half a drop: ah, my
Christ!

In this play, the blank verse speeches such as this show how Marlowe is inventing a new and immensely flexible poetic form, where the rhythm of the lines fit the ups and downs of the emotions of the characters. In the hands of Marlowe's contemporary, Shakespeare, this pliable blank verse matures into one of the wonders of world literature. It is also great for actors. Once again, Alleyn — this time wearing a surplice with a cross on the front and dominating the stage of The Theatre — makes the part his own. And *Doctor Faustus* is a big hit: the Admiral's Men perform it twenty-five times in the three years after October 1594 (at a time, Walter reminds us, when plays changed daily and many were only performed once). Elsewhere, a new production includes trapdoors springing open and shaggy-haired devils running across the stage while fireworks spout flames and the rumble of thunder is heard. It's a very daring play — before now, no one has been brave enough to write about alchemy and black magic, something that this god-fearing society thinks is no fit subject for entertainment. The play soon becomes a cause célèbre: one account claims that real devils appear on stage in a production in Exeter, with the actors stopping the performance in dismay. Shocking. But Marlowe's triumph is short-lived: at the age of twenty-nine he is dead, stabbed through the eye, ostensibly during a brawl about a bill. What a waste!

Bankside beckons

In 1587 London theatre gets a reshuffle. The focus shifts from Shoreditch, which is north of the river, to Bankside, on the south bank of the Thames, but crucially also outside of the jurisdiction of the City of London authorities, a place free of regulations. Bankside is London's prime entertainment zone, a place of bear-baiting and bull-baiting arenas, and brothels. Walter ferries us from north of the river across the Thames by wherry, quicker and easier than crossing by bridge, and less crowded. And we can see the huge numbers of little boats taking passengers up and down the river, with the boatmen's cries of 'Westward ho!' and 'Eastward ho!', indicating the direction of travel. Our boatman supplies the latest gossip and some blunt political opinions: he hates the Spanish Empire and wants to see all Catholics burnt.

On Bankside, new theatres are being built. The latest mover and shaker, Philip Henslowe, is a real entrepreneur. Originally a dyer, he is now a successful financier. Rumour has it that he keeps meticulous accounts of every penny he spends. In

1587, he decides to move into the entertainment business so he builds a new venue, The Rose. Costing about half as much as the Theatre, it is smaller and lies next to three of the biggest brothels in the area, but the site is quite boggy and the building always feels damp and smelly. As we walk around the place, we are glad of Walter's company because some of the narrow roads and evil-looking taverns feel positively dingy and downright dangerous. But, our guide assures us, 'You are safe with me.' Anyway, Henslowe's gamble pays off: the Rose is a great success.

Starting with a characteristic stroking of his beard, Walter now fills us in on the latest news. He twiddles with the skull on his ring and says that after the death of the superstar comedian Tarlton, the Queen's Men finally break up in 1594, and for the next few years London theatre is dominated by a duopoly of companies, the Admiral's Men and the Chamberlain's Men. While the Admiral's Men are still led by Edward Alleyn, the Chamberlain's Men are the new kids on the block. Founded in 1594 by the sixty-eight-year-old elder statesman Henry Carey Lord Hunsdon, Queen Elizabeth's new Lord Chamberlain, the company includes Richard Burbage, William Shakespeare (finally, he's made it to London) and Will Kemp, the great portly comedian who created the bard's comic roles. Family connections make these two competing companies strong. The Chamberlain's Men are led by actor Richard Burbage, whose father James runs the Theatre. The star of the Admiral's Men Edward Alleyn marries the step-daughter of Philip Henslowe, the man behind the Rose. To maximize audiences, they make a deal: the Admiral's Men have their base at the Rose, south of the river, while the Chamberlain's Men are based at the Theatre, north of the river. The Admirals have playwright Marlowe; the Chamberlains have Shakespeare.

We have arrived back near the edge of the River Thames. Walter leans against a stone wall, takes out a short clay pipe, fills it and begins to puff. We decline his kind offer of the rather acrid-smelling tobacco. As people walk past, he points out typical audience members and comments on what the penny admission to the theatre means to them. Look, there's a skilled craftsman, maybe a cobbler or wheelwright, whose daily wage is about fourteen pence. He can afford to take his wife to the theatre. But that one looks like an unskilled labourer, who only makes four pence a day so he can't afford the time off to see a show. If he does have time to go out it means he's unemployed. And if you don't work you don't eat. A penny can keep you fed on bread for a day or drunk on beer. 'A pipe of tobacco costs three pence,' says Walter, waving his pipe in the air. Next, he tells us about a very vocal social group: the London apprentices. They love going to theatres, where they made a lot of noise, but they also make their point in other ways — by rioting. Between 1581 and 1602, there are no less than thirty-five riots in the capital as unemployment rises and the gap between rich and poor grows. 'Gentlemen,' says Walter, 'are naturally worried

ELIZABETHAN THEATRE A & E

ACCIDENTS AND EMERGENCIES BESET LONDON VENUES, WHICH CAN BE DANGEROUS PLACES:

- IN 1583, AN OVERCROWDED GALLERY AT THE PARIS GARDEN BEAR-BAITING RING IN SOUTHWARK COLLAPSES AND EIGHT SPECTATORS ARE CRUSHED TO DEATH.

- IN 1587, DURING A PERFORMANCE BY THE ADMIRAL'S MEN ONE ACTOR FIRES A LOADED MUSKET, ACCIDENTALLY KILLING A CHILD AND A PREGNANT WOMAN IN THE AUDIENCE.

- IN 1599 SOME FORTY SPECTATORS ARE INJURED AND FIVE KILLED, INCLUDING — SAY REPORTS — 'TWO GOOD HANDSOME WHORES', WHEN A HOUSE IN ST JOHN STREET COLLAPSES WHILE A PUPPET PLAY IS BEING PERFORMED.

- WHEN A BAND OF SPANISH RAIDERS LAND IN CORNWALL, A GROUP OF ACTORS WHO ARE STAGING A BATTLE ARE MISTAKEN FOR REAL SOLDIERS. BUT INSTEAD OF RUNNING, THEY TURN ON THE INVADERS, WHO BEAT A HASTY RETREAT.

by disorder': Shakespeare has little sympathy for Jack Cade's uprising in the second part of *Henry VI* or for the food rioters in *Coriolanus*. 'And quite right too,' he says vehemently.

We are still on Bankside and Walter is looking for a wherry to ferry us back to the City. While we wait he carries on telling us about theatre's building boom. In 1595, the goldsmith and court official Francis Langley buys some land on Bankside, about half a mile to the west of the Rose, and builds the Swan. It boasts columns which have been painted in a marble finish and the place is large and beautiful. Two years later, Langley — who is a dodgy character suspected by the authorities of being a fence — challenges the duopoly of the Admirals and the Chamberlains by sponsoring Lord Pembroke's Men. At first all goes well. Then disaster strikes. When the company perform a satire called *The Isle of Dogs*, written by young Ben Jonson and the poet and pamphleteer Thomas Nashe, it is denounced as seditious, and Jonson is imprisoned. The two men have poked fun at Queen Elizabeth and her councillors. They have made some overtly critical political points. Now, because of this scandal, every copy of the play is hunted down and destroyed and the Privy Council, the top government ministers, issues a royal proclamation that all London theatres should be pulled down. Although this threat isn't carried out, it hangs as a warning over managers. After *The Isle of Dogs* debacle, the Swan falls into decay.

James Burbage is equally unlucky. The Theatre, now exclusive venue of the Chamberlain's Men, prospers but because it is open to the elements, it does less well on rainy days or during freezing weather. So Burbage does some wheeling and dealing, and builds an indoor theatre in an upstairs hall in the wealthy neighbourhood of Blackfriars, a City location. It costs the massive sum of £600. But then Burbage, the Bromley boy who has come so far, is hit by a double blow: the first is that the rich Blackfriars residents are not keen on a theatre in their neighbourhood because they know this will attract large crowds, and they are afraid of noise, disorder and criminal gangs. All they can think is: not in my backyard. So they petition the City authorities against it and get a ruling in their favour in

1596. The second blow is that the lease on the Theatre lapses in the same year, and the landlord Giles Allen refuses to renew it. No one knows why, shrugs Walter. Burbage has invested all his wealth in two theatres, and he can't use either of them. Heartbroken, he dies a year later.

Now his sons, Richard and Cuthbert, inherit the same problem. Not only has landlord Allen refused to renew the lease, but he also wants to keep the building. So the brothers decide to take matters into their own hands. They decide to break the rules and grab what's theirs. Walter knows the inside story: on 28 December 1598, during a winter so cold that the Thames partially freezes over, Richard leads a group of actors and other theatre investors to raid the Theatre. The men carry swords, daggers and axes, and are joined by day labourers commanded by Peter Street, a master carpenter. As the snow falls, they break into the theatre and demolish the wattle walls and dismantle the oak frame. Since it is Christmas, landlord Allen is away at his country estate, and although some of his neighbours protest, the raid goes unopposed. The actors look menacing with their weapons, and the labourers remove the valuable oak beams of the frame. These are transported by wagon to builder Street's warehouse. Several months later, when the weather is warmer, Burbage and Street use these same beams to construct the Globe theatre on cheap land south of the Thames. 'So the legendary Globe, which opens in 1599, has its origins, like many theatre enterprises,' says Walter with a twinkle in his eye, 'in a flagrant flouting of the rules.'

Sweet William

'It is time,' says Walter, 'to speak of Shakespeare.' We are in the Mermaid Tavern, on Cheapside, east of St Paul's. It is a dark building, with small windows through which the light comes fitfully, casting shadows on the whitewashed walls, oak paneling and hard wooden furniture. Here we drink ale, poured from pewter flagons, while Walter gives us a thumbnail sketch of the actor and playwright: he is courteous, unassuming and good company—a real gent. Born in the same year as Marlowe, Shakespeare takes longer to perfect his art, but this modest

WILLIAM SHAKESPEARE

Baptised: 26 April 1564.

Family: Son of John, a Stratford-upon-Avon glover and wool merchant, and Mary Arden, daughter of a landowner.

Education: King's New School, the local grammar school.

Private life: At eighteen, marries twenty-six-year-old Anne Hathaway (1582). She is already pregnant and baby Susanna is born in May 1583; twins Hamnet and Judith born in 1585. Leaves family in Stratford to work in London.

Career: Long-term member of the Chamberlain's Men, which he joins as actor and playwright in 1592. When theatres close due to plague, he writes poetry, *The Sonnets*. From about 1594, he produces roughly two plays a year until 1611.

Greatest hits: His early plays include *The Comedy of Errors*, *The Taming of the Shrew* and *Titus Andronicus*. He writes a cycle of English history plays, including two parts of *Henry IV*, plus *Henry V* and *Richard III*. He also dips into Roman history and classical times with *Julius Caesar*, *Coriolanus*, *Antony and Cleopatra* and *Troilus and Cressida*. Then come *Romeo and Juliet*, *A Midsummer Night's Dream*, *The Merchant of Venice*, *Twelfth Night* and *As You Like It*. His most famous tragedies are written in the early 1600s, including *Hamlet*, *Othello*, *King Lear* and *Macbeth*. His later plays, after 1605, include *The Tempest* and *The Winter's Tale*.

Collaborations: Later plays, such as *Henry VIII* and *The Two Noble Kinsmen*, written with John Fletcher.

Retirement: Spends his last few years in Stratford, with his family, by now a wealthy man, able to buy a large house and other property.

Scandal: None known.

Death: 23 April 1616.

Epitaph: 'He was not of an age, but for all time.' (Ben Jonson)

Afterlife: Iconic bard. The image of Hamlet holding a skull is a symbol not just of English drama, but of all theatre.

gent eventually becomes a one-man hit factory. At first he works as an actor, and as a long-term member of the Chamberlain's Men he has an insider's understanding of what makes a good play. When he starts writing, his earliest efforts are easy comedies and blood-and-gore tragedies. As he develops, the comedies become darker, the tragedies more nuanced and his history plays less reliant on stereotypical heroes and villains. His success is based on team work. He knows his actors and writes for them: the great tragic roles of Hamlet, Macbeth and Othello are written for Richard Burbage, who is noted for the sincerity and realism of his acting. As the young playwright John Webster says of him: 'What we see him personate we think truly done before us.' There are excellent boy actors in Shakespeare's company and he writes the complex parts of Lady Macbeth, Desdemona and Cleopatra specially for them. In *As You Like It* and *Twelfth Night*, he plays gender-bending games with women characters who disguise themselves as men. So in those plays audiences watch boys playing women pretending to be men.

Shakespeare doesn't care about being original: he steals stories, paragraphs of text and lines from other plays and books. In *Henry IV* part two he lifts two lines from Marlowe, turning 'Holla, ye pampered jades of Asia/ What can ye draw but twenty miles a day?' into 'And hollow pampered jades of Asia/ Which cannot go but thirty miles a day.' It's a theatrical in-joke that appeals to the poets and students in the audience. In each play he comes up with compelling stories, which combine comedy with tragedy, rudeness with piety, high with low culture. He increasingly understands his audience, and his work combines dense metaphors with farcical amusement. But there is one drawback to being a resident playwright for the Chamberlain's Men: the pay is not great, anything from seven pounds to ten pounds per play. So Shakespeare becomes really rich only when he, along with other company members, invests his money in the building of the Globe. He ends up as a well-off gentleman with a coat of arms.

Walter is amazed when we tell him about how today for us the bard has iconic status and is famous as the world's best playwright ever. Our idea that he is the most significant Englishman of the past thousand years raises more than one eyebrow. For Walter, Shakespeare is wonderfully talented, but he is only one of many other actors and playwrights in the business. He agrees that he has a marvellous facility with language, but also points out that the University Wits look down on him because he hasn't been to Oxbridge. What he does have is a deep understanding of human nature.

One reason for Shakespeare's enduring reputation is that he stays the course: his career lasts twenty-five years. Unlike Marlowe, he doesn't die young; unlike Jonson, he isn't quarrelsome; unlike his nearest rivals, more of his plays survive. Of his output of some forty plays (a handful written in collaboration with other playwrights), thirty-six are published in 1623, seven years after his death. This is a labour of love by two of his fellow company members, the actors John Heminges and Henry Condell. They choose a large format for this volume, which means it is a prestigious publication, and although its title is *Master William Shakespeare's Comedies, Histories and Tragedies*, it is known as the First Folio (Folio means large format). 'Actually,' says Walter, 'Jonson beats him to it: he produces a Folio edition of his own plays in 1616.'

Before we go any further, Walter is happy to confirm that the man from Stratford-upon-Avon wrote the plays credited to him — there is no conspiracy. They haven't been written by Marlowe, or the Earl of Oxford or Francis Bacon! His work is his indeed, and he is a supreme wordsmith, exploiting the flexibility of the English language, cramming nimble wit, vivid imagery and psychological truth into almost every speech. More than his rivals, he makes up new words to express new shades of meaning. In his lifetime he coins about two thousand new words. At his most inventive, he uses a new word every three or so lines. Words such as assassination, horrid and zany are his. He attaches the prefix 'un' to existing words: unhand, unmask, unveil. When we use expressions like 'to play fast and loose', 'the milk of human kindness', and 'more in sorrow than anger', we are quoting the bard. His phrases have become commonplace and a tenth of the most popular quotations in English are from his work: 'The quality of mercy is not strained'; 'If music be the food of love play on'; 'Is this a dagger which I see before me?' Sound familiar? We tell Walter that phrases from his plays have provided titles for novels, television programmes and music: *Brave New World* (*Tempest*), *To the Manor Born* (*Hamlet*), and 'Pomp and Circumstance' (*Othello*). There are more than a hundred examples!

William Shakespeare's *Hamlet* (1601)
Hamlet contemplates suicide:

To be, or not to be, that is the question:
Whether 'tis nobler in the mind to suffer
The slings and arrows of outrageous fortune,
Or to take arms against a sea of troubles,
And by opposing end them? To die, to sleep
No more; and by a sleep to say we end
The heartache and the thousand natural shocks
That flesh is heir to, 'tis a consummation
Devoutly to be wish'd. To die, to sleep;
To sleep, perchance to dream: aye, there's the rub;
For in that sleep of death what dreams may come
When we have shuffled off this mortal coil,
Must give us pause. There's the respect
That makes calamity of so long life;
For who would bear the whips and scorns of time,
The oppressor's wrong, the proud man's contumely,
The pangs of despised love, the law's delay,
The insolence of office, and the spurns
That patient merit of the unworthy takes,
When he himself might his quietus make
With a bare bodkin? Who would fardels bear,
To grunt and sweat under a weary life,
But that the dread of something after death,
The undiscover'd country from whose bourn
No traveller returns, puzzles the will
And makes us rather bear those ills we have
Than fly to others that we know not of.
Thus conscience does make cowards of us all,
And thus the native hue of resolution
Is sicklied o'er with the pale cast of thought,
And enterprises of great pith and moment
With this regard their currents turn awry,
And lose the name of action.

Shakespeare refines the blank verse that Marlowe used so brilliantly. This is iambic pentameter, which means that each line has a distinctive rhythm, consisting of five pairs of syllables, with the stress falling on the second of each pair: di-*dum*, di-*dum*, di-*dum*, di-*dum*, di-*dum*. It is copied from Italian verse but sounds natural in English. It works well in open-air theatres because its rhythm enables it to carry well. Typically, Shakespeare gives blank verse a twist: he alters its stately

William Shakespeare

rhythm whenever the speaker is under emotional pressure. In Hamlet's 'To be or not to be' speech, for example, the first four lines are irregular, with an extra syllable each. Hamlet's distress as he struggles with the temptation to end his life is expressed through this change of the regular rhythm.

One reason that Shakespeare's plays are both complicated yet popular is that many in his audiences have had the same grammar-school education as he did. So they recognize the classical references, the allusions and the jokes. Elizabethan education is focused on ancient Greece and Rome, and on the ancient art of rhetoric, which aims to use language in order to present an argument, and win it. It's a linguistic weapon. To give one example from many, Mark Antony's speech in *Julius Caesar* is pure rhetoric: 'Friends, Romans, Countrymen, lend me your ears./ I come to bury Caesar, not to praise him.' At the same time, like other playwrights, Shakespeare also uses prose, ordinary dialogue, often for characters who are lower class or who are saying comic things.

Many Shakespeare plays are familiar, but we have the chance of seeing how they were staged for the first time, with the actors they were written for. We can see *A Midsummer Night's Dream*, with the comic scene when Bottom is turned into an ass and is seduced by Titania, who has been fooled into thinking he's handsome. Or Jaques in *As You Like It*, taking his place on the stage and declaiming: 'All the world's a stage,/ And all the men and women merely players.' Or Shylock in *The Merchant of Venice* demanding his pound of flesh, but then appealing to our humanity: 'If you prick us do we not bleed?' Or in *The Tempest*, Ariel being hoist up in the air by using the backstage theatre machinery and Prospero's giving his 'We are such stuff as dreams are made on...' speech. Or the balcony scene from the star-crossed lovers of *Romeo and Juliet*, when she cries out: 'O Romeo,

Romeo, wherefore art thou Romeo?' *The Winter's Tale* includes the most famous stage direction in Shakespeare's work: 'Exit, pursued by bear.' Now how do they stage that?

Most thrilling of all, we can watch Shakespeare's great tragedies as they are first staged. We can watch the bearded Richard Burbage, Alleyn's great rival, playing King Lear on the blasted heath: 'Blow, winds, and crack your cheeks', and then see Gloucester, Lear's companion, being blinded on stage — how is that done? Or see the witches in Macbeth: 'When shall we three meet again?/ In thunder, lightning or in rain?' Although it is played in broad daylight, it's a play of dark deeds, with Burbage as Macbeth seeing a vision of the ghost of his victim Banquo slipping into his chair at the banquet scene, or the boy playing Lady Macbeth washing blood from her hands as she sleepwalks, her mind unhinged. In *Othello*, what do Elizabethan audiences make of seeing a black man as the tragic hero while the evil character, Iago, is white? We know that Burbage is applauded for playing the 'grieved Moor', and that a staging in Oxford in 1610 moves spectators to tears, but which boy plays Desdemona? And what about *Hamlet*, the bard's longest play and his masterpiece: in its printed version it lasts five hours so which bits are cut for a typical performance? Look closely at Burbage when he plays the Prince of Denmark delivering the most famous soliloquy in the history of theatre: 'To be, or not to be.'

Shakespeare never sets his plays in Elizabethan London, but he does make a unique contribution to the way we see ourselves. He writes ten history plays, about kings, wars and battles for the crown. As well as discussing the nature of power, they are also Tudor propaganda, the winner's version of history. His *Richard II* shows how the corrupt king is overthrown by Henry Bolingbroke, his cousin, who becomes Henry IV. The play includes a deeply patriotic speech by the dying John of Gaunt.

Then, in the two parts of *Henry IV*, Shakespeare creates the immensely popular figure of Falstaff, a hugely fat, cowardly and drunken knight. Falstaff becomes the friend of Prince Hal, the son and heir of Henry IV. They drink, make merry and get up to all kinds of disorder. Queen Elizabeth loves Falstaff, and asks Shakespeare to write a play about his love life (he obliges with *The Merry Wives of Windsor*). But Prince Hal, after the old king dies, rejects Falstaff, and becomes a conquering hero: Henry V. In the play that bears his name, he leads the English to a great victory against the French at Agincourt in 1415. On the way there Henry attacks the enemy at Harfleur, leading his soldiers: 'Once more unto the breach, dear friends, once more'; a speech which ends with the rousing 'Follow your spirit, and upon this charge/ Cry "God for Harry, England, and Saint George!"'

William Shakespeare's *Richard II* (1595)
John of Gaunt's deathbed speech:
This royal throne of kings, this scepter'd isle,
This earth of majesty, this seat of Mars,
This other Eden, demi-paradise,
This fortress built by Nature for herself
Against infection and the hand of war,
This happy breed of men, this little world,
This precious stone set in the silver sea,
Which serves it in the office of a wall,
Or as a moat defensive to a house,
Against the envy of less happier lands,
This blessed plot, this earth, this realm, this England.

But Henry V dies young. Then, after the bloody chaos of the Wars of the Roses, shown in the three parts of *Henry VI*, the last play of the history cycle is *Richard III*, which begins with the spine-tingling speech 'Now is the winter of our discontent made glorious summer by this son of York'. Richard III is one of theatre's most notorious villains, killing all rivals, including the young Princes in the Tower. But he ends badly, at the battle of Bosworth Field, when after failing to make his getaway — 'A horse, a horse, my kingdom for a horse' — he is killed by Henry Tudor, who becomes king Henry VII and is Queen Elizabeth's grandfather.

By the time he retires in 1613, Shakespeare has turned what was, for all its energy and gore, a rather crude form of theatre into a highly sophisticated and deeply expressive art form. His dramas are a theatre gold standard. Although little is known of his personal opinions, he does occasionally get his fingers burnt. When he writes the *Henry IV* plays, he names the fat knight character Sir John Oldcastle. The trouble is that there was a real Sir John Oldcastle, who was a Protestant martyr burned by the Catholics in 1417. And his proud descendants aren't happy with Shakespeare's portrait of him as a greedy drunk. They complain and the Master of the Revels Edmund Tilney forces the bard to change the name to Falstaff. Another play, called *Sir Thomas More*, to which Shakespeare contributed, is about a Catholic martyr, a dodgy subject in Protestant England, and the manuscript of the play has censorious notes by Tilney. On the first leaf, he writes: 'Leave out the insurrection wholly and the cause thereof.' In other words, he is censoring the opening scene, which is about riots against immigrants in London, because he thinks it might inflame audiences to attack other migrants.

'But wait a minute,' adds Walter suddenly, 'there's another story, this time about Shakespeare's sex life.' He rubs his hands. 'Actors have great sex appeal,' he says. Once, Richard Burbage is playing Richard III and a wealthy woman who fancies him invites him to her house discretely one night using as a password the name of his character. Shakespeare overhears the conversation, visits the woman and has sex with her. When a message is brought up that Richard III is at the front door, Shakespeare sends a note back saying that William the Conqueror came before Richard III.

We ask Walter more about Shakespeare. In all the biographies, there are several mysteries about his life: does he look like any of the portraits that have come down to us? What was he was doing in what the biographies call 'The Lost Years', 1585-92, and how did he get into theatre in the first place? What a chance to clear up one of history's great mysteries! What are his religious beliefs? What about his political opinions? How many plays did he collaborate on? Can we see the manuscript of *Cardenio*, his 'lost play'? And did he write a play called *Love's Labour's Won*? As an actor, did he really play the ghost of Hamlet's father? Walter fills us in on some of these secrets, but makes us swear to keep silent about them. And this we do.

Global triumph

It's Sunday morning and most people are at church as Walter walks us around an almost deserted Globe. In the yard in front of the stage a young man is sweeping up the rubbish left by the audience from the previous day. Walking around the Globe in the morning light, we can see that it's like the Theatre, whose massive timber beams were used in its construction, a polygon with an open-air yard and a platform stage that stays in the shade on summer afternoons to protect the actors. In order to save money, it has been built with a thatched roof.

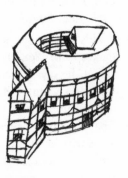

Walter takes us backstage to a room in the tiring house (the place where actors dress). The room is cramped, with stacks of baskets full of costumes. There are shelves with props — because the performances take place in broad daylight and there is no scenery, props are useful to help the audience understand what's happening. They include candlesticks (to illustrate night-time), skulls, crowns, parchment, plus assorted rapiers, halberds and muskets for battle scenes. Walter opens one of the baskets and takes out a cloak whose rich cloth and pearls take our breath away. He explains that these lavish costumes are a gift from a nobleman, and that they are worth a fortune. They need careful tending, but they are worth it. When an actor steps out dressed like this he draws all eyes. And one of the reasons people come to the theatre is its spectacle, especially royal spectacle. When Shakespeare's *Henry VIII* is staged at the Globe, there are some twenty-two actors on stage in some scenes, with trumpet blasts, gilded thrones, and pageantry. Audiences love it.

Walter shows us the scripts, which are the property of the theatre not the playwright (no copyright laws), and explains how each part is written out in full for each actor. Actors are overworked, performing between thirty and forty plays a year, learning their parts and often only giving one or two performances before the play is dropped if there is no interest. Every day a different play is staged. Only the very big hits — like Shakespeare's best — are constantly revived. This room is also where the boys in the company can change into their female costumes, which takes longer than for the men. And Walter draws our attention to the drums and pipes that provide the music.

But some of the things that happen to the Chamberlain's Men, resident company at the Globe, are no laughing matter. Leicester's stepson is the dashing Robert Devereux, the Earl of Essex, and although thirty years younger than the queen, he is a favourite until his headstrong disobedience causes his disgrace (in one incident the queen boxes his ears). In February 1601, he plans a comeback. One of his agents asks the Chamberlain's Men to stage Shakespeare's *Richard II* at the Globe for a special payment of £2. Essex uses this story of a king being deposed as a piece of propaganda to justify his attempt at a *coup d'etat*. The performance goes ahead, but Essex's uprising the following day attracts no popular support and the Earl is arrested, later beheaded. We notice that Walter fingers the skull on his ring again. Queen Elizabeth clearly understands the connection between political theatre and subversion. Walter reports that she is fond of saying, 'I am Richard II; know ye not that?' For a while, the fate of Shakespeare and the Chamberlain's Men hangs in the balance. But they are forgiven, and in the final years of Queen Elizabeth's reign they are the country's leading theatre company.

'Theatre entrepreneurs,' concludes Walter, 'are now in a good place.' They have a lot of freedom, and they follow the money: they stage plays that people want to see and which they will pay for; big crowds and big bucks. They are risk-takers of great practical experience and their companies — now numbering anything from twenty to thirty people — are commercial ventures. The manager makes the decisions, takes the risks and scoops the profits. Sometimes he owns the theatre, otherwise the main members of the company (playwrights and actors) invest in the building and become sharers, getting a cut of box office. They also hire a wider group of actors, who just get wages. And the boys who play all the female roles are employed by company members as apprentices. Around these members is a lot of activity: scriveners who copy out parts of plays (Walter smiles about this — it's a job he's done himself, in his younger days!); men and women who look after costumes; prop makers and painters; basket-makers who create wicker animal-head props; hands that provide food for actors; chaperones for the boys. 'It's time to drink a toast to all these men,' says Walter. We gladly join him and then accept his invitation to be introduced to his son, our next guide.

2
JACOBEAN THEATRE

2
Jacobean Theatre

Meet our guide: Wilt

Now our new guide, a young man in his early twenties whose name is Wilt Wickson, takes over from his father, Walter. There is yet another threat of plague hanging in the fetid London air and the old man has prudently decided to stay with family in the country. Wilt, who is a student of law at one of the Inns of Court, welcomes us just outside the fencing school at Ely Place in London's Holborn. He is a gentleman and has learned to fence here; he shows us the various kinds of swords and rapiers that are commonly worn and introduces us to his fencing master, an Italian called Giacomo. As we watch the maestro put a couple of students through their paces, we have time to acquaint ourselves with our new guide. He is dressed in sombre colours, wears a white ruff, and is full of restless energy, pacing up and down. He doesn't believe that the threat of disease is so serious, and says, 'I will stay in the capital to ride it out.' Something about his manner suggests that he finds living in the countryside a bit of a bore: the quiet pleasure of sitting in an orchard can't really compare to the fast pace of the capital's fleshpots. But his devil-may-care attitude is our gain. He has his ear close to the ground and is always on the look out for the latest theatrical news, or scandal. He dreams of being a poet, and finds inspiration in the rhythm of the verse he hears on stage. All of which make him a great guide to Jacobean theatre, telling us that on this trip we will be looking at the thespian scene from 1603 to the 1640s, from the reign of King James I to that of his son King Charles I.

Game of thrones

It's a new century, and the Scottish King James has come south to take his rightful place as the next monarch. Queen Elizabeth has died peacefully, at the age of sixty-nine, in March 1603, and because the Virgin Queen had no children James is next in line (from Margaret Tudor, Henry VIII's oldest sister). So it is that James VI of Scotland becomes James I of England. He is in his mid-thirties, the son of Elizabeth's rival and cousin Mary Queen of Scots, and is — Wilt informs us with a touch of glee — 'of slovenly appearance, with food stains on his clothes, and a habit of playing with his codpiece in public'. Wilt says that there are rumours that he is a tad too fond of his male favourites as well. There is gossip about his relationships with Robert Carr and George Villiers, whom he showers with gifts, including a peerage each. There's also an epigram in circulation: *Rex fuit Elizabeth, nunc est regina Jacobus*, which Wilt translates for us as, in everyday parlance, 'Elizabeth was king, now James is queen.' Wilt has seen the king and says that he walks in an odd, lurching motion and always looks awkward, but his mind is razor sharp. He has been king of Scotland from early childhood and has managed to survive the cut-throat politicking of that nation.

Wilt takes us to the City of London, now swelled to some quarter of a million people, to show us the fantastic triumphal arches that the authorities have built to welcome the new monarch in style. Although King James was crowned in July 1603, this ceremonial progress is staged on 15 March 1604 due to an outbreak of plague, which claims 30,000 lives, during the previous summer. So, after all, Walter, Wilt's father, was right to head for the country! The triumphal arches that Wilt shows us are amazingly elaborate constructions, carved with representations of London and allegorical figures depicting Divine Wisdom, British Monarchy and Father Thames. Several playwrights, such as Ben Jonson (though not William Shakespeare), write speeches that flatter King James and celebrate his accession to the throne.

One of the first things that King James does is to declare himself the patron of the nation's theatre. His cultural manifesto is to have more theatre at court and to support the most important theatre companies. His aim is to be a good patron of the arts. But he's also keen on control. As a result, the great nobles are no longer allowed to be patrons of their own companies and these companies in turn become the exclusive preserve of the royal family. Thus the

Chamberlain's Men get a name change. They become the King's Men. So Shakespeare's new patron is the king and the bard becomes a member of the royal household, with the right to wear the king's scarlet livery. Needless to say, the actors' status rises. The King's Men are often asked to perform at court, almost twenty times a year, more than Queen Elizabeth ever commanded. And Shakespeare writes *Macbeth* — the Scottish play — especially for the new Scottish monarch. King James's family also claim their share of the main theatre companies: his wife, Queen Anne, gets her own company of actors, the Queen's Men, and the couple's royal sons also have troupes named after them: Prince Henry's Men (formerly the Admiral's Men) and Prince Charles's Men. And finally their sister Princess Elizabeth gets a company of her own in 1610. Thus there are five companies under royal patronage.

Rare Ben Jonson

Wilt takes us to Bartholomew Fair, London's most important summer festival. It is August and we are in the precincts of the Priory at Smithfield in the parish of St Bartholomew the Great. All around us is a carnival atmosphere: we can see puppet shows, dancing bears, performing monkeys and caged tigers competing for attention with tight-rope walkers and fire-eaters. In one tent, an astrologer is casting a horoscope and in another a quack doctor offers medicines for all ailments. There is noise and confusion everywhere. Wilt, who is moving with his customary briskness, warns us to guard against pickpockets and says that any tent with the sign 'Soiled Doves' means prostitutes. The smell of roasting pork, beer and tobacco hangs in the air, while crowds of excited people buy toys, gingerbread, mousetraps, puppies and singing birds. At one point Wilt recognizes someone in the crowd and draws our attention to a stocky, sweating, dishevelled man who is moving between the stalls, with several books under his arm. 'He is Ben Jonson,' says Wilt, 'Shakespeare's leading rival, and the author of *Bartholomew Fair*, a comedy whose climax takes place at the very fair that we are enjoying.'

Blessed with the biggest and most quarrelsome ego in theatre, Jonson is a self-taught classical scholar, an opinionated satirist, a

BEN JONSON

Born: around 11 June 1572.

Family: Son of Protestant minister who dies before
Ben is born; mother remarries a London bricklayer.

Education: St Martin's parish school then Westminster
school, paid by an unknown patron. At Westminster he's
influenced by classical scholar William Camden and acquires
a passion for academic study.

Private Life: At seventeen works briefly as a bricklayer under his
stepfather, then serves in the army in the Netherlands. In 1594, marries
Anne Lewis; their four children die young.

Career: After marriage, begins work as a freelance playwright. Under
King James, Jonson receives royal favour and a substantial pension:
England's first Poet Laureate, with honours from Oxford
University. His admirers call themselves the Tribe of Ben.
In 1616 he publishes a folio volume of his works — shameless
self-promotion.

Greatest Hits: *Every Man in His Humour* (1597), *Volpone* (1605), *The
Alchemist* (1610), *Bartholomew Fair* (1614) and *The Devil Is an Ass* (1616).

Scandal: In 1598, Jonson kills actor Gabriel Spencer in a
duel; tried for murder. He pleads 'benefit of clergy'
(medieval loophole which allows you to escape hanging if you
can read Latin). Released but branded on thumb with a T
(for Tyburn, place of execution). Imprisoned other times for writing
political satires.

Death: 6 August 1637.

Epitaph: Crowds of mourners attend his burial at Westminster Abbey;
plain slab with engraving: 'O Rare Ben Jonson!'

self-advertising freelancer, and a poet and playwright of remarkable lyricism and vigour. He rocks! His poems include savage attacks on all the vices of society. One in particular is pretty forthright in his intentions: 'I am at feud/ With sin and vice.' Another poem criticizes a court lady for taking an abortion pill. When it comes to the stage, his best work is about contemporary London; his plays have the tang of the here and now. They are full of recognizable characters: puritans, servants, tradesmen, widows and mothers-in-law. He has a whole new theory of comedy and excels in showing confidence tricksters on stage. And he loves theatrical jokes. His *Bartholomew Fair* begins with the stage-keeper, broom in hand, chatting informally with the audience, telling them that the play will be worthless. Jonson also pens an 'Ode to Himself', which begins: 'Come leave the loathéd stage,/ And the more loathsome age,/ Where pride and impudence in faction knit/ Usurp the chair of wit,/ Indicting and arraigning, every day,/ Something they call a play.'

THEATRE THEORY: JONSON'S IDEA OF COMEDY

Ben Jonson pioneers the idea of the comedy of humours. He thinks of a stage character in terms of humours, which is the Renaissance word for a trait or passion, such as greed or lust, which defines a person's character. Because Jonson writes satires and comedies, he deliberately exaggerates these humours until his characters are solely motivated by them. Of course, he argues that he is doing this not just because he wants to entertain his audience, but also because he has a moral objection to vice, and he is on a mission to purge the vices and cure the bad behaviour of his age. His two key humours plays are *Every Man in His Humour* (1598) and *Every Man Out of His Humour* (1599). Jonson's example of comedy with a moral slant is much imitated by other British dramatists in the following centuries.

Among Jonson's best plays is *The Alchemist*, first performed by the King's Men in salubrious Oxford during yet another ugly outbreak of plague in London in 1610. The play is very topical, opening with an exposé of vice and folly. The story is this: a visitation of pestilence forces a gentleman, Lovewit, to flee to the country, leaving his house in the hands of his butler, who promptly assumes the persona of the fictitious Captain Face and proceeds to use the place for acts of fraud. As his partners in crime, he enlists the aid of Subtle, a fellow conman who pretends to be an alchemist, and Doll Common, a prostitute. The play opens at top speed with a violent argument between Subtle and Face concerning the division of the spoils: when threatened, Subtle tells Face: 'I fart at thee.' Jonson then shows how these three try to con various people with, among other inducements, the promise of turning base material into gold, thus exposing the folly of greed-induced credulity. *The Alchemist* becomes one of his most popular plays, although one member of the original audience, Henry Jackson (an Oxford fellow), records his disgust. He writes that although the play got 'great applause', the actors were 'not content with attacking alchemists, they most foully violated the sacred scriptures themselves'.

Ben Jonson's *Volpone* (1605)
Mosca describes his shape-shifting talents:
But your fine elegant rascal, that can rise,
And stoop, almost together, like an arrow
Shoot through the air as nimbly as a star
Turn short as doth a swallow; and be here,
And there, and here, and yonder, all at once;
Present to any humour, all occasion;
And change a visor, swifter than a thought!
This is the creature had the art born with him,
Toils not to learn it, but doth practise it
Out of most excellent nature: and such sparks
Are the true parasites, others but their zanies.

Ben Jonson

Likewise, *Volpone, or The Fox* (performed at the Globe in 1606 with Richard Burbage utterly convincing in the title role) is today regarded as a masterpiece. Despite being set in Venice, the real target of the play is the rising merchant class of London, some of whom are in the audience. A merciless satire of greed and lust, the play is full of rogues with animal names: Volpone (fox), Mosca (house fly), Voltore (vulture), Corbaccio (raven) and Corvino (crow). Here, human beings are as ferocious as animals. Volpone pretends to be at death's door in the hope of getting money from his friends, who in turn hope for a legacy after he dies. Mosca acts as go-between, but he too is deceiving Volpone and all the others who he pretends to serve. Mosca is the über parasite, adopting a different face depending on who he's dealing with. Jonson summaries the plot in an acrostic, which Wilt — who likes clever word play — appreciates. The play, which opens with Volpone literally worshiping gold as if it is a religious idol, is a satire on the obsessive pursuit of wealth in a society where rapid economic growth has led to more social inequality. Merchants prosper, but craftsmen suffer. The ending reveals Jonson's moral purpose: Volpone's possessions are confiscated and Mosca is sentenced to serve as a galley slave for life. Jonson explains that he made the punishment harsh to appease those who say that vice is rarely punished on stage. Needless to say, *Volpone* is an immediate and resounding success.

Ben Jonson's *Volpone* acrostic
V olpone, childless, rich, feigns sick, despairs,
O ffers his state to hopes of several heirs,
L ies languishing; his parasite receives
P resents of all, assures, deludes; then weaves
O ther cross-plots, which open themselves, are told.
N ew tricks for safety are sought; they thrive; when, bold,
E ach tempts th'other again, and all are sold.

Ego-heavy Jonson is so complacent that, despite being in King James's good books, in 1605 he collaborates with George Chapman and John Marston to write *Eastward Ho!*, a satire on social climbing which includes some jokes about the arrival of rough and smelly Scots in London in the wake of the new king. This causes a stir at court and the Master of the Revels arrests the writers and threatens to cut off their ears and noses. In the end, they are set free but it's a narrow escape. As for King James, he's just happy that these theatre laddies know who's boss. But other forces are also at work: Puritan disapproval is on the rise. The influence of religious fundamentalists is growing, especially after the foiled Gunpowder Plot — in which a group of Catholics planned to blow up King James and his entire parliament. With Catholics confirmed as enemies of the state, the Puritans appear as loyal defenders of Protestantism, the true religion. So their sensibilities must be appeased. In 1606 'An Act to Restrain the Abuses of Players' is passed and it bans swearing on stage — especially expressions such as 'God's wounds' or 'By God' — for being, er, ungodly. This is a blow against playwrights, many of whom now have to rewrite their plays, cutting out these oaths. Also under threat are the cheerful vulgarities of the past — typically, in Thomas Dekker's popular *The Shoemaker's Holiday* (a Rose Theatre hit from 1599), the hero Simon Eyre says to his wife, 'Where's Cicely Bumtrinket, your maid? She has a privy fault: she farts in her sleep.' But the Puritans aren't laughing, and their influence extends all over the country. In 1602 the authorities in Stratford-upon-Avon ban touring companies from playing there, and, nearer home, the Middlesex magistrates ban 'lewd jigs' at the Fortune theatre after complaints about them being obscene.

Theatreland expands

Now it's time to visit Bankside. Wilt leads us across London Bridge, an imposing hulk of an edifice of twenty arches, with six-storey houses and a hundred shops built on it. Think medieval, think Gormenghast. At its south end is the Great Stone Gate, where the decaying heads of executed traitors are displayed on pikes, to be picked at by birds. We shudder and hurry on. Our trusty guide takes us to a respectable-looking tavern in this otherwise seedy part of town, which is both a red-light district and a place of blood-sports. But Wilt knows us well enough by now to avoid suggesting a trip to view the bear-baiting. When we are seated around a wooden table, with cups of small beer (watered down ale that is safer to drink than water), he takes a piece of chalk out of his pocket and boldly draws an aerial view of the river Thames. We recognize its snake-like shape at once. Now Wilt takes a chess set from a nearby table and, using the pieces to represent the open-air venues, shows us how London's theatreland is developing.

South of the river, where we are at the moment, there's the Globe: Wilt puts down the chess-piece king — here's where the

PROTESTANTS AND CATHOLICS

In the early seventeenth century, the tensions between Protestants and Catholics escalate. They had emerged in the previous century, when Queen Elizabeth's older half-sister, Queen Mary, a Catholic, had vigorously persecuted Protestants, burning hundreds of them for heresy. Then, after Queen Mary's death in 1558, the Protestant Queen Elizabeth is excommunicated by the Pope, and plots against her life — with the plan of bringing the Catholic Mary Queen of Scots to the throne of England — became common. This means that Catholics are seen not only as heretical, but also as treacherous. These bitter conflicts are then fuelled by fears of invasion by the Catholic Spanish Armada in 1588. In King James's reign, the Gunpowder Plot — in which a group of Catholics, which include Guy Fawkes, conspire to blow up the Houses of Parliament — intensify these fears. After the king's death, the marriage of his heir, King Charles I, to the French Catholic Henrietta Maria leads to suspicions that the Popish religion is infiltrating the highest reaches of power. Meanwhile, the radical Protestants, or Puritans, militantly agitate for reform of the Church of England. These religious disputes lead to the outbreak of the Civil War, the dictatorship of Oliver Cromwell and the Puritans, and the execution of King Charles in 1649.

King's Men have their base. Nearby, there's the Rose, represented by a rook, and then there's a new venue, the Hope theatre, another rook, which Wilt tells us was built in 1605 as a multi-use venue that can be easily converted into a bear-baiting arena when there are not enough audiences for theatre. Turning to north of the river, Wilt uses a knight to show us where the Fortune theatre stands, a square-shaped venue built in 1600 at a location not very far from where the Theatre once stood. This is the venue of Prince Henry's Men (although his patronage doesn't last very long for he is struck down by typhoid fever at the age of eighteen). Another piece shows the position of the old Curtain theatre, where Prince Charles's Men move to. Charles is quite a serious, religious boy, so Wilt uses a bishop chess piece to represent this venue. The queen chess piece indicates the position of the Red Bull (1604), a conversion of an inn yard in Clerkenwell, another red-light district and a venue soon to be notorious for its rowdy audiences. This is the home of Queen Anne's Men.

London audiences, which once were fairly similar at each venue, a mix of gallants and grooms, wives and whores, are now becoming more diversified. North of the river, at the Red Bull and Fortune, theatregoers are more working class than those that go to watch Shakespeare's plays at the Globe on Bankside. They want conservative family values and cheery, brash patriotic plays. They are called citizen playhouses and become home to city comedy, a genre set in contemporary London usually concerning marriage and money, with, in Jonson's words, 'deeds and language such as men do use' in daily life. There, each show ends with a raucous jig. By contrast, the Globe's audiences are more classy, a mix of politicians, merchants and lawyers. And the jig has been dropped from each afternoon's programme because it is too rowdy for sophisticated tastes.

Built mainly of wood, these theatres are vulnerable to fire. Right on cue, on 29 June 1613, a spark from a turret cannon during a performance of Shakespeare's *Henry VIII* ignites a fire on the Globe's thatched roof and the venue burns down. 'Luckily there are no casualties,' says Wilt, 'although there is one man whose breeches catch fire, and he saves himself by pouring a bottle of beer on his legs.' The Globe is rebuilt the following year, this time with a tiled roof as a precaution. Wilt reckons that rumours have it that this fire is what persuades Shakespeare to retire from the stage. Then, on 9 December 1621, the Fortune burns down in the space of two hours. A risky business indeed.

At the same time, while British conquests are gradually making their mark on Ireland and North America, theatre becomes an exportable commodity. Over the water in Dublin, a British colony, there's the first performance of a play: it's *Gorboduc*, Britain's first Elizabethan drama in blank verse, staged at Dublin Castle. And already Shakespeare's work knows no bounds: in 1607, William Keeling, sea captain of the *Dragon* (bound for the East Indies), drops anchor off Sierra Leone in Africa. He orders his men to perform *Hamlet*.

Indoor theatres

The winter of 1608 is so cold that the Thames freezes solid and Wilt takes us on it by foot, showing us the various activities of the frost fair: the ice is thick enough for festivals to be held and there are booths selling food and goods, along with entertainment. We see the population in all its lively variety, from fine gentlemen and ladies in their capes and decorated hats, to ordinary artisans in coats and cloth caps, with the occasional beggar freezing in rags. Then we move into the City of London to discover the answer to the outstanding problem of London theatres: the weather. The drawback of open-air theatres is that if the weather is cold or rainy, the show becomes a painful endurance test for actors and audiences alike. So the idea of indoor theatre grows more and more attractive. In 1608, the actor-manager Richard Burbage finally succeeds where his father failed: he gets permission to stage shows at the indoor Blackfriars Theatre.

There had been indoor performances before, at royal palaces, at the Inns of Court, at the universities, but Blackfriars is the first permanent indoor theatre. As such, it is a blueprint for the theatre of the future. Entrance costs six pence — more than the penny at the outdoor venues — and the best seats are anything from one shilling and six pence (eighteen pence) to two shillings and six pence (thirty pence). So it attracts a more elite audience. With 600 seats, and lit by candles, it is a more intimate and magical place than the open-air yards that hold thousands.

When Wilt, who has changed into his best black clothes, takes us to see a show there, we are struck by how dark the auditorium is compared to today's electric-lit venues. The tallow candles cast a yellow light but it's hard to make out the faces of performers, so although it's more atmospheric than an outdoor venue, it's also more difficult to see. At the same time, it's more glamorous, with its finely dressed audience showing off the latest fashions: feathers, hair styles and so on. Jewels sparkle in the candlelight. The cheeks of the boys playing women shine with the dust of crushed pearls. Their costumes use glowing silver thread. Instead of trumpets blaring in the open air the indoor theatres have the sweet music of strings and woodwinds. And while the cheapest places in the open-air theatres are those nearest the stage, here the closest seats are the most expensive. Even better, for an extra payment, spectators can sit on a stool on the stage and be seen by everybody. 'But,' Wilt tells us in a conspiratorial whisper, 'at last night's performance things went too far. A nobleman got up and walked through the actors to greet a friend in the stalls. When an actor remonstrated, the nobleman slapped him — and the audience rose in uproar.'

In Queen Elizabeth's day, these indoor theatres had been home to boy bands, such as the Chapel Children, who played at the converted Buttery at Blackfriars monastery, and the Paul's Boys at St Paul's cathedral. Here plays were provided by professional playwrights, such as Ben Jonson. Such companies of boys, whose voices had not yet broken, were encouraged by the queen. Recruitment was sometimes a problem, with stories circulating about boys being sold into the job by their parents, or even kidnapped. The boys had to impersonate adults of all ages, wearing false beards and padded bosoms, and there was more than a touch of sexual ambivalence about seeing them playing nubile young women or corrupt grown-ups. Some boy actors, such as Nathan Field, later joined adult companies (in his case, the King's Men).

The Blackfriars theatre became home to the Blackfriars Boys, who could get away with performing sophisticated burlesques — full of satire and sexual innuendo — because they were more respectable than the common adult companies. But the

Blackfriars Boys are disbanded in 1608 when they overstep the mark by staging George Chapman's *Conspiracy and Tragedy of Charles, Duke of Byron*, a play about the French court, which includes a scene in which the French Queen slaps the face of her husband's mistress. The French Ambassador complains to the king about this outrage and the company is suppressed. Their demise gives actor and impresario Burbage his chance.

THEATRE THEORY: THE FIVE-ACT PLAY

The move to indoor theatres means that playwrights pay more attention to composing plays that have five acts (in imitation of classical examples such as Seneca). Between each act is an interlude, with music, for trimming candles. Each act has a different function: in Jacobean tragedy, the first act is Exposition (often by a ghost, who tells the avenger about the death he has to avenge); second, Anticipation (planning the revenge); third, Confrontation (avenger meets murderer); fourth, Complication (avenger runs into problems); fifth, dénouement (avenger kills murderer, often dying in the process). In the hands of a master penman, this scheme can be further complicated by the adding of various subplots (often comic). Or by playing with the form itself: in *Hamlet*, for example, Hamlet fails to immediately plan his revenge and instead delays things by pretending to be mad and trying to establish for certain the guilt of the murderer Claudius. Audiences appreciate these slight variations on the form of the play.

The acquisition of the Blackfriars indoor theatre by Burbage and the King's Men is a big financial boost: the company now has two venues, two potential audiences, two income streams, and somewhere to play when the weather is dire. Soon a pattern emerges with the company playing at the outdoor Globe in the summer and the indoor Blackfriars during the winter. This makes the King's Men the country's preeminent theatre company. It also means that Shakespeare's last plays are written with the new possibilities offered by indoor performance in mind. While outdoor theatres stage plays without a break, indoor theatre has to have short interludes between the customary five acts of a story to allow for the candle wicks to be trimmed. During these breaks, music is performed. Spectacular and magical effects, such as the colourful masque in *The Tempest* and the descent of Jupiter in *Cymbeline*, work better indoors.

There are other indoor theatres. In 1616, the former boy actor and by now rather dodgy entrepreneur Christopher Beeston opens the Cockpit Theatre in Drury Lane, the first theatre in the West End (an area of London which will have a great theatrical future), and moves his company from the Red Bull to this richer location. This copy of the Blackfriars theatre is soon the haunt of lawyers and students, and Wilt is a regular visitor there, spending many a cold afternoon warming his young bones at this venue. But disaster soon strikes. On Shrove Tuesday, a mob of apprentices breaks into the building and torches the place. They are angry because wideboy Beeston has transferred plays that only cost them one penny at the Red Bull to the Cockpit, where they now cost six pence. During the ensuing riot, one person is killed and many injured. Undaunted, however, Beeston rebuilds the venue, naming it the Phoenix (Greek mythical bird that rises from the ashes), but it is still frequently referred to as the Cockpit. Beeston carries on, offering strong competition to the Blackfriars by staging the work of fashionable playwrights such as John Ford and James Shirley. But, our guide reminds us, the brightest star of the new generation of playwrights is John Webster.

Webster's way

Like other playwrights of the time, Webster studied briefly as a lawyer, and Wilt has met him. He says, 'He's a very introverted bloke, and keeps himself to himself.' After collaborating with other playwrights on a series of comedies about everyday life in London, Webster turns to tragedy, writing two masterpieces: *The White Devil* and *The Duchess of Malfi*. Wilt, like some of his other contemporaries, is a bit puzzled by this change of course, which he puts down to the rather melancholic streak in the playwright's character. Webster is a bit of a punk, a rebel without a cause, who brings a punchy dark poetry to seventeenth-century theatre. In *The*

Born: Unknown, around 1579.

Family: Son of John, a London coach-maker, and
Elizabeth Coates, a blacksmith's daughter.

Education: Merchant Taylors School, London.

Private life: No image of him survives. Marries seventeen-year-old Sara
Peniall on 18 March 1606 in Islington. She's pregnant and their son,
John, born soon after.

Career: In his early twenties joins Philip Henslowe
at the Rose theatre.

Greatest hits: *The White Devil* (1612)
and *The Duchess of Malfi* (1613).

Scandal: None known.

Death: Unknown, around 1634.

Epitaph: In his poem 'Whispers of Immortality',
twentieth-century poet T S Eliot says that Webster always
saw 'the skull beneath the skin'.

White Devil, for example, the doomed protagonist Vittoria says: 'Know this, and let it somewhat raise your spite,/ Through darkness diamonds spread their richest light.' Both plays are set in Italy and *The Duchess of Malfi* tells the story of a young widow whose brothers — a duke and a cardinal — forbid her from remarrying. They order Bosola, a hit man, to watch over her. When she disobeys them by remarrying well below her station, Bosola tells them and they chase, torture and kill her, with the stage soon littered with bodies, including those of her husband and children. Like Webster's best work, it is a dark study of obsession, sex and madness. Memorable moments include the scene in which Bosola tests whether the Duchess is pregnant by giving her apricots (thought to induce labour) and a chorus of madmen, introduced by 'Oh Let Us Howl' — a fittingly discordant song. In another scene, the duke presents his sister with waxwork corpses of her family to convince her they have died, then he finally goes mad, believing he's a wolf man. The cardinal makes his mistress kiss the Bible and then reveals that it is covered with poison. Finally faced with death, the Duchess retains her dignity, saying, 'I am Duchess of Malfi still.' Likewise, in the end Bosola acknowledges the power of fate, 'We are merely the stars' tennis balls, struck and banded which way please them.'

In Wilt's view, Webster is cast into despair by the dismally tragic realization that our fault is in the stars.

> John Webster's *The Duchess of Malfi* (1613)
> *The Duchess of Malfi faces death:*
> What would it pleasure me to have my throat cut
> With diamonds? or to be smothered
> With cassia? or to be shot to death with pearls?
> I know death hath ten thousand several doors
> For men to take their exits; and 'tis found
> They go on such strange geometrical hinges,
> You may open them both ways: any way, for heaven-sake,
> So I were out of your whispering. Tell my brothers
> That I perceive death, now I am well awake,
> Best gift is they can give or I can take.
> I would fain put off my last woman's-fault,
> I'd not be tedious to you.

Although Webster labours long and hard to craft his plays, he soon learns that different theatre venues and different audiences can make or break your play. *The White Devil* is first staged in 1612 at the open-air Red Bull, and its mainly working-class audience is baffled by Webster's clever word play and refined sensibility. It's a flop. In exasperation, Webster calls the audience 'donkeys'. By contrast, his *The Duchess of Malfi* gets a good production by the King's Men at the indoor Blackfriars in 1614 and this indoor theatre's more intimate atmosphere and more educated audience appreciates his work. If Webster gives the genre of revenge drama a shot in the arm, he is not alone. With plays such as John Marston's *The Malcontent* and Thomas Middleton's *The Revenger's Tragedy*, Jacobean audiences can enjoy the spectacle of an avenger bringing justice to a brutally unjust world. As Vindice, the avenger in Middleton's play says, 'When the bad bleed, then is the tragedy good.'

Golden age of playwriting

Wilt is a bit of a bookworm, and a budding man of letters, so he spends one morning showing us how playwrights prepare their writing materials, trimming their goose-feather quills and preparing ink from ground oak-tree galls. Then he takes us to the best place in the capital where we can buy their printed play texts. So we go to St Paul's cathedral, a hub of sociable activity. The building is in bad repair, with crumbling masonry and soot-stained walls. Its gothic spire was toppled by lightning in 1561 and has never been rebuilt. The churchyard and the surrounding streets are like a gigantic market, with stall after stall selling all manner of goods. 'It's also the place where the Gunpowder plotters were executed,' says our guide, always on hand to provide such details. Now there's a crowd of people gossiping, talking and buying. Skillfully making his way through the throng, Wilt leads us to a nearby bookseller, at the Sign of the Gun, one of several local shops offering books and pamphlets. 'Book production,' he says, 'is booming': about three thousand books are published every year, double the amount of twenty years earlier. Bestsellers include the newly translated Authorised Version of the Bible, which is now read at home as well as in church, and *Foxe's Book of Martyrs*, which tells stories of the victims of the Catholic Queen Mary's persecutions.

As we walk inside the shop we see a large printing press. In the confined space, there is a heady smell of ink. The process works like this: the compositor arranges four pages of type in one block, called a form; the press man covers this with ink and prints it on the hand press; then he gives it to the proof-reader who checks it while the other man carries on printing. Paper is extremely expensive so even if the proof-reader finds some spelling mistakes, the printed sheets are still used in the final book. Although some playwrights, such as Ben Jonson, have a reputation for fanatical proof-reading, there are many copies of their books which include mistakes. On display in the shop are copies of printed plays. These are not the heavyweight Folio volumes but smaller, paperback-sized books called quartos.

On one table is a copy of *Arden of Faversham*, a tragedy about the murder of Thomas Arden, a businessman and mayor, by his wife and her lover, which dramatises a sensational real-life crime which happened in Kent in 1551. Another real-life case is a docudrama called *The Witch of Edmonton*, a collaboration by William Rowley,

Thomas Dekker and John Ford. This tells the 'true story' of Elizabeth Sawyer, an old woman shunned by her neighbours and finally executed for witchcraft. Like other plays about witchcraft, it is very popular. Then there is a popular satire, *The Knight of the Burning Pestle*, in which the upper-class toffs Francis Beaumont and John Fletcher mock the taste of the rising middle classes. Next to these is a printed version of Shakespeare's *Richard II* in which, Wilt points out, the king's involuntary abdication scene is absent. We gather that the Revels Office thought it might give people subversive ideas: if one monarch can be deposed, why not another? Our guide also tells us that in the first five years that Shakespeare's plays were published people didn't care who wrote what: his name did not appear on the title page. It's not until the second decade of the seventeenth century that plays become valued as literature, to be read as well as performed. Gradually, their authors become appreciated by a wider public. By now, as more and more young people read plays, some stage-struck students also keep engraved portraits of their favourite authors in their studies: the age of literary celebrity has truly begun...

This is a golden age for playgoing. About 20,000 Londoners visit theatres every week, and there is an enormous demand for new plays. Between 1560 and 1640, more than 3000 plays are written and it's hard to keep track of them all. Some playwrights claim to have written dozens of shows: the industrious Thomas Heywood says he's penned, or contributed to, 220 plays, but is mainly remembered for just one: *A Woman Killed with Kindness*, which is a popular domestic tragedy about an adulterous wife. Many plays are written by two or more playwrights in collaboration. The most famous writing team is Francis Beaumont and John Fletcher, who together pen about fifteen plays and fifty-five between them. Their collaboration is pretty intense: for six years, they share the same lodgings, the same clothes, the same bed and the same mistress. What's more, although the prolific Fletcher is fifteen years younger than Shakespeare, and comes from a higher social class, the two men collaborate on some of the bard's last plays. Then in 1611, Fletcher takes on the senior playwright by writing a sequel to the bard's *The Taming of the Shrew*, one of his most patriarchal plays. Calling it *The Woman's Prize; or, The Tamer Tamed*, Fletcher shows what happens to Petruccio, the main male character, after the end of Shakespeare's play. He changes the sexual politics of the original and shows women getting the better of men. Shakespeare doesn't mind, and he must have a sense of humour because this sequel is performed by the King's Men, his company. After Shakespeare's retirement, Fletcher becomes their house playwright.

ENEMIES OF THEATRE: THE PURITANS

The Puritans keep up the pressure on theatres and step up their campaign against all entertainments. In 1632 Puritan activist William Prynne attacks dancing as a 'Devil's Mass' and women actors as 'notorious whores' in his book *Histriomastix*. However, because women at the time are not allowed on public stages, who could he possibly have in mind? Most readers realize that this is a personal attack on King Charles's wife, Queen Henrietta Maria, who has been known to perform in court masques and is therefore a female actor. But the royals soon get their revenge: Prynne is taken to court, condemned to the pillory, and has his ears cut off.

Some collaborations achieve a legendary status: in 1607, Middleton and Dekker write *The Roaring Girl*, which celebrates the character of Moll Cutpurse, a cross-dresser, thief and brawler. Moll wears men's clothing and a woodcut shows this 'notorious baggage' holding a sword and smoking a clay pipe. Staged by Prince Henry's Men, she is based on a real character. A couple of years before, a court hears the case of Mary Firth, the real-life Moll Cutpurse, who appeared on stage in male attire at the Fortune theatre and sang bawdy songs while playing a lute. This makes her one of the first female performers in the history of British theatre. Mary becomes so notorious that audience members who have had their pockets picked come to her to see if she can get their property back. They really believe that Firth knows everyone who's anyone in London's shady underworld.

Among audiences, tragedy remains popular. A typical tragedy will have a self-destructive protagonist and will show corruption in high places. It will often feature the swordplay that Wilt showed us when we first met him. In 1622, *The Changeling*, by Thomas Middleton and William Rowley, is a murder story set among the Spanish nobility, and in 1629, *'Tis Pity She's a Whore*, by John Ford, is a story about incest among the Italian nobility. Both are staged at the Cockpit theatre. At all venues, the public, as well as loving poetry, has a delight in gore and in grotesque methods of mutilation and murder. The world of these tragedies is like a butcher's shop, a charnel house: constant revivals of Shakespeare's *Titus Andronicus* keep audiences glued to the stage as Lavinia is raped and then her tongue and hands are cut off to prevent her from revealing who did it. One of the play's grim stage directions reads 'Enter a messenger with two heads and a hand'; another character, the Queen of the Goths, has to eat a pie baked with the flesh of her two sons. In Marlowe's *Edward II*, the king is dispatched by a hot poker stuck up his rectum. In Middleton's *The Revenger's Tragedy* Vindice dresses up the skull of his dead lover, paints its lips with poison and then gets the Duke to kiss it. At the climax of Ford's *'Tis Pity She's a Whore*, Giovanni bursts onto the stage with his sister's heart speared on his sword. In Cyril Tourneur's *The Atheist's Tragedy*, the avenger dies when he raises an axe to kill the malefactor — but trips up and knocks his own brains out! It's a crazy, gory age.

A Swiss visitor, Thomas Platter, notes that many people also go to the theatre for news about current affairs. So when in 1624 the idea of a royal marriage between Prince Charles, King James's son and heir, and the Spanish Infanta is mooted, many disapprove because ever since the Spanish Armada that Catholic country has been viewed with suspicion. So crowds flock to see a play, Thomas Middleton's notorious *A Game at Chess*, because it is a political satire aimed at the Spanish ambassador. It is a sensation, playing to packed, rollicking houses at the Globe for nine days in a row, an amazing record. Taking the mickey out of foreign Catholics pays off. But after Spanish protests to the king, Middleton is imprisoned for breaking the rule that no living king or nobleman can be derided on stage. He is ruined: this is his last play.

The key achievement of this golden age of playwriting is the invention of the types of play that will be staged for the next few centuries: history plays and political plays, love stories and adventure fantasies, revenge dramas and farcical comedies, happy endings and sad ones. But playwrights also educate their audiences, making them pay closer attention to more emotional depth and more elaborate poetic imagery. At the same time, these plays show a troubled nation. Tragedies are set in Spain or Italy yet the message is unmistakable: courts and courtiers are corrupt. Back home, the great comedies about London life show a population well aware of class divisions, social inequalities, but also disrespectful of authority.

The Court Masque

After King James's death in 1625, his son is crowned Charles I. King Charles is prim, convinced of his Divine Right to rule, and, along with his French wife Henrietta Maria, a generous patron of the arts. At this point, Wilt takes us to the grand Banqueting House in Whitehall to chat about theatre in Caroline times. Inside this elegant building, with its classical columns and perfect proportions, we marvel at the swirling figures of the colourful ceiling. Painted by Sir Peter Paul Rubens, one of the court artists sponsored by the royals, it represents a breathtaking allegory which glorifies King James, Charles's father, as a supreme monarch. Here, Wilt acquaints us with the achievements of the building's creator Inigo Jones, the star architect of his day. Single-handedly he introduces the Continental classical style to London architecture, and if that is not enough he is also a great theatrical innovator. As the designer and director of dozens of masques for court audiences, Jones pioneers the use of the proscenium arch and realistic scenery. He's not just a big name; he's a pivotal figure. He's nothing less than the father of theatrical staging as we know it.

But these innovations are not for the likes of us. Masques are strictly private performances commissioned by the king to

Inigo Jones

be staged at royal palaces in front of members of the court. A cross between a play, a ball, amateur theatricals and fancy dress, they are immensely expensive and are timed to celebrate royal occasions such as weddings or births, and for Christmas festivities. Elements of the masque, however, had also been included in popular plays: there are masque scenes in *The Spanish Tragedy* and *The Tempest*. Under King James and King Charles, they include poetry recitals with music and dance, lavish costumes, gorgeous scenery and special effects. Jones invents machines to create clouds and other visual wonders. Royals and nobles take part, often playing gods or heroes, with regular actors playing minor roles. At one masque, at Theobalds Palace in Hertfordshire, in 1606, the participants are so drunk that many of them fall over. Masques are an import from Continental Europe, where the kings and queens revel in opulent display. They are a way of saying: 'You plebs, look at what fun we are having.'

Between 1605 and 1640, Jones — often in collaboration with wordsmith Ben Jonson — is responsible for staging more than 500 performances of masques and other elite entertainments. The first masque staged in the Banqueting House is their *Masque of Augurs*, performed on Twelfth Night in 1622, when the building is still not quite complete. Wilt has bought some of Jones's designs for costumes and we take a look at these lavish, elegantly drawn pictures. The last masque, performed here in 1635, is *The Temple of Love* by William Davenant, a playwright who claims to be Shakespeare's godson. But after a series of amazing successes Jonson and Jones have a bitter falling out in 1631: Jonson accuses Jones of exalting rich costumes and luxuriant sets at the expense of poetry. Wilt thinks he has a point: too much spectacle, not enough content. For example, in 1611, *The Masque of Oberon* costs more than £2000 (enough to pay for a warship), with the costumes costing half that gigantic sum — Jonson gets just £40 for writing the words.

'In the 1630s,' says Wilt, 'there is a feeling that the golden age of playwriting is over.' Still, new playhouses continue to be built, such as the small Salisbury Court indoor theatre, a barn conversion made at a cost of £1000 in 1630, and a handful of good plays are still written, like the comedies of Richard Brome, whose masterpiece is the rollicking *A Jovial Crew*, first staged in 1641. Other playwrights that people are talking about include John Marston, Philip Massinger and James Shirley. In the 1630s, the variety that they offer means that it is no longer necessary to stage a different play every day: the same play is now put on for several days at a time, which is easier on the actors and means that the quality of performance begins to rise. Revivals of older plays are as important as new work. Queen Henrietta Maria visits the Blackfriars theatre four times, giving a new respectability both to the venue and to the King's Men. She and her ladies act in the court masques — to the horror of the Puritans. And her husband King Charles maintains a healthy interest in plays, often making critical notes in his copies of the published texts. The Blackfriars becomes home to gallant playwrights who establish the fashion for exhibitions of wit as a chief ingredient of plays. By contrast, the north London outdoor venues, the Fortune and the Red Bull, continue to provide vigorous drum and trumpet plays, more vulgar, more backward-looking and yet more popular than the indoor stages. But all this is a last hurrah — the final curtain for theatre is about to fall.

The Banqueting House, we tell Wilt, is still standing today, and the building has another, more grim, significance: after his defeat in the English Civil War, King Charles is executed on 30 January 1649 on a scaffold set up outside this building so the beautiful ceiling is one of the last things he sees before he dies. By then, the Puritan killjoys have finally got their way. During the civil war, which lasts from 1642 to 1651, the Parliamentarians hold London, while King Charles's headquarters is Oxford. Since the Parliament and City government is dominated by religious zealots, the writing is on the wall for all theatres across the country. On 2 September 1642 Parliament issues an ordinance which bans all stage plays. In 1644, the glorious Globe theatre is pulled down. Four years later, a law is passed ordering all theatres to be dismantled, all actors to be whipped out of town, and anyone caught attending a play to be fined five shillings (sixty times the entrance price). The theatres remain closed for eighteen years. On this rather melancholy note, Wilt takes a deep bow and leaves us.

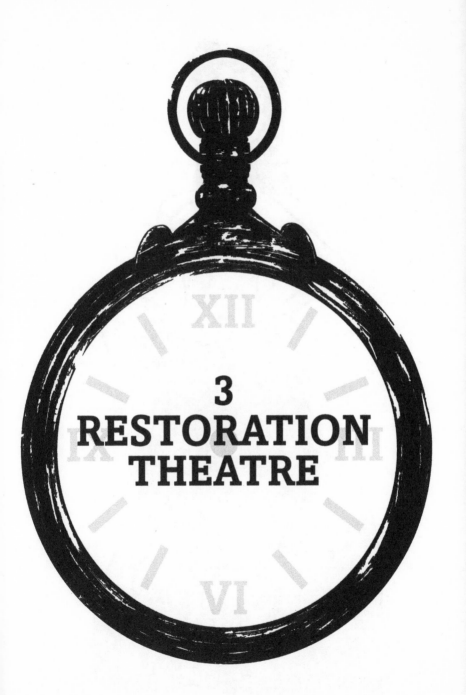

3
RESTORATION THEATRE

3
Restoration Theatre

Meet our guide: Moll

Our next guide, Moll Farthingale, is getting out of a sedan chair, in which two beefy men have carried her in elegant comfort to meet us. And, having dismissed the vehicle, she introduces herself as our new expert on theatre in the bawdy, colourful age of the Restoration of the monarchy, after the Civil War and the decade-long rule of the Puritans. Moll is wearing a light-blue satin dress, low-necked, and her skirt is open down the front, showing a laced underskirt. During this time, we gather, it is sexy for women's clothing to be a bit dishevelled, conveying a hint of wantonness. In defiance of Puritan strictures, Moll has a plunging neckline, which offers a precarious coverage of her ample bosom. She is a retired actress, now a widow whose advantageous marriage to a City merchant allows her to live comfortably. During her time as an actress, she was described as a great beauty, with dark ringlets, fine figure and exceptionally good legs (which delighted the men in the audience when she played the so-called breeches roles). What strikes us immediately is her vivacious manner, her lively eyes, and her footwear. These are a pair of embroidered light-blue satin shoes, totally unsuitable for walking the dusty and cobbled streets of London! She says that on this trip — which we hope for her sake will use some transport that protects her shoes — we will be looking at English theatre from the 1660s to the 1710s, from the reign of King Charles II up to Queen Anne.

Monarchy restored

London, since the early seventeenth century, has changed, mainly due to a population boom. Moll says, 'It's a rapidly growing city of about 400,000 — one of the biggest in Europe. And what a people live here!' As our guide takes us through the cramped streets of the old Square Mile and then along the more elegant avenues of the newly built West End, we see the grandees and ladies in their silks and velvets rub shoulders with young lads and lasses from the countryside, newly arrived to seek their fortunes as apprentices and servants. There are men in livery, African slave boys, craftsmen and sailors, street vendors and lawyers, ministers and financiers hurrying to parliament and the Exchange. Near the docks, foreign languages are heard; in the main streets carriages carry aristocrats to their destinations. Along the Strand, courtiers have built mansions such as Arundel House and Salisbury House. Spacious squares in Covent Garden and Lincoln's Inn are flanked by new houses for the wealthy, built in a Palladian style made fashionable by none other than the great architect Inigo Jones. In this noisy, smelly but exciting atmosphere, the new monarch sets the tone for the whole society. The thirty-year-old King Charles II has returned to London after being exiled on the Continent during the rule of Oliver Cromwell and the Puritans, who set up a republic and banned theatre, as well other entertainments. There is widespread public rejoicing at the Restoration of the monarchy: the dark days of religious bigotry are finally over. King Charles immediately makes a good impression.

Moll takes us to St James's Park, where we see King Charles, in the company of his courtiers, walking his spaniels, meeting members of the public and talking to all and sundry. It is a warm summer afternoon and the park, although just a quick walk away from parliament, looks quite rural, with its grazing deer and cows. The king is dressed in the latest French fashion, with a linen shirt, richly coloured waistcoat, every button neatly done up, a tailcoat and breeches, buckled shoes. His wig, another new Paris fashion, is thick and black, curly and long. He looks young and fit. As we stop under the shade of a large elm tree, Moll produces an amazing fan: it's a bunch of wispy ostrich feathers set in a heavy black handle. As she fans herself, she tells us that the king is quite informal and that when he loses one of his black spaniels, he appeals for its return in *Mercurius Publicus*, an ordinary newspaper. Although he's an autocrat, he's also the people's king.

King Charles likes going to the theatre. Not for him the sequestered performances of the palace; not for him the solemn pulpits of the Puritans. He prefers to venture into the bustling world of London, watching shows, meeting actors and actresses, especially actresses. He loves all kinds of entertainment — fairs, freak shows, tight-rope walkers and acrobats. At court there is an atmosphere of witty conversation, cheerful lechery and gallons of drink. Chief among a group of rakes and heavy drinkers, he notches up a fair number of mistresses, living up to his nickname: the Merry Monarch. He aims to set an example — his idea of theatre is fun.

The Restoration is the Year Zero for British drama. After a gap of eighteen years, during which the Puritans stopped all performances in London, this is a new beginning. While the Elizabethan and Jacobean past was a hurly-burly of movers and shakers, 'Restoration theatre,' Moll tells us, 'depends on one man: King Charles.' And he aims to control everything. No longer will common entrepreneurs be allowed to create theatre. King Charles decrees that there will only be two theatre companies. Aware that he owes a lot to the loyal royalists who kept him company during his long years of exile, he rewards two courtiers, who now become London's duopoly of theatre managers. Their names are Thomas Killigrew and Sir William Davenant. Since these names mean little to us, Moll gives us a brief sketch of their careers.

Thomas Killigrew

With his curly locks and lecherous moustache, Killigrew looks every inch a Cavalier. He is a veteran royalist. As a boy, he revelled in the blood-and-thunder shows at the open-air Red Bull theatre. Next, he was a page of honour to King Charles I, and then, after being imprisoned by the Puritans, joined King Charles II in exile on the Continent. He occasionally writes plays, the best one being *The Parson's*

William Davenant

Wedding, a dark take on sex and marriage. His specialization is telling merry stories and keeping the spirits of king and courtiers high. Apparently, confides Moll, on the ship bringing King Charles back to England, Killigrew tells risqué stories and sings a song about Moll Frith (the original Moll Cutpurse), which makes the monarch cry with laughter. So his appointment as manager of the King's Company — successor to the King's Men — is his reward for royal service.

By contrast to Killigrew, Davenant is a professional. He is widely thought to be Shakespeare's love child, and he never discourages this rumour. His first play, *The Cruel Brother*, was staged by the King's Men at the Blackfriars theatre in 1627, after which he had to take a career break due to a severe bout of venereal disease. He cures it by inhaling mercury and this results in the loss of part of his nose. Bouncing back, he stages masques for the royal court, and spends some of the Civil War in exile with the royals. His theatrical innovations started under Oliver Cromwell: having returned to Britain, in 1656 he stages *The Siege of Rhodes* privately at his home, Rutland House in London's Aldersgate Street. He gets around the law banning plays by calling it an opera. Among the performers is Mrs Coleman, one of the first women to appear on stage. King Charles appoints Davenant manager of the Duke's Company, whose patron is James, Duke of York, the king's younger brother.

King Charles makes theatre a royal prerogative. Actors are his majesty's servants: they wear the scarlet royal livery, and they have to sign the theatre book when they arrive for work — by order of the Lord Chamberlain. A royal official, the immensely imposing and influential courtier Henry Jermyn, the Earl of St Albans, is the Lord Chamberlain, who is responsible for the censorship of plays. Moll — no stranger to dark and intimate places — now takes us to the royal archives, kept in a dusty and damp cellar in the gothic Westminster Palace, to show us the Warrant that King Charles issues on 21 August 1660, proclaiming that only Killigrew and Davenant are allowed to create theatre in London. It gives them the power to set up companies, but also forbids them from staging any 'profanation, scurrility, or obscenity'. As she shows us this, Moll has a twinkle in her eye: the fun-loving King Charles and his courtiers don't really care about banning obscene jokes — but they need to keep up appearances. Two years later, Killigrew and Davenant both receive Letters Patent that confirm this Warrant. The most important thing, Moll points out, is that these Letters Patent make London theatre into a piece of property that can be inherited, and then bought and sold. The patent system lasts for almost two hundred years.

Anyone for tennis?

Killigrew and Davenant get to work. Moll — who has taken us to a nearby tavern to enjoy some refreshment after our dusty trip to the archive — tells us how the new system works. Because Killigrew manages the King's Company, named after the monarch, he gets the pick of professional actors and plays (a repertoire including the plays of Ben Jonson, Francis Beaumont and John Fletcher). By contrast, Davenant's actors are more inexperienced and he only gets a handful of old plays, 'Mainly Shakespeare,' says Moll, with a wrinkling of her nose. So he has a greater need for new plays and this drives the business of playwriting for the next thirty years. The differences between the two companies follow the temperaments of their managers: Killigrew leaves the day-to-day running of the King's Company to veteran actors Charles Hart and Michael Mohun, both old Cavaliers (supporters of King Charles I). Davenant leads from the front. But although it seems as if Killigrew has all the advantages, it is Davenant who is the most innovative. Both face challenges. The first problem is: what kind of theatre? Killigrew and Davenant don't want to use the old rowdy open-air venues — they have a different idea. Neither man can forget the sophisticated indoor theatre they enjoyed during their exile on the Continent. Killigrew remembers the French fashion for turning indoor tennis courts — open spaces sheltered from the elements — into theatres. So he sets up a stage in Gibbon's tennis court, in Vere Street, a small indoor space with a bare platform stage. Meanwhile, Davenant, itching to pursue the latest theatre trends, moves his company to Lisle's, another converted tennis court, this time near Lincoln's Inn Fields.

'Both venues,' Moll says, 'seat about four hundred people, which is okay because after a long gap the audience for theatre is small.' Prices are high so the audience is a select courtier coterie. One way of attracting customers, thinks Davenant, is to use realistic scenery, to make theatre a more visual experience. It's an inspired idea, and it gives him a competitive edge. Remembering the royal masques designed by Inigo Jones fifty years earlier, at Lisle's he creates a stage with beautifully painted scenery. Instead of the bare spaces of the past, his theatre features a proscenium arch, another of Jones's innovations. This means that the stage is framed like a picture, so the audience gets a sense of visual perspective. He also creates coloured lighting by putting tinted glass around candles. Thanks to such innovations, the theatre experience becomes more magical, a place for dreaming. He also uses backstage machines to fly in visual effects, such as airborne witches in his new version of *Macbeth*. Audiences love these 'scenes and machines' and they flock to see this new attraction. So successful is it that Killigrew is forced to do the same thing. So in 1663, he moves into a purpose-built new theatre in Bridges Street, next to Drury Lane. It is an address that will host theatre experiences for the next three and a half centuries.

While the duopoly of Killigrew and Davenant is the official set-up of London theatre, there is also one unofficial player, Moll informs us. George Jolly, who had led a touring company on the Continent during the rule of the Puritans, decides to challenge their dominance. He gets a licence to perform in London and moves into the old Cockpit theatre. Both Killigrew and Davenant are unimpressed, and act swiftly to suppress this challenge to their duopoly. In 1667, after some legal wrangling, they succeed. Jolly's Cockpit theatre is closed and turned into an academy for training actors. This turns out to be the first drama school in London, and its most outstanding graduate is Joe Haines. Although little is known of his early life, he catches the eye of Killigrew and becomes a comedian. Despite the fact that he is often insolent to those in authority, and frequently fired from the King's Company, he is loved by audiences, and just as frequently reinstated.

World of women

'Now,' says Moll, with a swish of her skirts, 'you have to remember one thing: during the Restoration, the London stage becomes for the first time a place for women.' To make her tale more real, she takes us to the Bridges Street, the entrance of Theatre Royal Drury Lane, home to the King's Company. The theatre is set back from the street, with access down a narrow passage. Because of the mud, Moll has pinned back the front edges of her skirt, which is so wide she has to walk sideways down this passage to squeeze through. We worry about her shoes! The building is a wooden structure, converted from a former riding school, and it has ample space. The main floor, the pit, has no roof so daylight can illuminate the shows. A glazed dome protects theatregoers from the elements, but it's not completely weatherproof, 'So if there's a bad thunderstorm, we might have to leave in a hurry,' says Moll with a chuckle. Then she takes us backstage and we see some of the props, here a wooden leg, there a ruff, here a hobby-horse, there a crown. 'Not very impressive in the cold light of day,' she admits, speaking from experience and with a toss of her locks, 'but when they are illuminated by candlelight on the stage they look magical.'

King Charles, in his 1662 Letters Patent, specifies that, since cross-dressing boy actors have caused offence, 'all the women's parts to be acted in either of the said two companies for the time to come may be performed by women'. Meanwhile, on the Continent, female actresses are the norm. But, here in England, to begin with boys still play the female roles. For example, the seventeen-year-old Edward Kynaston is much admired by the ladies in the audience, who invite him into their carriages for a spin around Hyde Park before he has even changed back into men's clothing. No one knows who is the first woman to appear publicly on the Restoration stage, although some say it is Margaret Hughes, who

Nell Gwyn

plays Desdemona in *Othello* for the King's Company in 1660. Moll coyly claims that she can't remember: maybe she doesn't want to admit that she has been around the block a few times.

Killigrew recruits several new female talents. Since there is no tradition of women actors, they have to be taught acting from scratch. One of them is Elizabeth Knipp, an actress who is married to a horse-trader, and who loves flirting with the audience. Moll says that Knipp once shared a coach with Samuel Pepys, the high-ranking civil servant (and known to us as a secret diarist), sitting on his lap and singing, while he fondles her breasts. Drink was involved. Other actresses include Rebecca Marshall and Elizabeth Boutell, about whom there is a verse in circulation, which includes the line 'chestnut-maned Boutell, whom all the town fucks'. Moll warns us not to take these libels as truth. Not all actresses, she points out, are loose women. When Davenant sees that Killigrew is using women actresses, he follows suit. Soon, he employs eight actresses, four of them living in his own house. A proper gentleman, he offers them protection because English actresses are often single, and seen as fair game. Theatre is sexy. Many actresses play breeches parts, in which they dress up as men, and this involves wearing tights which show off their legs, which the long dresses of the time usually hide. Here is the start of a theatre convention which leads up to today, when pantomime leads are still played by women.

As usual, it is the royals who set the fashion. King Charles II and his brother the Duke of York frequently go to the theatre. These court outings are part fashion show and part girl hunt. In their entourage are courtiers such as George Villiers, Duke of

Buckingham, and John Wilmot, the Earl of Rochester, a notorious rake, along with poets and professional dramatists such as John Dryden. Although the king is married, he has several flings with actresses. Most notoriously, he has a ten-year affair with Nell Gwyn. Her mother ran a brothel, and Nell might have been a child prostitute. She first comes to Killigrew's attention as a scantily clad orange seller at Drury Lane, and in 1665 she debuts in Dryden's play, *The Indian Emperor*. Three years later begins her affair with the very Merry Monarch. He commissions his court artist Sir Peter Lely to paint her nude portrait as a reclining Venus. She is a spirited individual: Moll tells us the story of her coach being jostled by a mob, who thought that she was the Duchess of Portsmouth, her Catholic rival. Gwyn pulls down the window and shouts, 'Good people, you are mistaken — I am the *Protestant* whore!' The rioters let her pass. She has two children by King Charles. When the older one, Charles, is six, Gwyn says, as the King arrives, 'Come here, you little bastard, and say hello to your father.' The King protests, so she adds, 'Your Majesty has given me no other name by which to call him.' In response, King Charles makes him Earl of Burford. The king's reputation as a libidinous libertine is well known, and Rochester, his companion in lust, has penned the following couplet: 'Poor prince! Thy prick, like thy buffoons at court,/ Will govern thee because it make thee sport.'

Thomas Betterton

Kings, Dukes and tragedies

The King's Company and the Duke's Company form a duopoly, but competition is fierce. Davenant has one big advantage over Killigrew: he employs Thomas Betterton, the greatest actor of the day. Betterton and his wife, actress Mary Saunderson, soon become the backbone of the Duke's Company. 'The athletic Betterton,' says Moll with a quick knowing smile, 'has great stage presence and his strong voice can command the attention of both fops and flower girls.' One of his star roles is Hamlet, a character he reprises for years. In the scene when the ghost of Hamlet's father enters Gertrude's bedroom, Betterton throws over a chair, a gesture entirely typical of his highly dramatic style. When Davenant dies in 1668, his royal patent passes to his son Charles — who is under age — and so Betterton takes over management of the Duke's Company. He is now London theatre's prime mover and shaker.

DRAMA THEORY: FRENCH MODELS

John Dryden's *An Essay of Dramatic Poesy*, published in 1668, is an account of what the Restoration poets and scholars valued in the plays of the day. Because many of them had been in exile on the Continent during the rule of the Puritans, they learnt a lot about French theatre and especially its neo-classical style, which values The Unities and the elegance of rhyming verse. Neo-classical drama is not only elegant, but also clear in its plotting and rational in its ideas. In Dryden's book, which is written as a discussion between four gentlemen on a boat trip on the Thames, the argument swings from praising the sophisticated style of Continental playwriting to appreciating the English tradition, exemplified by Shakespeare, of elaborate plots, powerful images and comic episodes. Dryden knows that Shakespeare's style is completely un-classical, but also realizes that his plays work well on stage. Still, he concludes that the messier aspects of the English tradition need to be modified by making the verse smoother, and the plots neater.

With the introduction of scenery and stage machinery, theatre becomes more visually exciting. But what about new plays? The man of the moment is the elegantly intellectual John Dryden: he is Poet Laureate, versifier and one of the first ever literary critics. 'Just as the fashions of the leading courtiers come straight from Paris,' says Moll, 'so British playwrights are influenced by the French.' Serious plays take the form of heroic tragedies, often in clunky rhyming couplets, which today are practically unwatchable (the language being too high-falutin' and the emotions too exaggerated) so we don't encourage Moll to take us to see one. For the Duke's Company, the market leaders in turgid tragedy are Dryden's two-part *Conquest of Granada* (1670-71) and Elkanah Settle's *The Empress of Morocco* (1673), 'Serious drama in rhyming couplets,' says Moll stifling a yawn behind her ostrich fan.

> Elkanah Settle's *The Empress of Morocco* (1673)
> *Muly Hamet is tragically smitten with the pains of exile:*
> Condemned never to see Morocco more!
> Thus am I doomed to quit all I adore:
> As profane sinners are from altars driven,
> Banished the temples to be banished heaven.
> Horror and tortures now my jailors be,
> Who paints damnation needs but copy me:
> For if mankind the pains of hell ever knew,
> 'Tis when they lose a mistress as I do.

But what is it that makes these tragedies so popular? 'One scholar, Thomas Rymer,' she says, 'comes up with the idea of "poetic justice", which stipulates that plays must have moral outcomes: the bad must be punished and the good must be rewarded. But as well as being morally good, these tragedies are spectacular to watch.' Visual effects in *The Empress of Morocco* include a masque scene representing Orpheus's descent to the underworld, showing the fires of hell and dancing demons, as well as a final tableau of dismembered bodies on spikes in a dungeon. When this play is staged, the rival King's Company responds with a parody, Thomas Duffet's *The Empress of Morocco: a Farce*, which replaces the kings and queens of the original with pimps and whores. The pomp of poetic justice, laughs Moll, is pricked by the laughter of satire.

Likewise, the courtier Buckingham can't resist easy laughter, and he persuades a group of playwrights to sneer at the genre of high tragedy in a play called *The Rehearsal*, which proves so popular that it is regularly revived, with updates, for several decades. One character, Drawcansir, is a parody of Almanzor, from Dryden's *The Conquest of Granada*. Drawcansir is 'a fierce hero that frights his mistress, snubs up kings, baffles armies and does what he will without regard to numbers, good manners, or justice'. A characteristic piss take is his rhyming couplet: 'I drink, I huff, I strut, look big and stare;/ And all this I can do, because I dare.' This is the first of a new kind of play — the burlesque. Aristocratic mockery is the distinct tone of the age. But when ordinary folk thumb their noses at aristocrats, they get punished. After Dryden makes a satirical joke against Rochester, the disreputable rake, he is beaten up in a back alley.

Dryden also pens a different kind of success. Well, Moll tells us with a wink, it's a new kind of sexy drama. His *Secret Love; or, The Maiden Queen*, is staged by the King's Company in 1667, starring Charles Hart (Celadon) and Nell Gwyn (Florimell) as the bantering well-matched couple. The play popularizes the joyful art of verbal sparring, a mix of warm affection and sexual antagonism. Here wit is the name of the game, and women give as good as they get. In this the pioneer has been Shakespeare's Benedick and Beatrice in *Much Ado about Nothing*. *Secret Love* has the first proviso scene in Restoration drama, in which the couple set out the rules of their marriage in a kind of prenuptial bargain. This type of scene will have a big theatrical future.

But new plays, however good, can't compete with old plays. Remixes of Shakespeare's plays are still firm favourites. The bard is seen as too rough and crude for the refined tastes of courtiers, who see elegant French culture as a must, so his plays are adapted, usually completely rewritten to suit the contemporary. Shakespeare's name is on the playbill, but the author is somebody else. Often these adaptations include singing, dancing and special effects. Two tragedies show that this highly artificial genre has some staying power: Dryden's blank verse play, *All for Love; or, the World Well Lost*, of 1677 is based on Shakespeare's *Antony and Cleopatra*. Dryden cleans up the original and sets it in one location, according to the theory of The Unities. Later, in 1681, Nahum Tate's *The History of King Lear* gives Shakespeare's cruel tragedy a happy ending: Lear recovers his throne, and Cordelia marries Edgar, who declares that 'truth and virtue shall at last succeed'. Poetic justice indeed. Also popular are plays by pre-Civil-War playwrights, such as Thomas Kyd's *The Spanish Tragedy* and John Webster's *The Duchess of Malfi*, which Samuel Pepys sees several times with Betterton in the cast. Other gimmicks to attract audiences back to the theatre include all-woman productions of plays: in 1672, Killigrew stages a revival of his own *The Parson's Wedding*, with an exclusively female cast. It's such a success that he produces an all-woman *Secret Love*.

In other parts of Britain, new theatre traditions are being started. In October 1662, John Ogilby — who had designed the ceremonial arches for King Charles's entry into London in 1661 — opens the Theatre Royal in Smock Alley near the River Liffey quays in Dublin, the first custom-built theatre in the city. Meanwhile, back in London, the Puritans joyfully fall to their prayers as two disasters suggest that God is unhappy with the fun-loving Restoration rulers: in 1665, the Great Plague kills 100,000. Then in 1666 the Great Fire of London burns everything down, including the medieval cathedral of St Paul's. It is a traumatic time, as London is reduced to a blackened ruin, with the loss of more than 13,000 houses and eighty-seven churches. Thousands of people are homeless. The damage is worse than the Blitz of 1940. For years after this cataclysmic disaster, London resembles a huge building site, as a new wave of architects, headed by Sir Christopher Wren, rebuild the City in a more Continental, classical style. By 1711, the new baroque-style St Paul's cathedral, whose dome soars above the skyline, is finished and London is reborn as a cleaner, safer city.

Dorset Garden versus Drury Lane

Moll looks absolutely gutted when she describes the horrors of the Great Plague and the Great Fire, and we understand that she may have lost friends in these disasters. But she is determined to shake off sad thoughts so she takes us to the Dorset Garden theatre. Built in 1671 for the Duke's Company, it's the most sumptuous playhouse in Britain. It is situated on the Thames waterfront, just below Fleet Street, and the white stone facade is beautifully proportioned in the Continental baroque style, with classical pillars and elegant windows. Moll says that Betterton, the manager, has rooms on the upper floors; living above the shop enables him to keep an eye on things. Outside, Moll points out the playbills, and tells us that the theatre costs about £9000 to build and has a capacity of 700. A popular play might gross £100 or more for a single performance. Ticket prices vary from day to day, and special offers include paying half price for arriving when the play is half over. Once inside, Moll asks us to sit on the backless benches in the pit and tells us some more about this venue, lit by its bright wax candles which, unlike the tallow candles of old, give a good warming light.

Dorset Garden has the latest stage machinery imported from Paris, and, in the 1670s, it becomes famous for its visually stunning productions. But while Betterton prospers at the Dorset Garden, Killigrew is less lucky. His Drury Lane theatre burns down in 1672, and all its expensive stage machinery is lost. Two years later, a replacement venue is built on the site, once again accessible only through an alleyway alongside the dingy Rose Tavern. The new Theatre Royal Drury Lane becomes a key venue. Of course, when Moll suggests that we pay a visit to see a typical performance there, we jump at the chance. Designed by Sir Christopher Wren, the building costs a modest £4000 but has a capacity of about 1000. Prices are much higher than the old open-air Elizabethan theatres, and we notice that the audience is more classy — fashionable men and women, the richer sort of merchant cram together in the pit. Around three sides of the auditorium are two tiers of boxes, where ladies and gentlemen sit together. That said, there are also some apprentices and servants in the cheap seats in the gods. There is no booking in advance. To get a good seat you need to come early and wait for the show to begin at three, passing the time listening to music being played by a small orchestra. Upper-class patrons send their servants to reserve their seats. It is warm inside the building and we are aware of the flutter of dozens of fans. Moll, who has brought her ostrich-feather contraption with her, explains that there is a language of fans: the way you hold and use your fan can indicate modesty, high spirits or intrigue.

It is a Saturday and a new play is being premiered. 'This means,' says Moll, 'that, unless it is a flop, the author has time to do rewrites on Sunday before the play is repeated on Monday.' If the play is successful and gets three performances, the playwright gets a bonus: the author's benefit, which means keeping the takings of every third performance. Looking at the stage, we can see the richly carved wooden proscenium arch. The stage is divided in two. The part nearest the audience is a platform that thrusts out in front of the proscenium; the other part is framed by the proscenium arch and displays the play's scenery. In these days, explains Moll, the actors stay on the projecting platform, very close to the audience. Behind them are brightly painted backgrounds, arranged to give a perspective effect. On the stage are seated several of the richer audience members — they have come to be seen as well as to watch the drama. Everywhere, people are arriving, greeting each other: it feels like an exclusive society party, more like a club than a theatre. We look out for King Charles or his brother James Duke of York. 'Look isn't that Samuel Pepys wearing his new style periwig?', says Moll, as she fans herself in the heat.

Suddenly there is the sound of violins, and we can see musicians high above the stage in a balcony box at the top of the proscenium arch. Then silence — almost; some people carry on chatting. An actor comes onto the stage to speak the play's Prologue. He addresses in turn the wits in the audience, then the gentlemen in the pit and finally other audience members in the boxes. He walks about confidently like a gentleman who feels perfectly secure because he is among friends. Later on, when the play's scenic background has to change, a whistle blows backstage and screens are slid along grooves in the floor to alter the picture. The actors wear the same clothes as the audience, the men in frock coats and the women in more elaborate dresses and hairdos.

We notice that the acting style is as mannered and exaggerated in its movements — elaborate bows and compliments — as that of the courtiers in the audience. Hand gestures are particularly important, with different signals for invitation, dramatic pause or to express extreme emotions such as shock or horror.

All the best actors of the company have a role and, Moll tells us, in between bouts of fanning, dramatists write with particular actors in mind. On this occasion, the playwright is well supported by a bunch of aristocrats who lead the cheers of his work. At the end, an actress comes on stage and delivers the Epilogue. Half tongue-in-cheek, half winningly, she hopes that the audience has enjoyed the play. Thunderous applause. Then the name of the play for the following day is given out. At this point Moll — our queen of gossip — tells us the story of Nell Gwyn's Epilogue from Dryden's *Tyrannick Love* of 1669. In this sad story, her character, Valeria, stabs herself at the end and lies dead on stage. Then, when the stage hands come on to carry her body off, she leaps up, crying: 'Hold, are you mad? You damned confounded dog,/ I am to rise and speak the Epilogue.' She says that she is 'the ghost of poor departed Nelly', and flirtatiously addresses the men in the audience: 'I'll come dance about your beds at nights/ And faith, you'll be in a sweet kind of taking/ When I surprise you between sleep and waking.' No doubt the king's mistress means it!

Restoration comedy

There are dozens of examples of rhymed heroic tragedies, but they have a short shelf life. By the 1670s the best new plays are comedies. Their subject is sex, sex and more sex. This is an era when rich men see nothing wrong with forcing themselves on women, especially when these are of a lower class. Maids beware. In this immoral age, when King Charles and his libidinous court set the tone, the best entertainments are comedies of manners. Three playwrights stand out: George Etherege, William Wycherley and Aphra Behn, the first female playwright.

Etherege is known as 'gentle George' and 'easy Etherege', and he is the acquaintance of courtier wits like Rochester, and privileged enough to be a dilettante playwright, penning only a handful of plays, while professionals such as Dryden sweat over dozens in order to make a living. You can't imagine Etherege sweating. His debut for the Duke's Company, *The Comical Revenge; or, Love in a Tub*, in 1664 features a faithless young charmer, Sir Frederick Frollick, who spars wittily with the Widow Rich. But despite its popularity — making £1000 in its first month — it is written in stilted rhyming verse which grates on the ear. Then, in his follow-up, *She Would If She Could* (1668), Etherege breaks decisively with the verse that has been drama's standard linguistic style and uses prose, ordinary conversation. From now on the best drama is

GEORGE ETHEREGE

Born: 1636, probably in Maidenhead, Berkshire.

Family: George Etherege and Mary Powney, George eldest of six children. After the death of his father, grandfather George is his guardian.

Education: Lord William's school, Thame, Oxfordshire. His grandfather sends him to study law at Clement's Inn, London, in 1654.

Private life: As a boy, stays in Paris with his father and the exiled Queen Henrietta Maria during the rule of the Puritans in the 1650s. After quitting theatre, he marries wealthy widow Mary Sheppard Arnold in 1680.

Career: In 1663 he leaves the law to write his first play *The Comical Revenge* (1664). In 1668 becomes secretary to Sir Daniel Harvey, ambassador to Turkey, and goes to Constantinople. Returns to London in 1671. After *Man of Mode*, quits writing for the stage and is knighted. In 1689, after the Glorious Revolution, he joins James II in exile in Paris.

Greatest hit: *Man of Mode* (1676).

Scandal: Part of the Earl of Rochester's circle; may have had a daughter by the unmarried actress Elizabeth Barry. Loses a fortune by gambling.

Influence: Invents the Restoration comedy of manners.

Death: In 1692 in Paris as a Jacobite exile.

written in ordinary language. We breathe a sigh of relief. Not bad for a dilettante!

Etherege's masterpiece is *The Man of Mode; or, Sir Fopling Flutter*, whose central character, Dorimant, is played by Betterton for the Duke's Company at Dorset Garden in 1676. A notorious libertine, Dorimant is modelled on Rochester, the king's pal, who boasts of being drunk non-stop for five years and dies of syphilis at the age of thirty-three in 1680. The play shows Dorimant running circles around his mistress, Mrs Loveit, in order to seduce her younger friend Belinda, before finally meeting his match in Harriet, who refuses to be seduced unless Dorimant marries her and leaves the city for the countryside, which for him is a fate worse than death. To the urban gentleman, the country is a place of bumpkins and yokels. When a dog bites Rochester he responds by telling it: 'I wish you were married and living in the country.' In the play, other sexual intrigues involve Young Bellair, a gentleman about town, and Sir Fopling Flutter, a newly arrived fop. The other women are Lady Townley, Lady Woodvil (Harriet's mother), and gentlewomen Belinda and Emilia. Their servants have names such as Handy, Busy and Pert. Deceit and disguise fuel the action.

Etherege's success comes down to his ability to weave several plots at the same time in a conversational language that sparkles with wit. He is a master of style. This is a world of people for whom life is a game and a series of poses. A person's quality is measured by the cut of their clothing, the elegance of their stance, and by their ability to be detached and witty. Pleasure is more important than morals; to consider the feelings of other people is bad form. Dorimant is a model of lecherous manhood, while Sir Fopling Flutter is a satire on affectation. Both characters are instantly familiar to audiences. The play is steeped in courtier values. Dorimant finally agrees to marry Harriet only because it's the only way to have sex with her — and because she has a huge fortune. Matrimony is a financial transaction. Etherege displays a great joy in the heartless actions of his characters, but there are subtle dark undertones: feelings of emptiness, even regret.

George Etherege's *The Man of Mode* (1676)

Dorimant is beaten in the game of love:

DORIMANT *(Aside)* I love her and dare not let her know it,
I fear she has an ascendant over me and may revenge the
wrongs I have done her sex.

But it's essentially a fun play. A great success when it is first performed, *The Man of Mode* is widely influential.

Etherege is great, but topping the charts for comedy is William Wycherley's *The Country Wife*, staged by the King's Company at Drury Lane in 1675. Nicknamed 'Manly Wycherley', he is part of Buckingham's circle of courtiers and another dilettante playwright who brings sexual intrigue centre stage.

His first play, *Love in a Wood* (1671), has a song at the end of the first act in praise of whores and their children. When Barbara Villiers, Duchess of Cleveland and mistress of King Charles, hears this, she takes offence and when her coach passes Wycherley's in Pall Mall, she abuses him as a 'villain', son of a whore. He answers, 'Madam, you have been pleased to bestow a title on me which belongs only to the fortunate.' According to gossip, the Duchess becomes his mistress and visits him at his chambers disguised as a country wife. In the play of that name, Horner is an upper-class rake who pretends to be impotent — as a result of a

William
Wycherley

WILLIAM WYCHERLEY

Born: 28 May 1641, Clive, Shropshire.

Family: Ancient Shropshire family. Parents Daniel, High Steward of the Marquess of Winchester, and Bethia, lady-in-waiting in the same household.

Education: Age 15, sent by Royalist father to study in France. Converts to Roman Catholicism. Age 17, returns to Queen's College, Oxford. Reconverts to Protestantism. By 1660 at the Inner Temple, studying law, but never completes his training.

Private life: Secret marriage in 1679 to the debt-ridden Countess of Drogheda loses him royal patronage. After her death in 1681 Wycherley in a fifteen-year lawsuit as her family dispute her first husband's will. At the age of 74 he marries again, Elizabeth Jackson, a young woman. He dies eleven days later.

Career: At 30, gets King Charles's patronage after success of first play *Love in a Wood* in 1671. His second play, *The Gentleman Dancing Master*, is a modest success, but his next two, *The Country Wife* (1675) and *The Plain Dealer* (1676) are triumphs. King James II loves *The Plain Dealer* so much that he pays Wycherley's debts and grants him a pension of £200 a year, but this stops in 1688 when King James flees.

Greatest hit: *The Country Wife* (1675).

Scandal: Imprisoned for debt in 1682 for four years.

Death: 1 January 1715, as a Catholic.

Afterlife: Coins the terms 'nincompoop' and 'happy-go-lucky'.

botched treatment for syphilis — in order to seduce the wives of other men. As his name suggests, he aims to cuckold husbands, putting horns on their heads (according to the imagery of the day). He succeeds with many ladies of virtuous reputation, especially the wives of upwardly mobile merchants, such as Lady Fidget, her sister-in-law Mrs Dainty Fidget, and her friend Mrs Squeamish. But he is almost undone by Margery Pinchwife, the country wife of the title, who is so naive that she almost gives the game away when she states openly that Horner can't possibly be impotent — since she has had him. Subplots show the married life of the Pinchwifes, and the love affairs of Harcourt, Horner's friend, and Pinchwife's sister Alithea. As the perspicacious maid Lucy says,

'Marrying to increase love is like gaming to become rich; alas, you only lose what little stock you had before.'

In the first production, the elderly Michael Mohun plays Pinchwife, while the younger Elizabeth Boutell plays his wife Margery, thus emphasising her youthful innocence. Charles Hart is Horner, while the comedian Joe Haines plays Sparkish, Alithea's official fiancé, and Edward Kynaston plays Harcourt. Elizabeth Knipp is Lady Fidget, who also speaks the Epilogue. In the story, two scenes stand out: the most notorious is the China Scene, in which Horner discusses his collection of china with two ladies, while the other characters nod along, unaware that the three are using double meanings.

William Wycherley's *The Country Wife* (1675)
The China Scene (Act IV, Scene 3):
Enter Lady Fidget with a piece of China in her hand, and Horner following.

LADY FIDGET And I have been toiling and moiling, for the prettiest piece of china, my dear.

HORNER Nay she has been too hard for me, do what I could.

MRS SQUEAMISH Oh Lord, I'll have some china too. Good Master Horner, don't think to give other people china, and me none. Come in with me too.

HORNER Upon my honour I have none left now.

MRS SQUEAMISH Nay, nay, I have known you deny your china before now, but you shan't put me off so. Come.

HORNER This lady had the last there.

LADY FIDGET Yes indeed, madam, to my certain knowledge he has no more left.

MRS SQUEAMISH Oh, but it may be he may have some you could not find.

LADY FIDGET What, d'ye think if he had had any left, I would not have had it too? For we women of quality never think we have china enough.

HORNER Do not take it ill, I cannot make china for you all, but I will have a roll-wagon [phallic-shaped china vase] for you too, another time.

Aphra Behn

The situation plays with the idea that a dirty mind is a joy forever. At the time, this is quite shocking and in some prim households 'china' becomes a taboo word! Likewise, the other stand-out scene shows Lady Fidget and her female friends getting drunk and singing bawdy songs. Showing the women to be as sex mad as the men also causes offence. In his next offering, *The Plain Dealer*, performed at the Theatre Royal Drury Lane in 1676, Manly Wycherley plays with the notoriety of *The Country Wife*, having one of his characters say that this play 'has quite taken away the reputation of poor china itself, and sullied the most innocent and pretty furniture of a lady's chamber'. In this, his last play, the central character is called Manly, and when he discovers that his mistress Olivia has stolen his money and married a fop, he decides to trick her into meeting him and avenge himself by raping her. During another episode a male character discovers the true sex of Fidelia, who is disguised as a man, by pulling off her wig and feeling her breasts. And this is not the only play to feature sexual assault. Violence against women is the dark side to these sexy comedies.

But not all playwrights are men. Aphra Behn, the first English woman to earn a living from writing, and, next to Dryden, the most prolific playwright of the time, hides the details of her life behind a mask.

APHRA BEHN

Born: Aphra Johnson, near Canturbury, Kent; baptised 14 December 1640.

Family: Bartholomew Johnson, a barber, and Elizabeth Denham, a wet-nurse.

Education: None known. In 1653, travels with Johnson to Surinam. He dies on the way, but Aphra grows up there.

Private life: Shortly after her return to England in 1664, she marries Johan Behn, a Dutch merchant. The couple separate. Never marries again.

Career: By 1666, Behn is connected to the court, and works as a spy for King Charles II in the Netherlands during Second Dutch War. But he doesn't pay her expenses so she is imprisoned for debt. Forced to write for a living. After the success of *The Forced Marriage; or, The Jealous Bridegroom* in 1670, Behn becomes resident playwright at the Duke's Company. She writes some twenty other plays.

Greatest hits: *The Rover* (1677). Novel: *Oroonoko* (1688).

Scandal: Her independence, artistic versatility and wit.

Death: 16 April 1688.

Epitaph: Buried in Westminster Abbey: 'Here lies a proof that wit can never be/ Defence enough against mortality.'

She is the mysterious masked lady of Restoration theatre. Her works include *The Forced Marriage; or, The Jealous Bridegroom*, staged in 1670. Its theme, loveless marriages arranged by domineering families, recurs throughout her work. She is concerned with the experience of women, but writes in the Restoration style (full of bawdy jokes). She writes better parts for women than most male playwrights; her characters are more likely to mock men. She's the only woman of her time to write (in her poem 'The Disappointment') about erectile dysfunction. She also writes *Oroonoko,* a novel set in the West Indies, a part of the world she knows well. Shortly after her death, the novel is made into a play.

Behn is an ardent royalist and her best play is *The Rover; or, The Banished Cavaliers.* Inspired by Killigrew's recollections of exile, Behn's play premieres in 1677, staged by the Duke's Company at Dorset Garden. A popular hit, it earns an extended run, enabling her to pocket the box office every third night and make some money. *The Rover* delights in the amorous adventures of a group of Cavaliers in Naples at Carnival time (which allows the characters to dress up as gypsies). The title character is Willmore, a rake who falls in love with a young woman called Hellena, sadly destined for a convent life by her family. At the same time, Angellica Bianca, a courtesan, falls for Willmore. Other cast members include pimps and goodtime girls. In the original production, Elizabeth Barry is Hellena and the Cavaliers are presented as free spirits, with an exuberant and appealing stage presence. Yet there's also a fear of rape in the air. At various points, Behn demonstrates her awareness of the plight of women in Restoration society: typically, Hellena argues that it is better to be a wife than a mistress because if she becomes a mistress, 'What shall I get? A cradle full of noise and mischief, with a pack of repentance at my back.'

Some new plays are more than just sex comedies. The future Poet Laureate Thomas Shadwell's *The Virtuoso*, first staged by the Duke's Company at Dorset Garden in 1676, takes up Ben Jonson's idea of humours comedy, in which each character symbolises a human folly. In this play, which is a topical satire on several subjects, including the newly formed Royal Society and the current interest in science, his characters are the virtuoso scientist Sir Nicholas Gimcrack, Sir Formal Trifle (crazy orator), Sir Samuel Hearty (pretentious wit), and Sir Nicholas's uncle Snarl (hypocrite). Within the usual confines of a love story, with subplots showing Lady Gimcrack seducing two of the other characters and Snarl's sexual fetish for being beaten by rods, Shadwell mercilessly mocks scientific crazes: Gimcrack experiments with swimming on dry land, and stores air from different parts of the country like wine in his cellar. He also searches for the philosopher's stone of the alchemists. An evening of poking fun at absurdity.

Plots and neo-Puritans

But the immoral court of King Charles, with its glittering wit, soon reaches its sell-by date. Towards the end of his reign, in 1678–81, the Popish Plot changes the whole atmosphere of the age, banishing forever the carefree world of the Cavaliers. The

nation's moral compass is about to be reset. To give us an idea
of the temper of the times, Moll takes us by hackney coach to
the White Horse tavern in the Strand, allegedly the scene of
a meeting between the mythomaniac Titus Oates and a group
of Jesuits during the Popish Plot. This meeting turns out to
have been a figment of Oates's fertile imagination. The tavern
is a dark place, with oak panelling and hard darkwood tables,
and Moll speaks in a low voice because of the gravity of the
situation. 'England,' she says, 'has become acutely unstable; the
Popish Plot creates an atmosphere of anti-Catholic paranoia.'
Some playwrights take sides: Aphra Behn, for example, is a
Tory and a supporter of James — in 1682 she writes an Epilogue
for the play *Romulus and Hersilia*, attacking Monmouth, the
Whigs' great white hope. But fear of a return to civil war leads
to a fall in box office. People are too scared to go out.

In this time of emergency, the Lord Chamberlain — the
theatre censor — is on the case. Before now, he has ignored the
sexual content of plays because he knows that they delight King
Charles. But he can't now ignore the danger of political sedition,
so Henry Bennet, Earl of Arlington — Lord Chamberlain — is
increasingly vigilant. 'He is instantly recognizable at court,'
says Moll, 'because he wears a black plaster on the bridge of his
nose, covering a scar he received while fighting for the Royalist
cause during the Civil War.' In 1680 this grandee casts his beady
eye on plays such as Nahum Tate's *The Sicilian Usurper*, which
adapts Shakespeare's *Richard II* into a Whig drama showing
how a tyrant is dethroned and replaced by constitutional rulers.
It gets a couple of public performances and then it's banned.
Because of stage censorship, there are few overtly political
plays. Playwrights prefer to write stories which refer obliquely
to current events. A good example is Thomas Otway's *Venice
Preserved; or, A Plot Discovered* (1682). Otway is an actor who
suffers so badly from stage fright that he only makes one stage
appearance! And turns instead to playwriting. *Venice Preserved*
is a tragedy which shows a failed revolt against Venetian rulers,
but audiences realize that it refers to the failed Popish Plot.
The play cleverly appeals to both Tories and Whigs, explains

POPISH PLOT, WHIGS AND TORIES

In the late seventeenth century, the tensions between Protestants and Catholics return in full force. James Duke of York is King Charles's brother — and a Catholic. He is heir to the throne because although Charles has fathered many children he has no legal offspring. So the fear of a Catholic king creates paranoia during the Popish Plot of 1678-81. This is a fictitious conspiracy invented by Titus Oates, a florid and ignorant clergyman and liar, who has already falsely accused a Hastings schoolmaster of sodomy. He claims that the Catholics plan to assassinate King Charles and place James on the throne. This results in an atmosphere of anti-Catholic hysteria, which precipitates the Exclusion Crisis, during which there is an attempt to pass an Act of Parliament to prevent James becoming king. This is unsuccessful and when Charles dies in 1685 James inherits the throne. But although he successfully puts down Monmouth's Rebellion (by James Scott, Duke of Monmouth, an illegitimate son of King Charles), his inept policies result in his forced abdication and the invitation of the Protestant William of Orange and his wife Mary, James's daughter, to be joint monarchs in the Glorious Revolution of 1688. The result of this — enshrined in the 1689 Bill of Rights — is the constitutional monarchy that in partnership with parliament has governed Britain ever since. Out of these conflicts emerge the first political parties: the Tories, who believe in tradition and support James as rightful king even though he is a Catholic, and the Whigs, who believe that the rightful king must always be a Protestant and rule with parliament.

Moll, who is now yawning behind her ostrich fan. We gather that she's had a late night so we suggest moving on.

Once again, we find ourselves in a hackney coach. It's raining so we're grateful for this mode of transport. We settle down as Moll takes up the story again. 'Theatre is in crisis,' she says, 'not only because of falling audiences but also due to incompetent management.' Killigrew proves to be a dud. After constant disputes with his actors, he completely loses their confidence. Hearing of this trouble, Betterton, manager of the rival Duke's Company, sees his chance. He waits and schemes. Then he makes a secret pact with Charles Hart and Edward Kynaston, the most important actors in the King's Company, and in 1682 merges the two companies under his leadership. Betterton chooses the Theatre Royal Drury Lane as his base, and plays safe by staging well-known favourites rather than looking for new plays. Now London only has one theatre company — the United Company.

King Charles dies in 1685 and his Catholic brother King James II abdicates in 1688, after a short but turbulent reign, to be replaced by the stoutly Protestant power couple of King William III and Queen Mary. They are models of piety and have little interest in theatre, so few of their courtiers attend shows and audiences are now dominated by the wealthy citizens of the City. 'Yet, despite such changes,' says Moll, 'the one thing guaranteed to bring in audiences is star actors.' The United Company's new draw is Elizabeth Barry. Known as the queen of tragedy, the greatest star of her day is plump, large-hipped and with an aquiline nose. Rumour has it that she was trained for the stage by the rake Rochester, who was also her lover. Moll is not sure about that but she does know that Barry started her career at Dorset Garden in 1675. In tragic plays, she stuns and captivates audiences. She means everything she says; she's intense; she's real. Yet at the same time she is melodious in her delivery of noble lines. Audiences have never seen anything like it. Her Belvidera in Thomas Otway's *Venice Preserved* — which he wrote for her — is complex and commanding. Her Monimia in the same author's *The Orphan* in 1680 is so memorable that it creates a fashion for so-called 'she-tragedies'. This genre of pathetic tragedy is concerned with the sufferings of a woman, sometimes innocent, sometimes guilty of sins of the flesh. Barry's career lasts thirty-five years. She is the first actor to be awarded a benefit performance, getting the box office for a show and thus boosting her income. And she gives Betterton a new lease of life — they play opposite each other throughout the 1680s. But although she earns £100 a year at a time when a gentleman can live on £50, it is still only half of Betterton's pay.

By contrast, Anne Bracegirdle is younger than Barry, more beautiful and more vivaciously expressive in her romantic and comic roles. She first appears on stage as a child, and later on her beauty attracts amorous interest from many quarters. This, Moll tells us, results in some dreadful incidents. Captain Richard Hill, a rake whose advances Bracegirdle has spurned, is determined to carry her off. Along with his dissolute friend Lord Charles Mohun, he tries to abduct her. This fails when William Mountford, her actor friend, intervenes. He is murdered by the would-be abductors. Ghastly! Throughout her life Bracegirdle has a particular reputation for virtue, being presented with 800 guineas from a subscription headed by Lord Halifax as a tribute to her morals, and her reputation is enhanced by her charity to the poor, of which there are many, around Drury Lane. Her greatest success is in the comedies of William Congreve and her good behaviour contrasts with that of some of the touchy characters in the audience. In one incident, Sir John Churchill, later Duke of Marlborough and hero of the Battle of Blenheim, insults an orange-selling woman, and the sword-prone Thomas Otway draws his blade on him. On another occasion, a Mr Scroop, being the worse for drink, insults one Sir Thomas Armstrong, and also draws his sword. This time they fight, and Scroop is run through the heart.

'Now,' says Moll as the coach sways alarmingly to our next destination, 'a new mover and shaker appears on the scene.' It's Christopher Rich, a financially savvy lawyer who fancies himself as a theatre manager (despite his complete ignorance of the business). In 1688, he buys a share in the Theatre Royal Drury Lane and becomes manager of the United Company. But he is bad news: he only wants to make money; he fails to invest; he cheats his actors. Things get so bad that they petition the Lord Chamberlain, claiming that Rich treats them like slaves. In 1695, a group of actors led by Betterton, Elizabeth Barry and Anne Bracegirdle — the breakaway Actors Company — obtain a new patent, split from Rich and move to a hastily refurbished Lisle's Tennis Court in Lincoln's Inn Fields. And so it is that London has two theatre companies again.

We now find ourselves in front of the Bank of England in Walbrook in the City. Moll shows us the sombre building and explains that it is founded in 1694 to act as the government's banker and is privately owned by stockholders. Standing in the

ENEMIES OF THEATRE: COLLIER'S ATTACK

After Jeremy Collier publishes, in April 1698, his vitriolic anti-theatre tract, *A Short View of Immorality and Profaneness of the English Stage Together with the Sense of Antiquity upon this Argument* (a book as longwinded — more than 280 pages — as its title), a pamphlet war breaks out. Dozens of publications attack or defend the theatre, which Collier denounces as 'intolerable' because of the playwrights' 'smuttiness of expression, their swearing, profaneness and lewd application of scripture, their abuse of the clergy, their making their top characters libertines and giving them success in their debauchery'. Collier argues that instead theatre ought to be moral: 'The business of plays is to recommend virtue and discountenance vice.' A Cambridge-educated neo-Puritan, he especially picks out the work of William Congreve and John Vanbrugh for condemnation. In this, he is supported by the various Societies for the Reformation of Manners, who send informers to see shows and scribble down any profane oaths or lewd lines. Then they prosecute the actors in the courts for speaking these words in public. Over the next three decades there are hundreds of such private prosecutions. These have limited success, but a climate of fear is created, and playwrights clean up their act.

dirty street, she quickly fills us in with some more details about theatre, assuring us that there is a connection with finance. 'In the 1690s,' she says, 'theatre experiences hard times as neo-Puritans, led by the ruling power couple, become ever more influential. This mood is symbolized by the new importance of finance. Money now talks louder than land.' This new economic universe means that the citizens of London want an orderly society and theatre, of course, is synonymous with disorder! They don't want their employees to waste time watching shows when they should be hard at work. The new moral order culminates in the Lord Chamberlain decreeing in 1697 that all plays must be licensed and cleansed of 'all obscenities'. A year later Jeremy Collier's *Short View of the Immorality and Profaneness of the English Stage* is published. Collier, an over-educated religious bigot, attacks playwrights for being dirty. But he has public opinion on his side, and plays are becoming much more sentimental and much less sexy.

Leading the change in taste is a man who will dominate London theatre for the next fifty years. Colley Cibber is a great actor-manager who begins acting at Drury Lane in 1690, although at first with little success. Then in 1696 he relaunches his career by writing a comedy, *Love's Last Shift; or, The Fool in Fashion*, which has a big flamboyant part for himself as the Frenchified fop, Sir Novelty Fashion. From now on, his forte is comedy dandies. *Love's Last Shift* is staged at Drury Lane and its title refers to a trick that a virtuous wife, Amanda, plays on her husband, Loveless, who prefers the brothel bed to the domestic hearth, and she manages to reform him in the course of one night by imitating a high-class courtesan. It's a big success with audiences and its virtuous ending is welcomed. But some see its moral uprightness as a challenge. In the same year John Vanbrugh, architect and playwright, writes *The Relapse: or, Virtue in Danger*, a sequel to Cibber's play in which the rakish husband ends up by succumbing to temptation and yet another extramarital affair. Cibber is as amused as anyone else in London at this response and doesn't mind — he gets to play another great monster of vanity: Lord Foppington. A year later, Vanbrugh does it again with *The Provoked Wife*, which shows a wife trapped in an abusive marriage. Its daring message is that she might consider leaving it or, if not, taking a lover. Mrs Barry plays the unhappy Lady Bute and the younger Bracegirdle her niece, while the starring role of Sir John Brute, the brutal husband, goes to Betterton, and is one of the peaks of his career. Similarly, two plays by Thomas Southerne — *The Wives' Excuse; or Cuckolds Make Themselves* (1691) and *The Fatal Marriage; or, The Innocent Adultery* (1694) — are she-tragedies in the pathetic tradition, and both feature suffering women. Audiences love sentimental stories, and exotic ones: his *Oroonoko; or The Royal Slave* (1696), based on the novel by Aphra Behn, is about a slave rebellion in Surinam that ends with the main characters committing suicide.

We are running out of time, and Moll looks tired, but she can't resist pointing out that Aphra Behn is not the only female playwright of these times. Although there are only thirty-three female playwrights to 345 male ones, they do make an impact — despite the prejudice that dismisses them as 'petticoat-authors'. And we all know what Moll thinks of that! One group, known collectively as the Female Wits, includes Catherine Trotter and Mary Pix, who both emerge during the 1695-96 season. Then there's Susannah Centlivre, the most successful female playwright of the new century, and Moll recommends her biggest hits: *The Busy Body* (1709), *The Wonder: A Woman Keeps a Secret* (1714) and *A Bold Stroke for a Wife* (1719). Her comedies are romantic in spirit and feature quick-witted women who are liberal in their attitudes. 'It makes a refreshing change,' laughs Moll.

Love in a new climate

The most outstanding playwright of the time is William Congreve, another dilettante whose masterpiece, *The Way of the World*, is staged by Betterton's company in 1700.

This quintessential comedy is set in fashionable London: St James's Park, the salons of the rich and the coffee-houses of the town. To tell us more, Moll takes us to Westminster Abbey, whose fine gothic edifice shines in the bright sunshine of a summer noon. Inside, she takes us down the echoing aisles, pointing out the burial places of Ben Jonson, William Davenant, John Dryden, Aphra Behn and Congreve.

Because of the changes in moral climate, *The Way of the World* has more romance than the lecherous fare typical of the earlier Restoration period. At its heart is a story about a couple learning to love and respect each other. Mirabell (his name suggests that he admires women), a young man about town, is in love with Millamant (her name suggests a thousand admirers). But to marry her he must first win over her aunt, Lady Wishfort, who controls the young woman's estate. (Arranged marriages are still the norm.) Mirabell tries to please Wishfort until Mrs Marwood,

WILLIAM CONGREVE

Born: 24 January 1670, Bardsey, Yorkshire.

Family: Ancient and respected. In 1674 Congreve's officer father William and mother Mary join garrison at Youghal, Ireland. After the Glorious Revolution of 1688 they move to Stretton, Staffordshire.

Education: Kilkenny College, then Trinity College, Dublin. In 1691 moves to London to attend Middle Temple. Never a serious student, he writes plays instead.

Private life: Never married but rumored to be involved with the actress Anne Bracegirdle. Later embarks on a long affair with Henrietta, Duchess of Marlborough. She has a daughter, Mary, in 1723.

Career: His first comedy, *The Old Bachelor*, at Drury Lane in 1693 is an enormous success. Writes three more plays. Holds numerous government posts, including Customs Collector at Poole.

Greatest hit: *The Way of the World* (1700).

Death: 19 January 1729, after a coach accident.

Afterlife: In his own words: 'Heaven has no rage like love to hatred turned, nor hell a fury like a woman scorned.'

rejected earlier by him, threatens to expose his scheming. Further complications are introduced in a tortuous plot, plus other characters with delightful names such as Fainall, Witwoud and Petulant, and servants called Waitwell, Foible and Mincing. In the end, Millamant accepts Mirabell's proposal and rejects Witwoud, Lady Wishfort's candidate for her hand. Its excessive complexity might explain why the play is relatively unpopular with its original audience — despite its thrilling cast: Betterton plays Fainall, the villain, the great Elizabeth Barry plays Mrs Marwood and the charming Anne Bracegirdle plays Millamant, 'Nay' — says Moll, her eyes suddenly sparkling — 'she is her.' Mirabell is played by John Verbruggen.

With its elegance, sophistication and exquisite lightness of tone, the play revels in its London air: at one point, Millamant says, 'I nauseate walking: 'tis a country diversion; I loathe the country and everything that relates to it.' Much of the dialogue is memorable, as in Mrs Marwood's 'But say what you will, 'tis better to be left than never to have been loved.' Central to the pleasure of the play is Congreve's delicate handling of the love game as played by Mirabell and Millamant. They embody the ideal attitude, intense yet balanced, love based on both mutual esteem and pride in self. In the Act Four proviso scene, Mirabell and Millamant wittily discuss a prenuptial agreement. Central to Millamant is her independence: 'My dear liberty, shall I leave thee? My faithful solitude, my darling contemplation, must I bid you adieu?' she asks before stating 'I can't do it, 'tis more than impossible.' She asserts her right to be lazy: 'I will lie a-bed in a morning as long as I please.' She also objects to being addressed by such names as 'wife, spouse, my dear, joy, jewel, love, sweetheart; and the rest of that nauseous cant in which men and their wives are so fulsomely familiar.' She refuses to be belittled. She forbids public displays of intimacy, and reserves the right to write to whoever she pleases, wear what she wants and to be 'sole empress of my tea table'. Mirabell has conditions of his own: his wife should not hang around with

William Congreve

women of bad character, nor wear make-up or masks to disguise her appearance in public. She is warned to have 'no she-friend to screen her affairs', no fop to take her secretly to the theatre, 'to wheedle you a fop-scrambling'. Mirabell criticizes the use of tight dresses during pregnancy, and forbids excessive drinking. Both parties itemize the conditions in a spirit of fun, but the mutual agreement is also a political metaphor: the relationship between monarchy and parliament also has to be negotiated, as it is during the Glorious Revolution.

If Congreve's play is not an immediate hit, other plays show the public appetite for stories about moral reform. As we leave Westminster Abbey, Moll tells us that in 1704 Colley Cibber stages *The Careless Husband* by Richard Steele, the Irish soldier, journalist and Whig politician. In it Sir Charles Easy is unfaithful to his wife until she discovers him asleep in a chair next to her maid. When Lady Easy sees him she doesn't make a fuss; she simply puts her neck cloth on his bare and wigless head to keep him warm. When Charles realizes that he has been found out, he promptly changes into a loving husband. 'It's not very convincing,' says Moll, 'but it shows that the trend for comedies of moral reform has arrived.' What audiences now want is theatre that resets your moral compass.

While Betterton's Actors Company competes with Rich's United Company for audiences, an Irish playwright briefly lights up the scene. We are now walking towards Covent Garden as Moll tells us about George Farquhar, the Derry-born son of an Irish clergyman. Quitting his studies for a life in the theatre, he moves to Dublin, but while performing in John Dryden's *The Indian Emperor*, he forgets to use a blunt sword and badly wounds a fellow actor. Shocked by the accident, he gives up acting and leaves for London in 1698, travelling with Robert Wilks, an actor who later becomes the manager of Drury Lane. Both men are among the first Dubliners to make their fortunes in London, heading a wave of Irish migrants who will transform the British stage during the next three centuries. Despite suffering from tuberculosis,

Farquhar writes like a fury. His 1698 playwriting debut, *Love and a Bottle*, is widely praised for its wit. A year later, his *The Constant Couple* at Drury Lane is a great success, helped by his friend Wilks's portrayal of Henry Wildair, a dashing baronet who is one of several suitors of Lady Lurewell, the scheming protagonist. He's a new type of theatre hero, more a man of honour than a fop. It's a role that becomes Wilks's signature and makes him a heartthrob.

Farquhar's best play is *The Recruiting Officer*, staged in 1706 at Drury Lane. Set in Shrewsbury, where two years previously the playwright had been a military man, it is a rural comedy and, with it, British drama temporarily abandons the town and takes a stroll around other parts of the nation. While Sergeant Kite, the recruiting officer, tries to fool the impressionable men of Shrewsbury into enlisting in the army, the womanizing Captain Plume — whose motto is 'she was for the wedding before consummation and I was for consummation before the wedding' — and his friend Worthy, a local gentleman, pursue Sylvia, a young lady, and Melinda, her cousin. Both women have recently come into fortunes, which means that their parents want to control who they marry. Sylvia's father sends her away, but she returns dressed as a man (a classic breeches part) and offers to enlist in the army. In a good-tempered satirical spirit, Farquhar creates the character of the cowardly Captain Brazen, who is also smitten by Melinda. Some smart plotting deals with sexual intrigue, but with a light-heartedness that is fresh and entertaining.

The first production of *The Recruiting Officer* stars Anne Oldfield, an actress discovered by Farquhar and with whom, say the town gossips, he is having an affair. We turn to Moll for confirmation, but she is non-committal. The part of the foppish Brazen proves to be a notable role for Colley Cibber. The delightful play is an immediate hit, and some performances result in memorable incidents. On one evening in 1710, the actors insert a ballad mocking John Churchill, Duke of Marlborough, the famous general and favourite of Queen Anne, for his avarice. The crowd erupts with applause, which intensifies when people spot the Duke's daughter, the Duchess of Montagu, in a box. She is blushing bright red. Elsewhere, the play goes on to become one of the most frequently performed plays of the eighteenth century, the first play to be performed in Australia and likewise the first to be staged at the Dock Street Theatre in Charleston, South Carolina.

In 1707, despite the success of *The Recruiting Officer*, Farquhar is short of cash, and Wilks encourages him to write another play. The next day Farquhar delivers the plot for *The Beaux' Stratagem*, which is then performed six weeks later. The play is a hit, but Farquhar does not live to enjoy his success. He succumbs to tuberculosis after the third performance. Meanwhile, the first Theatre Royal outside London, in Smock Alley, Dublin, Farquhar's old stomping ground, grows in popularity, even though its repertoire relies on staging London hits. Nearer home, Bath builds a small theatre in 1705 and Norwich, the second largest city in Britain, soon follows suit. By now we find ourselves outside Drury Lane theatre again. Moll is going to see a tragedy this afternoon. It's not to our taste so we leave her to it. With a swish of her skirts, she disappears inside.

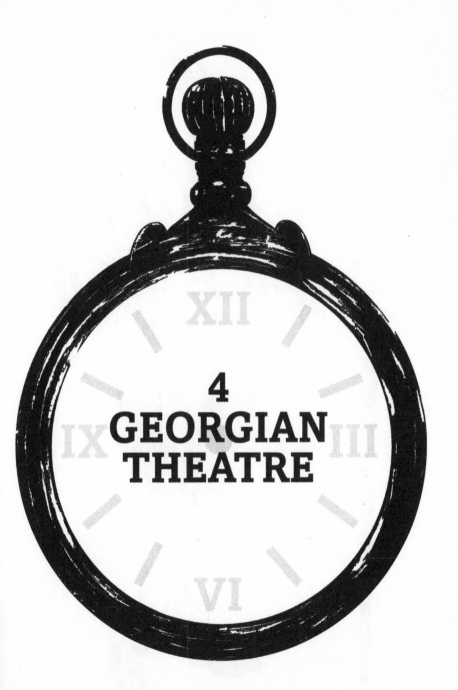

4
GEORGIAN
THEATRE

4
Georgian Theatre

Meet our guide: Edgcott

We meet our new guide, Henry Holme Lord Edgcott, in Old Slaughter's coffee house in St Martin's Lane, one of the fashionable meeting places that have sprung up in London. It's a convivial place, with a warm fire, and wooden settles and tables. We are invited to enjoy the latest exotic imports: coffee, tea or hot chocolate. Edgcott is rather on the plump side, but well dressed in a tight-fitting embroidered coat, plain waistcoat and breeches fastened below the knee. His shirt is frilled at the cuffs and he sports a knotted lace cravat. His powdered wig is tied back with a ribbon. He carries a cane, and exudes an air of being a man about town. We've been told that he is a member of the Kit-Cat Club, a group of well-connected Whig politicians, patrons of the arts and artists, who sponsor plays and attend the theatre regularly. They even paid for the funeral of playwright and critic John Dryden, although they never agreed with his Tory views. The name of this talking shop comes from Christopher (Kit) Catt, keeper of a pie-house in Grays Inn Lane, where the club originally met. 'His mutton pies are,' says Edgcott, 'a treat.' After he has slurped down his coffee, Edgcott takes out a long clay pipe. We're a bit awed by the fact that he is a real-life lord, with a country seat in Buckinghamshire and a town house in Mayfair, and he has the gruff manner of someone who doesn't suffer fools gladly. He leans back, gets comfortable in his seat, takes a deep puff of tobacco, and tells us that on this trip we will be looking at English theatre from the 1710s to the 1780s, the Georgian era.

Georgian England

We leave Old Slaughter's, and Edgcott takes us for a stroll in the streets of Mayfair, newly laid out with neat red-brick terraced housing. After the Great Fire of 1666, London has been rebuilt, with more than a hundred streets widened and two new avenues, King Street and Queen Street, laid out in the City. As the habitations of Londoners expand towards the west, aristocrats build elegant squares in Mayfair and St James's. The swelling numbers of the new middle-classes — manufacturers, tradesmen and financiers — live near them in what is today called the West End. Although there are no street lights, no paving, no sewage system, no paid police, no effective fire brigade and no regulation of alcohol or tobacco, the place is buzzing. Everywhere, there's the stink of horses and the smell of coal. We hear the sound of street vendors and ballad singers. This is the age of music, where opera for toffs is heard side by side with street pop songs. We see black servants and maimed ex-soldiers, a grim reminder of slavery and wars. 'London is also,' says Edgcott, 'a city with enormous numbers of poor,' who live in appalling conditions in dilapidated garrets, courts, alleys and tenements — 'death rates,' he growls, 'far exceed birth rates, and infant mortality is particularly high.'

Welcome to the Georgian era, when for more than one hundred years four kings called George rule Britain. In 1714, the new king, George I, is Elector of Hanover, a principality in Germany. Although he is fifty-four, and doesn't speak English, he is offered the throne because he is the closest Protestant relation of the late Queen Anne, who dies on 1 August. Under the 'Act of Settlement' of 1701, only Protestants are allowed to wear the crown so her Catholic relatives are barred. Because of the difficulties of travelling, King George does not arrive in London until September and is crowned in Westminster Abbey a month later. In public, he is quite wooden and shy; apart from state occasions, he wears a normal frockcoat and ordinary clothes; his favourite pastime is playing cards informally with friends. Because he is a foreigner and supports the pro-Protestant Whigs in government, King George is not universally popular. Around the country, celebrations of his coronation are disrupted by pro-Tory protests and riots. To combat such disturbances, the 'Riot Act' is passed, which means that officials can order any noisy group of people to disperse. If they don't, the army is called in. Even more serious than rioting is the Jacobite claim, supported by the Tories, to the throne by the Catholic James Stuart (Old Pretender), son of the exiled King James II. In 1715, the first Jacobite Rebellion takes place, but fails. All this turmoil seems a long way away from elegant Mayfair, with its fancy carriages and well-dressed gentlemen and ladies, but Edgcott warns us to be on our guard as these are tempestuous times.

Yet the theatre system is stable. Where once royal courtiers dominated the scene, it is now the theatre-makers who call the shots. Although King George is a great patron of music, and supports George Frederick Handel — a German musical genius who comes from Hanover to London — he is something of a theatre philistine. Spoken drama bores him because he doesn't understand the language very well.

So the top man in London theatre is the Irish-born Sir Richard Steele — journalist, playwright, boss of the Theatre Royal Drury Lane, and a prominent Whig MP. Well-fed, affable and determined to do the right thing, Steele is very hands-off, leaving the day-to-day running of Drury Lane to three actors: Colley Cibber, Robert Wilks and Barton Booth (who ran away to join the theatre instead of taking holy orders). Led by them, Drury Lane becomes identified with the Whigs. In 1722, Steele's most important play, *The Conscious Lovers* is staged here. As Edgcott takes us to Drury Lane, walking past the noisy Covent Garden market, he tells us the story of the play and explains its significance. *The Conscious Lovers* is about Bevil Junior, who is encouraged by his father, Sir John Bevil, to marry the wealthy Lucinda, daughter of Mr Sealand. He doesn't love her, but his best friend Myrtle does. Instead, Bevil loves Indiana, a young woman of good family who is apparently poor (in fact she is Sealand's lost daughter). So Bevil and Myrtle devise a scheme, involving lots of disguises, to marry the women they love. 'The thing about *The Conscious Lovers*,' says Edgcott, 'is that its hero is a model of good sense and good manners.' For example, he disapproves of the fashion for dueling. And symbolically the union of Bevil and Indiana represents the joining of the old gentry with the new merchant class in an entertainment which, as Steele explains in a preface, inspires 'a joy too exquisite for laughter'. But although *The Conscious Lovers* is a success, it also attracts criticism. One review, by playwright and critic John

Dennis, contrasts the traditional idea of comedy — that it should mock evil deeds — with Steele's more sentimental type of comedy. The play is a massive blockbuster. With an initial run of eighteen consecutive nights, it makes more money than any other Drury Lane play. This new style of sentimental comedy will last for the rest of the century.

THE CRITIC'S VIEW: THE CONSCIOUS LOVERS

John Dennis reviews *The Conscious Lovers* (1722):

How little do they know of the nature of true comedy, who believe that its proper business is to set us patterns for imitation: for all such patterns are serious things, and laughter is the life, and the very soul of comedy. It is its proper business to expose persons to our view, whose views we may shun, and whose follies we may despise; and by showing us what is done upon the comic stage, to show us what ought never to be done upon the stage of the world.

As well as being a theatre manager and politician, the affable Steele is also that new kind of social animal — a journalist. Newspaper censorship lapsed in 1695, so the British press is now the most lively in Europe. Steele, in collaboration with his friend, the essayist and playwright Joseph Addison, founds *The Tatler* and *The Spectator* in the early years of the century. They also publish the first theatre magazine — *The Theatre*. Edgcott shows us a copy of *The Tatler* and we can see how gossip from coffeehouses sits alongside articles which aim to improve taste, manners and teach polite conversation. These publications are also the first to include theatre reviews. Edgcott reckons that at least a tenth of London's population reads them regularly. Addison, who excels at the classics (his Latin verses are much admired) also tries his hand at playwriting. His breakthrough is *Cato*, which plays at Drury Lane in 1713. It's a heavy tragedy about the life and death by suicide of a Roman orator, neo-classical in style and obedient to The Unities. So it's more Continental than English. However, although its verse has great decorum, it is also immensely tedious. Nothing happens. Still, both Whigs and Tories in the audience applaud the republican Cato's stoical defence of Roman values against the tyranny of Julius Caesar. On one occasion, Barton Booth, the actor playing Cato, is called to the box of the Tory Viscount Bolingbroke, who rewards him with the princely sum of fifty guineas.

Bourgeois respectability

'These days,' Edgcott tells us, striding along with his cane swinging, 'respectability is becoming the chief criterion for audiences.' Rapidly expanding on the back of wealth created by merchants trading with new colonies in the West Indies, north America and India, the middle classes become avid consumers not only of imports such as sugar, tea, coffee and chocolate, but also of the arts. Learning to appreciate new tastes, this social group not only provides the audiences for theatre, but also a growing readership for novels, poetry and printed plays. More women than ever before are literate, and interested in the arts. Now admission to a theatre depends on being properly dressed: if you are scruffy, you can't come in. In the 1690s, theatre performances started at 4pm. By 1720, start times are 6pm. The rising middle class, headed by busy civil servants, industrious merchants and professional gentlemen, have work to do during the day. Theatre becomes an evening event.

It is a summer afternoon, and we arrive at Drury Lane. As we walk around the empty and echoing theatre, Edgcott mentions some plays which are quite significant, but not worth dwelling on too long. In his brusque way, he dismisses the tragedies of the Poet Laureate Nicholas Rowe as a parade of weepy women: *Jane Shore* (1714) and *Lady Jane Grey* (1715) are she-tragedies about doomed historical figures. 'Rowe's greatest contribution to drama,' says Edgcott argumentatively, 'is not his pathetic plays but his six-volume edition of the work of William Shakespeare, which makes the bard instantly available to a new generation of actors.' For the first time, his spelling is modernized and the plays are divided into acts and scenes. Rowe also includes a biography of Shakespeare, based on research done in Stratford-upon-Avon. Edgcott gives us a sharp look, and asks if we have any questions? We don't so he moves on. It is a very tempestuous time politically, he reminds us, so Colley Cibber's play, *The Non-Juror*, at Drury Lane in 1717, is worth a mention. Just two years after the failed Jacobite Rising of 1715, it has a Papist spy as the villain and the play is a propaganda piece directed against Roman Catholics and their Tory apologists. But although audiences are more respectable than ever, they still respond strongly to this kind of provocation, erupting into so much noise that performances are abandoned. Shaken by this experience, Cibber never writes another political play. Edgcott says that this is an early warning of the many theatre riots to come.

A more typical Drury Lane play is George Lillo's *The London Merchant; or, The History of George Barnwell*, first staged in 1731. The story concerns George Barnwell, a hardworking apprentice, who is seduced by the scheming Sarah Millwood into robbery, murder and finally ends up on the scaffold. A quote from Trueman, Barnwell's fellow apprentice, gives a flavour of this self-righteous drama: 'He who trusts heaven ought never to despair. But business requires our attendance — business, the youth's best preservative from ill, as idleness is his worst of snares.' But although Lillo lectures his audience, the great thing about the play is that the characters are ordinary middle-class folk. Unsurprisingly, this becomes a hardy perennial on the eighteenth-century stage. But what does Edgcott think of it? 'Bah,' he says as he takes a long snort of snuff, 'tedious drivel.' The new middle classes are too pushy for his taste.

Although the affable Steele is the top man, he is not the only mover and shaker. As in the Restoration times, there are two patents, and the other one is held by John Rich, son of theatre manager Christopher Rich. Unlike his incompetent and heavy-handed father, John Rich is an immensely successful actor-manager. His career spans some forty-seven years, beginning at Lincoln's Inn Fields in 1715. Here, he creates something completely new — an evening full of entertainment, a good night out. He does this by adding an 'afterpiece' to the main play. These afterpieces are short plays in a variety of forms: satires, sketches or burlesques. He also writes himself into history by promoting what will become that most English of shows: the pantomime. At this date panto is a short episode of humorous slapstick. It features stock characters from the Italian *commedia dell'arte*: the wily Harlequin, the lovely Colombine and her strict father Pantaloon. Plots are based on Harlequin's attempts to get Colombine. Rich makes a name for himself by playing Harlequin, and such pantomimes — which have few words but lots of knockabout — regularly sell out. Rich is also pretty eccentric, deliberately mangling the surnames of his actors and keeping more than two dozen cats in his house. Edgcott wrinkles his nose in disgust.

Ballads and beggars

Without knowing the politics of Georgian England, we would struggle to understand the deeply satirical theatre of the time. So to fill us in, Edgcott takes us to the Cheshire Cheese pub, off Fleet Street, hoping that some beer will help us swallow the lesson. He leads us up the creaking stairs and along a narrow corridor until we finally find a table in an upstairs room. There's a heavy scent of sawdust mixed with ale. He takes out his long clay pipe again. 'The most important political figure,' he says, 'is Sir Robert Walpole, the big Whig.' This Eton- and Cambridge-educated pot-bellied man is coarse, corrupt and cynical, but he dominates politics through his personal connections, and grasp of detail. He is expert at screening King George I from political attack, earning the nickname Screen-Master General. We chuckle, recognizing an early example of spin. Although our guide is a Whig, he doesn't approve of Walpole's corruption and the 'Robinocracy', a system of hangers-on paid by bribery. 'The man's a scoundrel and a genius, all in one,' he says. And Walpole rules as Britain's first and longest-serving prime minister for more than two decades from 1721. In 1735, King George II is so pleased with his work that he makes him a gift of the house at 10 Downing Street — still the residence of British prime ministers today.

'The existence,' says Edgcott, tapping his pipe on the table, 'of two competing companies (Steele's Drury Lane and Rich's Lincoln's Inn Fields) means that anyone with a new play has a choice of which theatre to take it to.' So when John Gay, an overweight scribbler of pastoral verse and friend of the poet Alexander Pope, is rejected by Steele, he takes his new play, *The Beggar's Opera*, to Rich. Gay has had his ups and downs: enjoying a success with *What D'Ye Call It?* (a short satire on tragedy) and suffering a failure with *Three Hours after Marriage* (a comedy which isn't funny). He's also lost all his money — including about one thousand pounds raised by subscription for his poems — in the South Sea Company, whose collapse in 1720 is the greatest financial scandal of the age. (Colley Cibber is another of its victims.) As always, finance and speculation go hand in hand, leading to spectacular crashes.

JOHN GAY

Born: 30 June 1685, Barnstaple, Devon.

Family: Orphaned at ten and brought up by uncle Reverend John Hammer.

Education: Barnstaple Grammar School.

Private life: Never married.

Career: Secretary to Duchess of Monmouth and Lord Clarendon. Writes poems, plays and ballad operas. In 1729, *Polly*, sequel to *The Beggar's Opera*, is banned by Lord Chamberlain, but its publication earns Gay money.

Greatest hit: *The Beggar's Opera* (1728).

Death: 4 December 1732.

Epitaph: Buried in Westminster Abbey. Inscription from *The Beggar's Opera*: 'Life is a jest, and all things show it:/ I thought so once and now I know it.'

Afterlife: Invented the ballad opera and is thus the father of modern musicals.

The Beggar's Opera opens at Lincoln's Inn Fields on 29 January 1728. This three-act tale of the London underworld is a completely new thing: a ballad opera sung in English. Edgcott hums a couple of tunes, but they are unfamiliar. 'For this music,' he says, 'Gay has raided the world of broadsheet ballads, church hymns and folk tunes, a welcome contrast to the serious Italian opera arias of the time.' By recycling popular songs, Gay is saying that English music is every bit as good as Italian imports. Loosely based on the notorious real-life story of highwayman Jack Sheppard, the musical is set in Newgate, London's chief prison, which prompts poet and pamphleteer Jonathan Swift to label it ironically a 'Newgate pastoral'.

John Gay's *The Beggar's Opera* (1728)
Peachum sings his first air, 'An Old Woman Clothed in Gray':
Through all the employments of life
Each neighbour abuses his brother;
Whore and rogue they call husband and wife:
All professions be-rogue one another.
The priest calls the lawyer a cheat,
The lawyer be-knaves the divine;
And the statesman, because he's so great,
Thinks his trade as honest as mine.

Peachum — a fence and thief catcher — and his wife discover that their daughter Polly has secretly married Macheath, a highwayman. Peachum is sceptical about marriage, saying: 'Do you think your mother and I should have lived comfortably so long together if ever we had been married?' Upset at losing Polly, they decide to capture Macheath, who is betrayed by two whores, Jenny Diver and Suky Tawdry. Imprisoned in Newgate, and guarded by Lockit the jailer, Macheath asks the latter's daughter Lucy — who also fancies him — to help him escape. But when four more women claim him as their husband, he gives up, and says he's ready to hang. The Beggar, who acts as the show's narrator, says that although a moral conclusion would see Macheath being executed, the audience demands a happy ending, and so Macheath is reprieved. The evening ends on a dance of celebration. Although the show is full of fun, it is clear that while the characters are petty criminals, their crimes pale into insignificance when compared to those of Walpole. Certainly, the buzz in the newspapers emphasizes the show's criticism of political corruption.

The Beggar's Opera takes the town by storm. It runs for some sixty-two nights, the longest run in London theatre so far. And it's regularly revived. In February 1728, *The Craftsman*, a newspaper, describes its impact: 'This week a dramatic entertainment has been exhibited at the theatre in Lincoln's Inn Fields, entitled *The Beggar's Opera*, which has met with a general applause, insomuch that the wags say it has made Rich very gay, and probably will make Gay very rich.' And so it does. It's also part of a cross-media interest in criminals and tarts. In 1729 the artist William Hogarth paints scenes from *The Beggar's Opera*, and is inspired by the fate of Polly Peachum to create Moll Hackabout, the whore in his *Harlot's Progress* series. Likewise that new literary form, the novel, gets a shot in the arm from Daniel Defoe's *Moll Flanders*, which is also about low lifes. As always, the world of the wild and desperate is a subject that fascinates the respectable and the comfortable.

Drury Lane and Covent Garden

Following the sensational success of *The Beggar's Opera*, John Rich builds a new 1400-seat Theatre Royal in Covent Garden, which opens on 7 December 1732. Designed by Edward Shepherd (architect of many London mansions), it is located in the Covent Garden Piazza, just around the corner from Drury Lane, on the same site as the Royal Opera House today. Edgcott takes us to have a look but as the winter night has already fallen we don't get a good sight of the building's exterior. The inside, however, takes our breath away. The proscenium arch is very tall, and the three tiers of side boxes look sumptuous, painted in gold and cream. The whole theatre glows in the light of a thousand candles. In the stalls, the fashionable audience sits on backless benches. The tiers of boxes are occupied by the more well-off patrons. At the very top there is a gallery of cheap seats. In front of the proscenium arch is the platform which juts out into the stalls, and the shape and atmosphere of the theatre is essentially the same as in Restoration times. When the building is officially opened, Rich is carried shoulder-high by his actors, with onlookers shouting 'Rich for ever'. His first show is a popular favourite: William Congreve's *The Way of the World*. But plays are just one part of his repertoire: the first ballet is performed here in 1734, and George Frederick Handel presents a season of Italian opera the following year.

So now the two official theatres in London are Drury Lane and Covent Garden. These large buildings are the inheritors of the patent system, which stipulates that London can have only two theatres. But there is a loophole in law and so it is that other theatres flourish, injecting a dash of competition into the system. Edgcott sits us down on one of the backless benches in the pit and says that the most important of these is the King's Theatre (formerly the Queen's Theatre under Queen Anne) in Haymarket. It was built by polymath John Vanbrugh, the architect of Blenheim Palace and Castle Howard who is also a playwright. On the other side of the same street is the Little Theatre Haymarket, a small venue built by John Potter, a young carpenter, in 1720. Other semi-legal London venues include the Irish actor Henry Giffard's Goodman's Fields theatre, in Ayliffe Street in the working-class district of Whitechapel. In Greenwich and Richmond, William Penkethman runs summer seasons. These semi-legitimate ventures create a lively theatre culture.

In terms of programming, this is the age when seasons run from September to May, the majority of plays being revivals. But ordinary straight dramas are just one part of the entertainment. In fact, the vitality of the British stage comes from the variety of entertainment on offer. A typical evening lasts between four and five hours, beginning with a musical overture, followed by the main play (a five-act tragedy or a comedy), which is then followed by an afterpiece, usually a shorter comic play, to round off the evening. These short plays are often mischievous in content. The burletta, basically a comic opera, is a popular form of afterpiece. Other gimmicks to attract audiences include dancers, contortionists and singers. In between the acts of the play, you can watch dancing or listen to music.

Edgcott also takes this opportunity to tell us that, in the same month that *The Beggar's Opera* opens, Colley Cibber's last comedy, *The Provoked Husband; or, A Journey to London* (adapted from an unfinished play by John Vanbrugh), is a popular success, running for an impressive twenty-eight nights at Drury Lane. Cibber is the most performed playwright of the age, although he's rarely original. And here our guide acidly quotes the judgment of critic and essayist Alexander Pope that Cibber's drastic adaptations of the classics 'crucify Molière' and betray 'hapless Shakespeare'. Instead of such travesties, it would be more fun to sample some outdoor entertainment so, with a swing of his cane, Edgcott takes us to the Vauxhall Pleasure Gardens, the most happening venue in town.

Acquired by Jonathan Tyers in 1728, the gardens have been turned into a paradise of long walks, shady trees and thick hedges. As we walk along the dusty avenues with Edgcott, we can hear music from every corner: opera arias, ballads and even organ music. Ahead of us we see the new statue, made by French rococo sculptor Louis-François Roubiliac, of Handel, languidly playing a lyre. We see print sellers hawking their song sheets: 'Rule Britannia', with music by the hugely popular Thomas Arne, is a favourite. Edgcott takes us to a supper box, a pop-up gazebo, and says that as night falls these places are used as assignations for lovers, and the dark alleys offer plenty of places to meet ladies of the night. Edgcott also tells us about the rival Ranelagh Gardens, in Chelsea, which holds massive masquerades — the equivalent of today's raves. In 1749, Elizabeth Chudleigh — an impoverished upper-class beauty — appears as Iphigenia at a masquerade, wearing only a leafy set of briefs. 'This exploit,' harrumphs Edgcott, 'is gossiped about for years.'

Censorship revived

On our next trip, Edgcott takes us to Westminster Hall, where the House of Commons is sitting in the warmth of early summer in 1737. 'This is one year you should never forget,' he tells us, the smell of hock thick on his breath, 'because it changes theatre for more than two centuries.' These are turbulent times. In the previous year, the 'Gin Act' raises the tax on gin — 'a drink popularly known as "mother's ruin",' says Edgcott, with a grim smile — and provokes riots in London. Property is damaged and looted, and magistrates read the 'Riot Act'. To quell discontent, the government reduces the tax. 'Yes,' says Edgcott, 'there are limits to state power.' Take the Lord Chamberlain, for example. It soon becomes apparent that he is powerless — several semi-legal theatres thrive. 'Damn,' scoffs Edgcott, 'this royal official is a toothless tiger.'

As we linger just outside the gothic Westminster Hall, Edgcott says that it is at around this time that Henry Fielding emerges as the sharpest satirist in British theatre. This hook-nosed, lanky, Eton-educated law student turns to writing for the stage when he runs out of money to continue his studies. In his twenties he pens a number of short plays mocking the theatre of the time: based at the Little Theatre Haymarket, he stages *Tom Thumb* (a satire ridiculing tragedy) in 1730. Then he moves on to attacking George II, the new monarch, with *The Welsh Opera* in 1731. Using the now fashionable ballad opera style, he imagines a hen-pecked monarch with his pretentious queen and impotent heir. Walpole appears in the guise of a pilfering butler called Robin. When news leaks out that Fielding wants to expand this short play into a full three acts, Walpole has the work — now titled *The Grub-Street Opera* — banned from the stage. So Fielding publishes it instead, and gets a handsome income from sales. Then in January 1736, he turns his hook-nose on Walpole and the Robinocracy. He stages *Pasquin*, a satire sniffing out electoral corruption. Frederick, the Prince of Wales, who has fallen out with his father, attends the play, thus supporting Fielding's oppositional stance. *Pasquin* runs for sixty nights and is watched by a glittering array of high society.

Henry Fielding

Now Frederick and a group of discontented aristocrats form the Rumpsteak Club — named because King George II has 'rumped', or turned his back, on them. While Fielding stages *The Historical Register for the Year 1736*, yet another satirical show, the opposition to Walpole publishes disrespectful cartoons of King George II's rump, caricatured as hugely fat and farty — and called *The Golden Rump*. These antagonize Walpole so much that he promptly drafts a censorship bill and rapidly steers it through parliament. In order to guarantee the royal assent, he gets a ghost writer to draft a play called *The Golden Rump*. 'He may even have written it himself,' says our guide, with a malicious look.

We quietly slip into the public gallery in time to see Walpole, looking particularly bloated, steering the 'Licensing Act' through the house. The act has two main provisions: first, it restricts the production of plays to theatres that have a royal patent (Drury Lane and Covent Garden) and, second, it insists that all plays have to be licensed by the Lord Chamberlain before they can be performed. To convince the MPs of the need for this kind of censorship Walpole reads excerpts from *The Golden Rump* to the assembled house. According to him, the set is a huge pair of buttocks, with characters arriving on stage through the arsehole. The plot scandalously suggests that the Queen administers enemas to the King. It is, claims Walpole, full of scatalogical passages about King George's piles and his flatulence. Some MPs are visibly outraged at the passages Walpole reads out. As we watch, Walpole's 'Licensing Act' is approved by the Commons — 185 votes to 63 — and later gets passed in the Lords, where only one person, Lord Chesterfield, tries vainly to defend freedom of speech. It gets royal assent on 21 June 1737. This new policy of strict censorship means that the Lord Chamberlain finally gets some teeth.

The results are devastating. Most of the smaller illegitimate theatres are prosecuted if they put on text-based plays rather than musical entertainments. So theatre managers prefer to stage safe old plays rather than risk new ones. Needless to say, anti-government satire falls silent. No more jokes about the monarchy; no more attacks on corruption; no bad language; no sex. A big chill descends on anyone who wants to write for the stage. (Fielding throws in the towel and takes up novel writing instead!) The rude vitality of English playwriting goes underground, where it stays for a very long time.

An actor's life

Out of the blue, Edgcott suggests we attend a different kind of spectacle. He wants to take us to witness the public hanging of a convicted highwayman, an event that is sure to attract thousands of spectators. When we say that we'd rather not, he looks visibly put out, but soon recovers. Instead, he takes us to painter and engraver William Hogarth's house in Leicester Fields (today called Leicester Square). Here we will see gory visions of England at a safe distance. Edgcott knows the family and although the artist is away at his country house in Chiswick, we are admitted and shown his studio. Above the fireplace is a large engraving of his picture of *Strolling Actresses Dressing in a Barn*.

Here touring players are portrayed satirically as slatterns with tawdry costumes and poor hygiene (in one corner a pet monkey pisses into a stage helmet). 'But the picture,' says Edgcott, 'also shows a way of life that is dying out because of the new "Licensing Act".' Now actors are forced to tour to Ireland and Scotland, where the law is poorly enforced. In these countries local heroes create local theatres. In Dublin, the rebuilt Smock Alley theatre competes with the new Theatre Royal in Aungier Street, which opens in 1735 with George Farqhuar's *The Recruiting Officer*. Smock Alley is managed by Dublin-born impresario Thomas Sheridan, but the audience is too small to support two theatres and in 1745 they merge, with Smock Alley presenting plays while Aungier Street is used for balls. Sheridan is a reformer and bans aristocrats from sitting on stage, but when he enforces this in the face of a drunken Trinity College student, about fifty gents rip up the theatre in what are known as the Kelly riots. When normal service resumes, it is evident that in Dublin theatre taste is formed by the London patent theatres, and the same is true of British theatre outside London.

Edgcott takes out an engraved map from one of Hogarth's drawers, and prods various towns with his fat finger. Here is Norwich, England's second largest city, where in 1768 Thomas Ivory gets a royal patent for his theatre, which becomes a centre for a local touring circuit which covers East Anglia. There is York, where in 1769 the comic actor Tate Wilkinson gets a patent for a theatre, and another local touring circuit develops. And there is Birmingham, where in 1774 the New Street Theatre is built — in the teeth of opposition from local businessmen who fear it will encourage workers to be idle. Most of these venues rejoice in patents that give them the right to call themselves a Theatre

Royal, and they put on versions of London hits, thus creating a national repertoire. Another example is the grand Theatre Royal in Bristol, built in 1766 on the model of Drury Lane (another stab of the finger). Today called the Bristol Old Vic it is the longest continuously running theatre in the country. One jewel, another rare survivor, is the tiny Georgian Theatre Royal in Richmond, Yorkshire. Further afield, Edgcott spreads the map out, Edinburgh acquires a Theatre Royal in 1769. About time too since the city already had a thriving theatre culture. In 1756, audiences watched *Douglas*, a verse tragedy set in Viking times by John Home, a minister in the Church of Scotland. Nationalistic audiences were thrilled by this high-flown play because they identify with its fighting folk and see in them an echo of the bloody struggle of Bonnie Prince Charlie (the Young Pretender, and son of James Stuart) against the English army in the 1745 Jacobite rebellion. At one performance, a proud audience member calls out: 'Whaur's yer Wullie Shakespeare noo?' But the fact that Home is a minister is a local scandal and a furious pamphlet war breaks out, another example of neo-Puritanism! Home is forced to quit the church, but gets a London production of his play at Covent Garden because of the influence of the Earl of Bute, Scottish mentor to the future George III. Home is Bute's secretary.

In London, the duopoly of Drury Lane and Covent Garden creates a stable system, 'and draws' — says Edgcott, taking a seat in Hogarth's studio and motioning us to do the same — 'on a pool of some 300 eager actors.' At Drury Lane about seventy-five are regularly employed. But it's hard work: a typical actor needs to know anything between twenty-five and sixty roles word perfect. At this point, Edgcott takes out a pack of playing cards which have been decorated with pictures of famous actors of the time. The first one he puts on the table shows Theophilus Cibber, Colley's son, who boasts of knowing one hundred and sixty parts off by heart. Then Edgcott produces another card with the image of actress Lavinia Fenton, who became a star overnight after playing Polly in *The Beggar's Opera*. She is so popular that she ends up marrying the Duke of Bolton. Once despised, actors now rub shoulders with the aristocracy. Edgcott then puts down three cards which show pictures of the best tragedians of the age: Barton Booth, James

Quin and Charles Macklin. Since the death of Booth in 1733, Quin is the unchallenged star actor. His style is declamatory, and the sound of his speeches is orotund and stentorian, as he struts across the stage, captivating audiences as Macbeth, Othello or Lear. Equally impressive is the Irish Macklin, who finds success rather late in his career with an amazing performance as Shylock at Drury Lane, giving him a serious tragic stature. Macklin has a dark countenance, moves heavily across the stage and his first line — 'Three thousand ducats' — is delivered in a slow, deliberate articulation. His more natural style is an exception. Other old-school actors tend to concentrate only on their own performance: they come onto the stage, ignore the other actors, and speak directly to the audience, assuming stylized postures and a mannered delivery. But in 1741 all this changes. Edgcott takes out his trump card — the name is David Garrick.

Garrick fever

Garrick is the megastar who will dominate British theatre for thirty-five years after 1741. Born in 1717, the son of a Litchfield army captain and named after his Huguenot migrant grandfather, David is educated at a local school by the lumbering Dr Johnson — who is destined to become the intellectual heavyweight of the age. After Johnson's Litchfield school goes bust, this odd couple travel together to London to seek their fortunes. At first Garrick tries working as a wine merchant. When this fails, he contacts Henry Giffard at Goodman's Fields, and starts acting, appearing under a pseudonym to avoid upsetting his respectable family. Although the theatre is unlicensed, Giffard gets around the law by selling tickets to a music concert and offering a free play in the interval. On 19 October 1741,

David Garrick

Garrick's performance as Richard III, in Colley Cibber's adaptation of Shakespeare, is a sensation. A small man, he is nevertheless agile and is blessed with a melodious voice and penetrating eyes. On stage, he doesn't just stand and deliver his lines, but moves around, using his whole body to make the character more human. Soon everyone is talking about this sellout show; everyone claims to have seen it; everyone praises it. Fashionable carriages jam the streets around the theatre. Garrick is twenty-four. And he has had no training.

THE CRITIC'S VIEW: GARRICK'S DEBUT

London Daily Post and General Advertiser reports on David Garrick's incognito debut (1741):

Last night was performed, gratis, the *Tragedy of Richard the Third*, at the theatre in Goodman's Fields, when the character of Richard was performed by a young gentleman who never appeared before, whose reception was the most extraordinary and great that was ever known on such an occasion; and we hear he obliges the town this evening with the same performance.

A year later, Drury Lane hires Garrick, and his career instantly takes off, his performances becoming the template of good acting. Inspired by Charles Macklin he rejects booming declamation, striking a pose and formal speaking, preferring a more natural manner of speech and movement. More realistic, more vital, more compelling. The moment he comes on stage, he generates a feeling of intense energy and powerful emotion. He's dynamic. Following Hamlet's advice to the players, he suits his actions to the words he's saying. Today, we'd call it Method Acting. Away from the theatre, his party trick is to put his head between two doors so that only his face is visible and then alter his expression rapidly to represent a variety of different emotions.

During the next thirty years, he acts ninety-six roles, appearing on some 2400 nights. In the 1746–47 season, he is paired with the great James Quin in a series of acting duels at the rival Covent Garden, drawing huge crowds, including royalty, to watch the spectacle of two amazing, but very different, talents. Quin is slow and ponderous; Garrick light and fleet-footed. In November, they play opposite each other in Nicholas Rowe's pathetic tragedy *The Fair Penitent*. At one point, Quin is heard to mutter: 'If this young fellow is right, I and the rest of the players must have been all wrong.' It's a prophetic statement. Garrick soon works with the best actors of the time: Peg Woffington (daughter of a Dublin bricklayer who began her career at Aungier Street and then debuted at Covent Garden in the breeches role of Sylvia in *The Recruiting Officer*), Kitty Clive (specialist in pert parts), Spranger Barry (Dublin-born actor and Covent Garden manager) and Anne Street Dancer (later Mrs Barry). His tragedy queens are the frail Susannah Cibber (daughter of Thomas Arne and wife of Theophilus Cibber) and the robust Hannah Prichard (memorable as Lady Macbeth). Crowd pleasers include revivals of John Vanbrugh's *The Provoked Wife*, in which he plays Sir John Brute in a memorable scene in drag, and Ben Jonson's *The Alchemist*, in which he plays Abel Drugger, a tobacconist cheated by Subtle and Face. In the Duke of Buckingham's *The Rehearsal*, he plays the fictional playwright Bayes more than fifty times. His most requested part is Ranger, a Restoration charmer, in Benjamin Hoadley's 1747 play *The Suspicious Husband*. But his most celebrated roles are Shakespearean: an unforgettable King Lear, which he models on close observation of a man who had killed his infant daughter and gone mad with grief. Then Hamlet, for which he contrives a special wig that makes the character's hair stand on end. So in the scene where the ghost of Hamlet's father appears, he staggers in horror, knees buckling, face going pale — and his hair seems to rise. Audiences are both terrified, and enthralled.

As well as being a star, Garrick is also a hack — after 1740, when his first play, a short satire called *Lethe; or, Aesop in the Shade*, is staged at Drury Lane, he writes some twenty plays and one hundred prologues. One of his best, co-written with George Colman in 1766, is *The Clandestine Marriage*, which is inspired by William Hogarth's *Marriage-à-la-Mode* series of prints, and offers a comment on class: it tells the story of a businessman's daughter who tries to avoid marriage to an aristocrat she doesn't love. But Garrick's stubborn refusal to play the elderly Lord Ogleby leads to a row with his co-author, who then moves to the rival Covent Garden. Curiously enough, Garrick's most popular work is the afterpiece farce called *Miss in Her Teens; or The Medley of Lovers* about a young woman, Miss Biddy Bellair, and her suitors, in which he himself plays one of them, Mr Fribble, in an extravagantly farcical way.

In 1747, Garrick becomes the manager of Drury Lane, and Dr Johnson — now a famous man of letters — writes him an ode which sets out his formula for popular mainstream theatre. Garrick appears on stage and recites the ode, which includes the lines: 'The drama's laws, the drama's patrons give;/ For we that live to please, must please to live.' It's a crowd-pleaser manifesto. As a highly successful manager, he balances artistic excellence with the need to sell tickets. But he is essentially conservative: he puts on few new plays and wouldn't dream of challenging the 'Licensing Act' or offending the Lord Chamberlain. As Dr Johnson says, 'His profession made him rich and he made his profession respectable.'

Garrick introduces other reforms that create a better theatre-going experience. He banishes aristocrats from sitting on the stage in 1763, and realizes that his new style of acting means that he must train his actors to move across the stage more and respond to each other. It's a major innovation. He also pays actors more fairly and works with the same team for years, which leads to better performances. Lazy actors are fired. He uses the latest know-how to get more elegant costumes, sharper stage lighting and improved stage design. Employing Philippe Jacques de Loutherbourg, the Strasbourg-born painter and master of romantic and gothic mise-en-scène, he breaks decisively with the old style of scenery which has ruled the stage for more than a century. Out go perspective flats and in come realistic stage pictures. It's a mighty moment: as the action of the play moves behind the proscenium arch, Drury Lane becomes the first modern theatre of illusion.

But Garrick also has his eye on popularity. In 1745, in response to Bonnie Prince Charlie's rebellion, he plays the new national anthem 'God Save the King'. In patriotic respect, everyone in the audience stands up, beginning a tradition of audiences rising to their feet at the end of every show that carries on until well into the 1960s. He also writes the words of 'Heart of Oak', the march of the royal navy, with its chorus that ends on the proud promise that 'We'll fight and we'll conquer again and again.' The age of Empire has found its voice!

Unable to sit still, Garrick is a hyperactive manager. He does everything, dashing around, supervising all aspects of running Drury Lane, from auditioning new actors to checking the accounts. He is also a frantic networker, always meeting dukes, duchesses and fashionable people, flitting from one appointment to another, in a social whirl. He becomes an international star, visiting Paris, and then embarking on a Grand Tour of Italy. And he cannily manages his image through the press, investing his own money in several newspapers. More than 250 portraits are made of him, both in private and in character, outnumbering those of any other actor. Prints spread his image far and wide; little china statues of him are made. Although frantically active, he does find a measure of calm when he marries Eva Maria Veigel, a charming Viennese dancer, in 1749.

Garrick is instrumental in creating a veritable Shakespeare industry. To show us more about the new cult of the bard, Edgcott suggests that we travel out of London to take a look at Shakespeare's birthplace in the sleepy little town of Stratford-upon-Avon. The journey takes about three days, and Edgcott organizes inns for us to stay at along the way. We travel in a coach — which we note is better sprung and more comfortable than the ones we used in the Restoration period — along the new system of turnpike roads, which charge tolls to raise money for repairing potholes. On the way, we notice that already people drive on the left, and that — although most of the fields are still divided into strips of different crops as they were in medieval times — some tracts of land have been enclosed by improving landlords. These large fields are typically surrounded by hedgerows and trees, and they look like our own familiar landscape: rural England.

When we finally reach our destination, Edgcott takes us around to Shakespeare's home. This was his family's residence from 1597, and we are told that he died in the main bedroom here. It is a timbered structure with a five-gabled frontage facing the street and a courtyard, with a well in the middle. The house Edgcott shows us was rebuilt around 1700, but we happen to know that because its present owner is so fed up with Shakespearean tourists turning up at his front door he pulls the whole place down in 1759. Not wishing to antagonize anyone, we don't linger for long! Instead we repair to the White Lion, Stratford's only decent inn, to drink some ale and eat cold meat.

While discussing the Shakespeare industry, Edgcott — with a snort of snuff — tells us that one in six performances in London is of a Shakespeare play. Of the ninety-six roles in Garrick's career, sixteen are Shakespearean. The actor not only excels in tragic roles, but also buys copies of the original Elizabethan publications of Shakespeare's plays, and revises the plays, restoring many lines that have been cut in their Restoration adaptations. He venerates the bard and this culminates in the Shakespeare Jubilee, which he organizes.

THE SHAKESPEARE INDUSTRY

Shakespeare's plays are performed in adaptations which have very little in common with the original versions, which are too dark or edgy for respectable ears. So various Restoration versions hold the stage: Nahum Tate's *King Lear*, with its happy ending; William Davenant's *Macbeth*, with its cuts of anything too graphic, including Macbeth's death. But, gradually, during the eighteenth century, the bard's words are rediscovered. Starting with Nicholas Rowe, numerous edited editions of the plays are published, including one by Samuel Johnson. Garrick improves the texts of twenty-two Shakespeare plays. And his Shakespeare Jubilee makes a tourist destination out of Stratford-upon-Avon, popularizing the idea that Shakespeare is a genius, a secular god, a symbol of British national identity. Shakespeare becomes an industry; statues, ceramics and pictures of him and his characters become commonplace, and his name is evoked as the patron saint of theatre. The spin-offs are many, one example being John Boydell, an enterprising engraver and print-seller, who in 1789 opens his Shakespeare Gallery in Pall Mall. Here he displays paintings of scenes from the plays by artists such as Sir Joshua Reynolds and Henry Fuseli — and he sells thousands of engravings of them.

This is held at Stratford on 6 September 1769, which is alas about five years too late given that 1764 was the two-hundredth anniversary of Shakespeare's birth. Never mind. Garrick writes an ode to the bard, and plans songs, processions of the playwright's characters and other events, including a horse race. On the banks of the Avon, an octagonal wooden amphitheatre, the Rotunda, is erected. Medals are struck and boxes are made out of the wood of a mulberry tree once planted by Shakespeare. Enormous excitement is generated, but on the day torrential rain leads to the cancellation of most of the events. The Rotunda is flooded. Garrick manages to recite his ode, set to music by Thomas Arne, but the jubilee is a failure, losing a massive £2000. Because of the weather, most of the visitors want to leave, but not enough coaches are available. The Edinburgh-born James Boswell, Dr Johnson's biographer, sums up: 'After the joy of the Jubilee came the uneasy reflection that I was in a little village in wet weather and knew not how to get away.' But Garrick bounces back, staging *The Jubilee* as an afterpiece on the Drury Lane stage, recycling poems, songs and other celebrations. This afterpiece is a big deal — getting a record 152 performances in three years and constant revivals for at least a century.

Back in London, Edgcott takes us to the Adelphi buildings, just south of the Strand and next to the Thames, where in 1772 Garrick buys a house. Built by the Scottish brothers Robert and James Adam (Adelphi comes from the Greek word for brothers) this is a terrace of neoclassical buildings, white, elegant and the best address in London. Having been on the Grand Tour, the Adam brothers bring motifs inspired by ancient Rome and Greece to their intricate designs. Below the terrace, we can hear the sounds of sailors and warehousemen unloading boats and the flap of sails on the Thames. Seagulls cry. Inside, Edgcott takes us to a beautifully proportioned day room, and, when we are comfortable, he tells us a bit more about Garrick's management style, which can be pretty brusque. The Revd William Hawkins, a professor of poetry at Oxford university, has five of his plays turned down. When he complains, Garrick answers: 'I have the same right to reject a play, which I think is a bad one, as you have to compose it.' At Christmas, Garrick also pioneers the evergreen seasonal pantomimes, which always give a boost to the box office. As does news of his retirement, and the last time he plays his most famous roles Drury Lane is sold out, dangerously crammed with spectators. At his farewell performance on 10 June 1776, the auditorium is awash with tears.

Theatre riots

Eighteenth-century audiences know how to make their feelings clear. Edgcott reminds us of the caricatures of boisterous audiences which he showed us at Hogarth's house. They are, according to him, a cross-section of society. Outside Drury Lane and Covent Garden, prostitutes are present in large numbers; inside, some are picking up their customers. 'This is so common,' Edgcott laughingly tells us, with an emphatic nod of his bewigged head, that it's reflected in the slang of the time: 'Covent Garden abbess means bawd, Covent Garden nun means whore, Drury Lane vestal the same, and the Drury Lane ague is syphilis.' We can understand why religious Evangelical Christians see theatre as a flesh market of debauch. Inside the theatres, the audience is voluble and sometimes violent. Once, during a performance of *Hamlet*, when the heavy-footed Quin pauses too long while delivering Horatio's line 'I'll meet thee there', a voice from the top gallery calls out: 'Why don't you tell the gentleman whether you will meet him or not?' General laughter. While fashionable people in the boxes spend much of the show sizing each other up, and gossiping, the galleries ring with cheers, songs and are sometimes the source of pelted fruit. Yes, the audience is a power to be reckoned with. Its weapon of choice is the riot.

Because of what Edgcott calls the Roast Beef wars in Europe, the French are enemy number one. So perhaps it is not a good idea that, at Drury Lane in 1755, Garrick employs Jean-Georges Noverre, a Swiss ballet-master, and his French company, to perform *The Chinese Festival*, a fashionable piece of, er, chinoiserie. Every night a riot breaks out — with people hissing and pelting the stage with oranges, apples and peas (so that dancers will slip on them). At one point a passionate speech is heard: 'Oh Britons! Oh my countrymen! You will certainly not suffer these foreigner dogs to amuse us.' After several nights of disorder, which includes the smashing of windows at Garrick's Southampton Street house, the show is stopped. Some years later, a comic opera called *The Blackamoor Washed White* — written by Henry Bate, a cleric and journalist nicknamed The Fighting Parson because of his quarrelsome articles — is similarly stopped. Audiences particularly object to a scene where an Englishman, Sir Oliver Oddfish, replaces his untrustworthy servants with 'foreign' black servants. For four nights in a row, people shout 'No more! No more!', jump on stage, exchange punches, and make such a noise that the play can't continue. Eventually Garrick pulls the plug. 'Such riots,' says Edgcott, 'occur so often that both Drury Lane and Covent Garden have to be redecorated regularly to repair the damage.'

ENEMIES OF THEATRE: EVANGELICALS

Throughout the eighteenth century, the neo-Puritan opposition to theatre is alive and well, given encouragement by the growth of Evangelical Christianity. As usual, the City aldermen are suspicious of theatres, especially the unlicensed semi-legal ones. In 1735, Sir John Barnard, a City MP, introduces a parliamentary Bill 'to restrain the number of playhouses'. He is supported by various moralists, such as the novelist Samuel Richardson, but the bill fails through lack of political support. But many other voices are raised against theatrical entertainment. In 1757, for example, a typical pamphlet, the anonymous *Players' Scourge*, states: 'Play actors are the most profligate wretches, and the vilest vermin, that hell ever vomited out. They are the filth and garbage of the world.' Charming!

In 1763 there are serious riots at both Drury Lane and Covent Garden against the abolition of half-price late admission. This is the system which allows audience members, who might still be at work when the show starts or don't want to sit through the main piece, to pay half price when they arrive after act three. For this they get to see the afterpieces: pantomimes, farces and dances. When Garrick abolishes the half-price late admission, more disturbances force him to back-peddle. Sometimes, disturbances also happen backstage. In 1735, Charles Macklin quarrels with fellow actor Thomas Hallam about a wig, and stabs him in the eye with his stick. Hallam dies the next day, and Macklin stands trial for murder. In a society that hangs boys for petty theft, he gets off lightly, with having his hand branded. Phew, that was close!

In the 1760s, a new crop of illegitimate theatres begin to challenge the great duopoly. In 1768, the six-foot-tall and intensely patriotic ex-cavalry officer Philip Astley, and his wife Patty, open a riding school south of Westminster Bridge. Here they hold equestrian entertainments and their son John becomes a popular horseback performer, doing daring acrobatics. Other guilty pleasures at this venue include comedy acts and dancing dogs. Astley is one of a new breed of cultural entrepreneur. By 1795, he is so successful that he builds a Royal Amphitheatre, which has a round sandy ring. This is the forerunner of today's circus shows. Another illegitimate theatre is Sadler's Wells, which is revamped in 1765 by its manager Thomas Rosoman, who turns it into a venue for opera. The site, just outside Islington village, is a mineral spring where Richard Sadler built a wooden Music House in 1683 to rival the entertainments of the fashionable Tunbridge and Epsom watering holes. By the 1750s, visitors to Sadler's Wells can see jugglers, tumblers, wrestlers and a singing duck. However, we suspect that the beer brewed from the spring waters is the primary attraction. Other players on the fringes of the Georgian theatre scene are equally eccentric. Take Samuel Foote, a Cornish-born actor, dramatist and theatre manager, who spends years running the Little Theatre Haymarket, illegally staging shows and playing cat and mouse with the authorities. He is a maverick, mimic and occasional drag artist. His 1760 play, *The Minor*, is a satire on the new evangelical Methodist movement, and fills this venue for thirty-eight nights. In 1766, Foote is injured in a horse riding accident while with Prince Edward, King George III's brother, and his leg is amputated. Perhaps in compensation, Edgcott isn't really sure, he is given a licence to stage plays at the Little in the summer season while the two patent theatres are closed.

Meanwhile, in Dublin, in 1754 a riot destroys the Smock Alley theatre. The audience is antagonised when Thomas Sheridan and the lively Peg Woffington star in the French philosopher Voltaire's tragedy, *Mahomet*, which tells the story of the hero Alcanor, who not only sacrifices his children, but also dies fighting the tyrant Mahomet. The Irish public, increasingly nationalistic, resent Sheridan's support of British rule. When the Irish parliament is suspended, a riot breaks out, with the audience smashing up the venue. In response, Sheridan quits the city for London, taking his son Richard Brinsley with him.

Entertain us

The 1770s are glory days for London's two big patent theatres. Edgcott, despite his gruff ways, has been very generous to us, showing us London sights such as the royal barge processing down the river Thames, with its forest of ship masts. He now invites us to his town house in Mayfair. He wants to tell us about two uplifting comedies so this sunny spring day seems ideal. His house has large, light and airy reception rooms, with liveried footmen and the discrete bustle of behind-the-scenes activity. Once we are seated in his salon, he is ready to tell us about a couple of magnificent plays by two exiled Irishmen who save British theatre from the gush of sentimental comedy.

At Covent Garden, the Irish author Oliver Goldsmith's *She Stoops To Conquer; or, The Mistakes of a Night* opens on 15 March 1773. 'Goldsmith is a strange character,' says Edgcott, 'a great talker prone to stuttering, a social butterfly uneasy with women and a debt-ridden gambler who is compulsively generous.' His play is immediately recognized as brilliant. By this time, Goldsmith has already published his popular novel, *The Vicar of Wakefield*, about the joys and sorrows of a country minister, and a long poem, *The Deserted Village*, which is a protest about the depopulation of the countryside in the wake of the Enclosures. As with these works, and other popular novels such as Henry Fielding's *Tom Jones*, *She Stoops To Conquer* is set in the countryside, among the country gentry in their fine houses. It is a play of mistaken identities, practical jokes and farcical confusion. Squire Hardcastle, a

Oliver Goldsmith

country gentleman, plans to marry off his daughter Kate to the well-bred Charles Marlow. But when Charles visits him for the first time, he is fooled by Tony Lumpkin, Kate's half-brother and a practical joker, into believing that Hardcastle's country house is a mere inn. So Charles thinks his host is a landlord and Kate a barmaid. But because he can only relax among low-class lasses, becoming tongue-tied in the company of refined gentlewomen, this enables him to talk freely and allows the self-possessed Kate to find out if he will make a good husband. As the title of the play indicates, she must stoop socially before she can conquer Charles's heart. Other complications are subplots in which Charles's travelling companion, George Hastings, and Constance Neville, Tony Lumpkin's cousin, plan to elope, and Tony's mother, Mrs Hardcastle, plots to keep some valuable jewels, which belong to Constance. Needless to say, all ends happily.

Goldsmith's play is not only merry, it is also a theatre manifesto. Up until now, sentimental comedy, a trend kicked off by Richard Steele's *The Conscious Lovers*, is all the rage in theatre. But there is one problem with sentimental comedy — it's not funny. It may be improving, but it doesn't make you laugh. With *She Stoops To Conquer*, Goldsmith is saying that sentimental comedy is full of out-of-touch aristocrats, insipid dialogue and contrived emotions. By contrast, true comedy, aptly called laughing comedy, is about ordinary people, satirical dialogue and real down-to-earth humour. For the first production of *She Stoops To Conquer*, Garrick provides a Prologue in which an actor appears on stage dressed in black, holding a handkerchief and in mourning for comedy, a sick

THEATRE THEORY:
LAUGHING COMEDY

Oliver Goldsmith's *She Stoops To Conquer* and Richard Brinsley Sheridan's *The School for Scandal* are comedies of manners, written in the broad tradition of William Congreve and the Restoration playwrights, although without their sexual explicitness. They are called laughing comedies as opposed to the sentimental weeping comedies that are the norm. In a 1773 essay for the *Westminster Magazine*, called 'Laughing and Sentimental Comedy', Goldsmith says that laughing comedy uses humour to criticize the behaviour of upper-class society. It is down to earth and true while sentimental comedy is artificial and false. The origins of laughing comedy go back to French playwright Molière and Ben Jonson's satirical comedies, and a variety of comic situations are used to show the shortcomings of stock characters, such as the flirt, the gossip, the wastrel, the bore, the rich uncle, the country cousin and so on. And Shakespeare's influence can also be seen in the comedy of errors and vulgar but big-hearted characters such as Tony Lumpkin.

patient dying of sentimentality. Throughout the play Goldsmith parodies the language of sentimental comedy, as when Hardcastle says, 'Modesty seldom resides in a breast that is not enriched with nobler virtues.' Or when Constance refuses to elope with George, saying, 'Prudence once more comes to my relief, and I will obey its dictates. In the moment of passion, fortune may be despised, but it ever produces a lasting repentance.' In this way, Goldsmith is having a laugh at the moralistic clichés that saturate Georgian theatre.

Like George Farquhar's *The Recruiting Officer*, *She Stoops To Conquer* is written with clarity, great pace and is full of hilarious moments, as when Tony persuades his mother, Mrs Hardcastle, to hide in the mud of her garden, by pretending that her husband is a highwayman. This is both a well-made play that obeys The Unities, more or less, and a story with great generosity of heart in which love conquers all. Marlow's initial flirting with Kate, when he thinks she's a barmaid, is predatory but he redeems himself by becoming more honorable: 'I can never harbour a thought of seducing simplicity that trusted in my honour,' he says. In the end, it is Kate's play. An unusually spirited heroine for the time, she understands Charles perfectly: 'He said some civil things of my face, talked much of his want of merit, and the greatness of mine; mentioned his heart, gave a short tragedy speech, and ended with pretended rapture.' If this young couple is well-matched, it is Kate who is in control. When the *Morning Chronicle* reviews the show it makes much of the gales of laughter that shake the theatre: 'The audience are kept in a continual roar.' The play has had the same effect ever since.

'When Garrick retires in 1776,' says Edgcott, 'he leaves Drury Lane in a good shape.' It is the premier theatre in Britain and the envy of Europe. The dizzying decade is capped by the arrival of Richard Brinsley Sheridan, the extravagant and frequently penniless Dublin-born son of Thomas, who ran the Smock Alley Theatre. Having arrived in London, with a young wife and little cash, Richard is desperate for money and in 1775 his debut play, *The Rivals*, gives us Mrs Malaprop, one of the great comic characters of the English language, who hilariously mangles her words: when she wants to say, 'If I apprehend anything in this world', she actually says 'Sure, if I reprehend anything in this world'; for 'a nice arrangement of epithets' she says, 'a nice derangement of epitaphs!'; for 'obliterate him quite from your memory' she says, 'illiterate him'; and for 'he is the very pinnacle of politeness' she says, 'the very pineapple of politeness'. But the play's first performance is a flop, so Sheridan recasts the part of Sir Lucius O'Trigger — sacking the quarrelsome John Lee and giving it to the Irish-born Lawrence Clinch — for the second performance eleven days later, and the play is a huge hit. Then Sheridan, along with his father-in-law — composer Thomas Linley — stage a charming opera, *The Duenna*, which proves to be very popular. It plays for seventy-five performances. In 1776, Sheridan — along with Linley

RICHARD BRINSLEY SHERIDAN

Born: 30 October 1751, Dublin.

Family: Third son of Thomas Sheridan, Smock Alley
actor-manager, and Frances, novelist and playwright.

Education: In Dublin, the English Grammar School.
The family moves permanently to England in 1758 and
he is sent to Harrow. Father gives him elocution lessons.

Private life: Moved to Bath in 1770 and falls in love
with Elizabeth Ann, sixteen-year-old daughter of composer
Thomas Linley.

Scandal: In March 1772, Sheridan elopes with Miss Linley to
France, then returns and fights two duels with Major Mathews,
one of her disappointed suitors. In April 1773 he marries her at
Marylebone Church, London.

Career: Sheridan's first comedy, *The Rivals*, is at Covent Garden in 1775.
Writes other plays and succeeds Garrick as manager of Drury Lane.

Politics: Sheridan enters parliament for Stafford in 1780,
as friend of Charles James Fox (prominent Whig and opponent of
George III). Excels as an orator. Minor
success as a minister.

Greatest hit: *The School for Scandal* (1777).

Death: 7 July 1816.

Resting place: Buried in Poets' Corner, Westminster Abbey,
near David Garrick.

and another partner — buy a half share in Drury Lane, which he now manages. It is here that he stages his masterpiece, *The School for Scandal*, in 1777.

Set in London, the play is a comedy of upper-class manners, and opens with a scene in the dressing room of the aptly named Lady Sneerwell. She is a prime mover of the school for scandal, a club of gossip mongers who put down all and sundry. The story centres on the fortunes of two very different brothers, Charles and James Surface. Charles is good-natured but appears extravagant,

Richard Brinsley
Sheridan

while James is a hypocrite who appears to be highly moral. Charles is in love with Maria, the ward of Sir Peter Teazle, whose young wife Lady Teazle is trying to block this relationship because she wants to have an affair with Charles. Meanwhile Joseph has his eye on the fortune that will one day come to Maria and is backed in his suit by Teazle, who has been fooled by the young man's righteous appearance. Meanwhile, Charles and James's uncle Sir Oliver Surface, who has made his fortune as a Nabob in India, arrives unexpectedly. He hears conflicting reports of his nephews and so decides to spy on them. In the auction scene, he approaches Charles in the guise of a money-lender to buy his family portraits, and is impressed with Charles' sense of honour. When he approaches Joseph as a poor relation asking for help, Joseph rejects him. Then, in the screen scene, Teazle suspects his wife of having an affair with Charles and visits Joseph to ask for advice. Lady Teazle, who is enjoying a tryst with Joseph, hastily hides behind a screen. When Charles unexpectedly arrives, Teazle, in turn, hides in a closet. Charles inadvertently reveals Lady Teazle behind the screen and Teazle realises what kind of man Joseph really is.

Sheridan wants to write a comedy in the style of William Congreve, but he knows that the public won't tolerate any indecency. So this is a sex comedy with practically no sex. What it does have is enormous energy and a terrific glee in satirizing high society and its love of malicious gossip. As Snake, one of Lady Sneerwell's set, says: 'To my knowledge, she has been the cause of six matches being broken off, and three sons being disinherited;

of four forced elopements, and as many close confinements; nine separate maintenances, and two divorces.' Another theme is that of hypocrisy: Joseph pretends to be honourable while trying to destroy his brother's love of Maria. But goodness does prevail as Maria opposes the slanderous behaviour of Lady Sneerwell and her friends: 'Wit loses its respect for me when I see it in company with malice.' The play deals very effectively with the corrosive nature of slander, the fragility of reputation, and the differences between appearance and reality.

Richard Brinsley Sheridan's *The School for Scandal* (1777)
Charles pulls down the screen:
SIR PETER He had a girl with him when I called.
CHARLES What! Joseph? You jest.
SIR PETER Hush! A little French milliner. And the best of the jest is — she's in the room now.
CHARLES The devil she is!
SIR PETER Hush! I tell you. *(Points to the screen.)*
CHARLES Behind the screen! 'Slife, let's unveil her.
SIR PETER No, no, he's coming.
CHARLES Oh, egad, we'll have a peep at the little milliner.
SIR PETER Not for the world! Joseph will never forgive me.
CHARLES I'll stand by you.
SIR PETER Odds, here he is!
(Joseph enters just as Charles throws down the screen.)
CHARLES Lady Teazle — by all that's wonderful.
SIR PETER Lady Teazle, by all that's damnable!
CHARLES Sir Peter, this is one of the smartest French milliners I ever saw. Egad, you seem all to have been diverting yourselves here at hide and seek — and I don't see who is out of the secret. Shall I beg your ladyship to inform me? Not a word! Brother, will you be pleased to explain this matter? What! Is morality dumb too? Sir Peter, though I found you in the dark, perhaps you are not so now? All mute.

But it mixes compassion with satire, and with hilarious results: at one point a minor character makes up the story of an indoor duel: 'Sir Peter forced Charles to take one pistol, and they fired, it seems, pretty nearly together. Charles's shot took effect, as I told you, and Sir Peter's missed; but, what is very extraordinary, the ball struck

> ## THE CRITIC'S VIEW: THE SCHOOL FOR SCANDAL
>
> William Hazlitt on *The School for Scandal* (1777):
>
> *The School for Scandal* is, if not the most original, perhaps the most finished and faultless comedy which we have. When it is acted, you hear people all around you exclaiming, 'Surely it is impossible for anything to be cleverer.' The scene in which Charles sells all the old family pictures but his uncle's, who is the purchaser in disguise, and that of the discovery of Lady Teazle when the screen falls, are among the happiest and most highly wrought that comedy, in its wide and brilliant range, can boast. Besides the wit and ingenuity of this play, there is a genial spirit of frankness and generosity about it that relieves the heart as well as clears the lungs. It professes a faith in the natural goodness as well as habitual depravity of human nature.

against a little bronze Pliny that stood over the fireplace, grazed out of the window at a right angle, and wounded the postman, who was just coming to the door.' If sentimental comedy flatters the middle classes, Sheridan finally makes them laugh.

The first production opens on 8 May 1777 and runs for twenty nights, and within three years clocks up 261 performances. On the first night a twelve-year-old boy is passing Drury Lane and hears a frightening roar. Thinking that the building is collapsing, he puts his hands over his head and runs for safety. In fact, the noise is the audience applauding the climax of the play, when the screen falls to reveal Lady Teazle hidden in Joseph's room. Perdita Robinson plays Maria but has to give up the part when she becomes visibly pregnant (she later becomes the Prince of Wales's mistress, as Edgcott informs us, in a manner not unlike that of the gossip mongers in the play). Mrs Abingdon plays Lady Teazle with a knowing sharpness despite being twenty years too old for the part. Many audience members know that she is the mistress of the Earl of Shelburne. So her innocent lines are even funnier. After his success on the opening night, Sheridan goes for a celebration and gets so drunk that he is told off by the constables for his rowdy behaviour in the street.

In the 1770s, apart from Goldsmith, Sheridan's only real rival is Richard Cumberland, whose sentimental comedy *The West Indian* is about Belcour, a rakish Creole plantation owner who, with his slaves and huge wealth, has 'rum and sugar enough belonging to him to make all the water in the Thames into punch'. In this play, Cumberland has the high-minded idea of taking a social type — the Empire colonial — and challenging the metropolitan tendency to mock them. But as well as being highly moral, he is also a jealous personality. When Cumberland takes his children to see *The School for Scandal*, he is so envious that he pinches them to stop them laughing. Sheridan has the last word: in his 1779 play, *The Critic; or, A Tragedy Rehearsed* — a spirited rewrite of the Duke of Buckingham's Restoration satire *The Rehearsal* — he bases his character Sir Fretful Plagiary (the name says it all) on none other than Cumberland.

While audiences laugh at the comedies of Goldsmith and Sheridan, and it seems as if, in the words of Pangloss from Voltaire's 1759 satire *Candide*, 'All is for the best in the best of all possible worlds'. But there are storm clouds on the horizon. Not for the first time, Edgcott shoots us a dark look. We know that look: it says that we need to pay attention. Here comes a history lesson. 'Beginning in 1775,' he says, 'the American Revolutionary War is well under way by 1780, and the Thirteen Colonies — led by George Washington — soon achieve independence.' While British redcoat armies try in vain to defeat him in battle, Washington spends the freezing winter of 1777-78 in a camp at Valley Forge in Pennsylvania. To keep up morale, he orders his troops to perform Joseph Addison's *Cato*, an improving tragedy. The American war is also the low point of a very unusual playwright: General John Burgoyne, nicknamed Gentleman Johnny, is forced to surrender his 6000 men to the Americans at Saratoga in 1777. On returning to London after this military disaster, he becomes a part-time playwright. When Edgcott tells us this, we can feel that he disapproves of this dilettante style of playwriting. Yet Gentleman Johnny's best comedy, *The Heiress*, is a big hit in 1786. It is a love story that evokes the life of the upper-classes, where marriage is made for money rather than love, traditional gentility contrasts with new money, girls are not expected to be educated and French valets speak in a hilarious Franglais. But what Edgcott doesn't know is that Burgoyne achieves immortality not through his military leadership, nor through his plays, but by becoming a character in George Bernard Shaw's 1897 play *The Devil's Disciple*. Meanwhile, the incompetence of George III, whose ministers Lord Bute and Lord North are not up to the job, results in the loss of the American colonies, and other problems are brewing. 'But,' says Edgcott, as he shows us out with a generous broad smile, 'that's another story.'

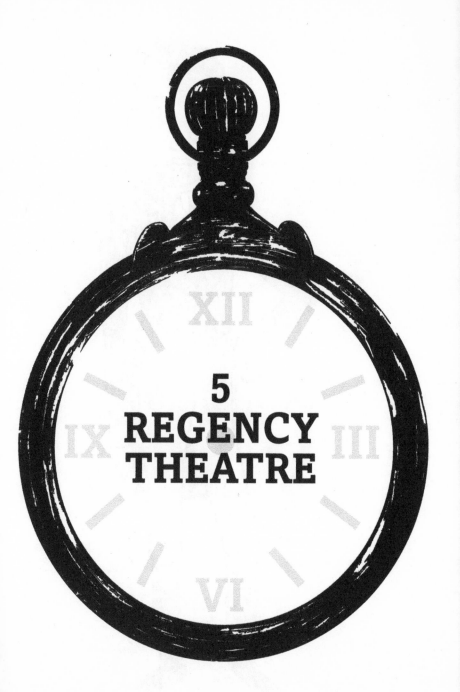

5
REGENCY THEATRE

5
Regency Theatre

Meet our guide: Gabriel

We meet our new guide, Gabriel Freeman, in a brand-new elegant town house in London's Marylebone Park district. It's a fashionable abode, in an area where the rich and famous live. He welcomes us in a spacious and sunny reception room decorated with neo-classical motifs. Gabriel is a young black man, impeccably dressed in a green frock coat, white shirt and cravat, with an embroidered waistcoat of orange, picked out in gold thread. He tells us that he was once a plantation slave in Jamaica, before being brought to London by his owner, who was very wealthy and had connections in high places. Like other slaves who were lucky enough to be favoured by their master, Gabriel was educated, in his case, at the Greycoat School in Westminster. This allowed him to gain the confidence of a prominent duke, to whom he had been sold to work as his valet. The duke took him under his wing, encouraging him to read, write and go to the theatre. When the old duke died, Gabriel was left with a sizable annual income — and his freedom. Since then, he mixes in cultivated company, but only among reformers and those sympathetic to the struggle for the emancipation of slaves. He has become a political activist, capable of giving fiery speeches in support of the cause, yet at the same time he's at home in fashionable society. As he paces energetically up and down the room, he says that on this trip we will be looking at British theatre from the 1780s to the 1830s, the age of the Regency, a time of reform, revolution and war.

Regency England

To give us a better idea of this age, Gabriel walks us down the newly built Regents Street, part of a development masterminded by architect John Nash, its gleaming white neoclassical columns embodying an aspiration to elegance. 'By 1800,' says our guide, 'the population of London is about one million, having doubled in the past sixty years. It's a proper metropolis.' And we can see the improvements. Streets are now paved and cleaned, lit by oil lamps at night, with piped water and sewers running underneath. It feels wealthier than ever before. Instead of one bridge over the Thames, Gabriel tells us, six new bridges are built between 1750 and 1827. The construction boom results also in new gentlemen's clubs, banks and insurance companies in nearby St James's. Typically, the respectable middle classes of merchants, traders and administrators have moved to the squares of Islington, Bloomsbury and Bayswater. They emulate upper-class taste, buying books and pictures, and of course patronising the theatre. But the big change is the growth of the working classes, who live in the poorer areas of the East End. 'As their wages rise,' says Gabriel, 'they demand better living conditions and more entertainment.'

Outside London, things are similarly busy. To give us a flavour of fashionable life in the playgrounds of the rich, Gabriel takes us to Brighton. It's a lovely day in autumn and, after an early start, we travel down to this seaside resort in a comfortable carriage — lighter and faster than its Georgian model — on well-maintained roads. Arriving in Brighton in the evening, we are put up at an inn, where, after some awkwardness about Gabriel's status, and skin colour, we have a hearty meal, and then retire for the night to small but comfortable rooms, lit with single candles. The next morning, Gabriel takes us to the Brighton Pavilion, a wonderfully ornate pleasure palace built by John Nash in 1787 for George, Prince of Wales, the oldest son of King George III. King George, explains Gabriel, suffers from bouts of mental collapse, and during the last and longest of these, between 1811 and 1820, his son becomes Prince Regent. The Pavilion is far enough away from court life in London to give him a discreet location for his liaisons with Maria Fitzherbert, his lover. 'Unfortunately,' says Gabriel, 'he cannot marry her because she is a Roman Catholic, and the heir to the throne must marry a Protestant.' In fact, he points out, Catholic Emancipation has been as hot an issue as the abolition of slavery. He then takes us inside to look around the palace, which has been enlarged by Henry Holland (designer of the Prince Regent's Carlton House in London) and redecorated in a medley of Chinese and Indian styles, with Mughal and Islamic motifs evoking Britain's colonial possessions. In these lush surroundings, we catch a glimpse of the Prince Regent, a rather plump but exquisitely dressed man. In fact, he, along with the trend-setting dandy Beau Brummell, becomes the model for men's fashions, introducing dark coats, full-length trousers, linen shirts and elaborately knotted cravats. These stylish changes go hand-in-hand with a giant expenditure on a lavish lifestyle: the Prince Regent has a gargantuan appetite. A cartoon of him by James Gillray shows a fatty sprawling after a massive meal, surrounded by empty bottles, unpaid bills, cures for venereal disease and an overflowing chamber pot: the title is *A Voluptuary under the Horrors of Digestion*.

Unsurprisingly, the Prince Regent's behaviour makes him unpopular with the British people, who have to pay for his extravagances. Against his father's will, he supports the aristocratic Whig Opposition to the Tory leader William Pitt the Younger, who becomes prime minister at the age of twenty-four in 1783, the youngest to hold that office. Pitt, however, is popular with the public because he is incorruptible — in fact, he's nicknamed Honest Billy. In parliament, the Prince Regent's allies include Whigs such as Charles James Fox and Richard Brinsley Sheridan, manager of the Theatre Royal Drury Lane. The Whig political programme promotes the supremacy of parliament over monarchy, Catholic Emancipation, abolition of slavery and reform of the corrupt voting system. Many of the Whigs meet at Brooks, a beautiful Palladian-style club in St James's Street, which Gabriel points out to us when we are back in the capital.

Our guide also explains that respectable society is ever-more afraid of the unruly masses. In 1780, these fears are realised when London is convulsed by the anti-Catholic Gordon Riots, in which huge crowds protest against a parliamentary bill in favour of Catholic Emancipation. This reform, explains Gabriel, aims to remove the disabilities imposed on Catholics by the Popery Act of 1698, which prevents them from holding public office. During the Gordon Riots, an initially peaceful demonstration gets out of hand and the so-called King Mob runs amok, burning down buildings and looting. Covent Garden theatre is attacked because it employs 'papists and Frenchmen'. Rioting lasts for days, Newgate prison is burnt down, the houses of rich Catholics are looted, and the Bank of England besieged. London is shrouded by a huge pall of acrid smoke. Gabriel tells us that the poet William Blake, at the time a mere artist's apprentice, is caught up in the riots, but escapes unharmed. The 'Riot Act' is read and the redcoats shoot 285 people. But this is just a prelude to momentous events across the Channel in Paris.

Age of revolution

It is the best of times, it is the worst of times; it is the age of wisdom, it is the age of folly; it is the season of enlightenment, it is the season of fear. Yes, the French Revolution begins with the storming of the hated Bastille prison in 1789. At first, this event is welcomed in Britain as the triumph of liberty over tyranny. Gabriel can barely hide the excitement in his voice as he tells us the story, miming a trumpet blast and a roll on the drums. Charles James Fox and the Whigs call it 'the greatest event it is that ever happened in the world! And the best!' To introduce us to the radical temper of the times, our guide takes us to the Welsh nonconformist minister Richard Price's Newington Green meeting house, in the village of Stoke Newington just north of London. It is a small, but neatly proportioned, white stucco building, with large windows that symbolise openness. Inside, the white-washed walls and simple wooden pews are gleaming, and the pulpit is much more prominent than the simple altar table. Like other nonconformists, such as the Joseph Priestley, Price is a political radical. It is here that in November 1789 he preaches a sermon that hails events in France as the dawn of a new era: 'Behold all ye friends of freedom; behold the light you have struck, after setting America free, reflected to France and there kindled into a blaze that lays despotism in ashes and warms and illuminates Europe.' 'The ardour for liberty in these heady days also extends to the rights of women,' says Gabriel, his voice echoing slightly in the little church, as he tells us that Mary Wollstonecraft, a feminist pioneer, is one of Price's congregation.

RADICALS AND REACTIONARIES

The events of the French Revolution — which unfold from the Storming of the Bastille on 14 July 1789 until 9 November 1799, when Napoleon Bonaparte stages a coup — inspire passionate debate in Britain. On the side of the revolutionaries are radicals such as Tom Paine, son of a Norfolk Quaker who advocates American independence in *Common Sense* in 1776 and then in *The Rights of Man* defends the French Revolution against its critics in 1791. Richard Price's 1789 sermon attracts the anger of Edmund Burke, a leading Whig MP uncomfortable with the idea of reform, who writes the conservative *Reflections on the Revolution in France* (1791). This sparks a pamphlet war, which tops three hundred publications, debating fundamental questions of politics, and spills over into novels, poetry, popular song and caricature. The controversy energizes reform societies, such as the Society for Constitutional Information, and inspires the formation of the London Corresponding Society in 1792. All of these want reform of the old corrupt parliamentary system, and an extension of the franchise. But in May 1792, the Tory government fights back: it issues a royal proclamation against seditious writing and actively persecutes any radical it can find. This results in mass arrests and treason trials.

The age of revolution creates a hunger for news, and the illegitimate minor theatres on the fringes of London — Sadler's Wells, Astley's Amphitheatre and the Royal Circus — soon cater for this need. They are the newsreels of Regency London. Gabriel loves his subject and positively glows as he describes these intoxicating events. At Sadler's Wells, a play called *Gallic Freedom; or, Vive la Liberté* celebrates the storming of the Bastille. At Astley's you can see *Paris in an Uproar; or, The Destruction of the Bastille and the Triumph of Liberty*. Both are early examples of documentary theatre. In such times, it is perhaps inevitable that a manager would emerge to challenge the duopoly of the patent theatres, Drury Lane and Covent Garden. And so it happens. In 1787 John Palmer — a comic actor known as Plausible Jack, who played Joseph in the first production of Sheridan's *The School for Scandal* — attempts to establish an alternative theatre. After all, there is plenty of evidence that people want to see more shows, and the lure of profit is strong. Armed with permission to build from the Lord Lieutenant of the Tower he chooses Wellclose Square, situated within the Liberties of the Tower of London, and builds the Royalty Theatre. With a capacity of 2600 seats, sixty per cent of which are affordable, the aim is to bring in a working-class audience from the East End. But although the opening night of 20 June draws a huge crowd, Palmer's staging of straight plays (Shakespeare's *As You Like It* and Garrick's *A Miss in Her Teens*) is deemed illegal because only the patent theatres are allowed to perform spoken drama. Faced with the threat of prosecution, Palmer abandons straight plays and turns to dancing dogs, dancing humans and musicals.

At Drury Lane and Covent Garden, meanwhile, the manager is king. Richard Brinsley Sheridan rules Drury Lane, but he prefers making orations in parliament to the day-to-day affairs of the theatre. At Covent Garden, Thomas Harris and George Colman the Elder manage the theatre, until they quarrel over an actress, Jane Lessingham, a lover of Harris's. When he tells us this, Gabriel raises his eyebrows: 'Typical!' Anyway, the London patent theatres are creating a nationwide repertoire and a tradition that elevates the spoken drama as the peak of theatrical experience. This means that all new actors have to play the big roles in the repertory in order to be taken seriously. At the same time, British theatre now enjoys a global reach: in 1789, George Farquhar's *The Recruiting Officer* is performed at Port Jackson in Australia by convicts, who have been transported there by a brutal justice system.

New faces

In the 1780s, a new generation of actors arrives. Gabriel now takes us on a brisk walk in Hyde Park, towards Rotten Row (the king's private road), hoping that we might spot some of the stars of the stage. It is late afternoon, but despite the chill in the air there are many groups of elegant men and women promenading up and down the avenues. While Gabriel looks out for recognisable faces, he brings us up to speed. The biggest star is Sarah Siddons, the queen of tragedy. Born in Wales, she is the eldest of the twelve children of Roger and Sarah Kemble, who lead a troupe of touring actors. In 1773, at the age of eighteen, she marries William Siddons, also an actor. Her first Drury Lane appearance in 1775 is not a success and she returns to the provinces. Then in 1782 she triumphs at Drury Lane in the title role of David Garrick's adaptation of Thomas Southerne's tragedy, *Isabella; or, The Fatal Marriage*. This time her career takes off, and her

Sarah Siddons

tragic heroines mesmerize audiences with their striking eyes, dignity of demeanour and utter conviction. As Lady Macbeth, she breaks with convention in the sleepwalking scene by putting down the candle she is carrying so that her hands are free to mimic the washing of the blood. Then her body convulses with horrible shudders, and Gabriel tells us that one audience member, the Irish playwright James Sheridan Knowles, exclaims: 'Well sir, I smelt blood! I swear that I smelt blood!' And William Hazlitt, critic and essayist, notes that she seems inhuman, 'a being from a darker world, full of evil'. It is a sublime performance. So realistic is her acting that when, in the role of Aphasia in Christopher Marlowe's *Tamburlaine*, she falls senseless to the floor, audiences believe she really is dead, and the manager is forced to come on stage to reassure them. The attitudes that Siddons strikes become models for artists and her iconic status is confirmed when her portrait is painted by Thomas Gainsborough and Sir Joshua Reynolds, the Fabio Testino of the time. On 29 June 1812 she gives an extraordinary farewell performance. She plays Lady Macbeth, and the audience, applauding rapturously, refuses to let the play continue after the end of her sleepwalking scene. The curtain is brought down. Eventually, the curtain rises and Siddons is seen sitting on a chair in her everyday clothes. Now, no longer Lady Macbeth, she gives an emotional farewell speech that lasts eight minutes. Gabriel, who swears that he has seen her perform countless times, wasn't there on this occasion, but he says that hundreds of people now claim to have been there — so many that they could have filled the theatre ten times over!

As we continue our bracing walk, Gabriel introduces some other names. There's Frances 'Fanny' Abington, who was born in a slum and began her career as a street singer before working at the Little Theatre Haymarket and then Drury Lane. She is not only an actress, but also a fashion icon. She promotes the wearing of loose-flowing gowns and a cap which is soon known as the Abington cap. Then there's Elizabeth Farren from Ireland, a one-time child actress, who marries into the peerage in 1797 when she bags the Earl of Derby. 'Theatre circles are hotbeds of intrigue,' Gabriel says, with Georgiana Cavendish, Duchess of Devonshire, persuading

THE CRITIC'S VIEW: KEMBLE AS HAMLET

Critic Richard Sharp describes Kemble's Hamlet:

He is a very handsome man, almost tall and almost large, with features of a sensible but fixed and tragic cast; his action is graceful, though somewhat formal, which you will find it hard to believe, yet it is true. Very careful study appears in all he says and all he does; but there is more singularity and ingenuity, than simplicity and fire. Upon the whole he strikes me rather as a finished French performer, than as a varied and vigorous English actor, and it is plain he will succeed better in heroic, than in natural and passionate tragedy.

actress Mary 'Perdita' Robinson, who excels in breeches parts, to sleep with prominent Whig politicians such as Charles James Fox and Richard Brinsley Sheridan. Perdita rises so high that she becomes mistress to the Prince Regent, thus swapping breeches for silk underdrawers. Then there's the exuberant Dorothy Jordan, another Irish actress who also excels in breeches roles and as the boisterous Priscilla Tomboy in the musical farce, *The Romp*. She has a twenty-year affair with the Duke of Clarence, third son of King George III and the future King William IV, bearing him no less than ten children. Eventually, the government persuades him to pay her off: 'Not very nice,' says Gabriel.

Look, is that John Philip Kemble? We hurry across, but are just too late to get a proper look at Siddons's brother, as he clambers into a carriage and is gone. When Gabriel gets his breath back, he says that Kemble was brought up a Catholic with the intention of becoming a priest, but chose the stage instead. He first acts in the provinces in Tate Wilkinson's York company before coming to London, making his Drury Lane debut as Hamlet, one of his best roles, in 1783. Often performing opposite his sister, he is the age's foremost tragic male. Kemble's speciality is Shakespeare, and his Macbeth is memorable. Likewise, his statuesque dignity suits the Roman characters in the tragic repertoire: Coriolanus, Brutus, Cato. His style is all about aloof coolness, precision of articulation and elaboration of minute details, founded on a thorough psychological study of the character. In comedy, he flops. But Kemble also is significant in another way: in 1788 he becomes manager of Drury Lane; in 1803 he gets the same job at Covent Garden.

Then a small group of women, dressed in flowing gowns with their hands in muffs to protect them from the cold, pass by. 'Ah,' says Gabriel, indicating a lively dark-haired woman, 'that's Elizabeth Inchbald.' Who? The most successful female playwright of the time, he answers. After an acting career lasting a decade, she turns to playwriting. Starting in 1780, she has twenty plays staged. Her distinguishing feature is rapidity of composition: Gabriel says that when she is at work on her fifth play in two years journalists joke about her 'dramatic progeny', her 'pregnant pen' and her 'fertile conception'. But she has the last laugh. At her death, she leaves an estate worth £6000, a sum far beyond any journalist's dreams. She's also quite a radical: in plays such as *I'll Tell You What*, *Such Things Are* and *Every One Has His Fault* she questions why women should submit to their husbands and fathers. Her plays frequently mention current crazes, such as gaming, ballooning and mesmerism, and most of them include the 'Inchbald woman', who is — like the playwright — independent but loving, with more common sense than the men around them. As well as her original plays, she enjoys great success with her adaptations. Her version of German-playwright August von Kotzebue *Lover's Vows* is first performed at Covent Garden in 1798, and runs for forty-two nights, before being performed in fashionable Bath, Bristol and Newcastle. It is the play that the young gentry in Jane Austen's 1814 novel, *Mansfield Park*, choose for their home theatricals. Inchbald is the first British female theatre critic, and a friend of William Godwin, the radical political philosopher, novelist and free thinker, her life being marked by tensions between her instinctive love of freedom and the stricter dictates of her Catholic beliefs. She supports the ideals of the French Revolution, but not its excesses. In 1792, she writes an incendiary play called *The Massacre*, inspired by the September Massacres in Paris where, panicked by the idea of inmates rioting, the French National Guard liquidates half the prison population without trial. There is no chance that the Lord Chamberlain will approve such a political play — the British elite are already jumpy about revolution, fearing the contagion from across the Channel. So she just circulates the text among her radical friends, including Godwin, playwright Thomas Holcroft and revolutionary Tom Paine, currently in exile in France because of his radical opinions.

Gabriel is quite diffident when talking about Inchbald, and we get the feeling that he's a bit out of his depth with female thespians. But he does say that there is one other female playwright worth mentioning: Hannah Cowley. Her *The Belle's Stratagem* is performed at Covent Garden in 1780. Its title is a riposte to George Farquhar's *The Beaux' Stratagem* and it is a romantic comedy of manners. Its view of the ups and downs of the marriage market is a hit with both the general public and the royals, with Queen Charlotte insisting that it is revived for the royal family at least once a year. When this play is staged in Paris in the early 1830s, the actress playing the ingenue, Letitia, is Harriet Smithson, who inspires composer Hector Berlioz's *Symphonie Fantastique*. But romance goes hand-in-hand with a feminist sensibility in Cowley's work. In her first play, *The Runaway*, she has Bella, the friend of Emily Morley, the mysterious runaway, challenge the wording of the marriage vow: 'I won't hear of it, "love" one might manage that perhaps — but "honour, obey"! — 'tis strange the ladies had never interest enough to get this ungallant form amended.' Yes, concludes Gabriel, there is much that needs reforming!

Slavery on stage

On which note, Gabriel now takes us to a printer and bookshop at 2 George Yard, a tiny place off Lombard Street in the City of London, where the Society for the Abolition of Slavery was formed in 1787 by a handful of Evangelical Protestants and Quakers. They waited until all the workers had gone home so they could have the place to themselves. We do the same. In the back, a heavy printing press dominates a dingy room. There's a strong smell of ink in the air. In the front, the shop sells books, pamphlets and prints — all vital instruments in the propaganda war against slavery. Gabriel tells us that about 15,000 black people live in Britain, half in London. Some are slaves, others sailors or soldiers who have served the country. As well as telling us some statistics — such as, three million Africans were transported across the Atlantic — he also describes some of his own experiences. And then passionately puts the case for abolition. In parliament, the anti-slavery campaign is supported by Whigs like Charles James Fox, but is led by William Wilberforce, a Cambridge graduate, religious convert and friend of the Tory prime minister William Pitt. After various attempts, which are blocked by rich merchants, Wilberforce finally succeeds in convincing parliament to abolish slavery in Britain in 1807, although it remains legal across the colonies until 1833. Although Gabriel commends the good work of these Evangelicals, he points out that grassroots black campaigners have been equally active. For example, Olaudah Equiano is a prominent member of the Sons of Africa, a group of twelve black men who campaign vigorously for abolition.

Gabriel also reveals the history of black characters — as played by white actors on stage. Isaac Bickerstaffe's comic afterpiece opera, *The Padlock*, is staged at Drury Lane in 1768, and is the first entertainment to feature a blackface comedian, Mungo, who is played by actor and song-writer Charles Dibdin as a caricature of a black servant. It is so successful that Dibdin turns it into a one-man show, in which he does impressions of black people and sings songs. This means that in the popular imagination the name Mungo rapidly becomes synonymous with any 'uppity' black man. Gabriel ruefully admits that he himself has been called this on countless occasions. Throughout the century, there are stage adaptations of Aphra Behn's novel, *Oroonoko*, which is set in Surinam, as well as plays about slavery, such as Archibald McLaren's *The Negro Slaves; or, The Blackman and the Blackbird* (Edinburgh, 1799) or John Fawcett's *Obi; or, Three Fingered Jack* (Little Theatre Haymarket, 1800), which features an escaped Jamaican slave. But the most popular of all, and the hit of the 1787-88 season at the Little Theatre, is George Colman the Younger's *Inkle and Yarico*. Colman, who is well known for catering to popular taste, creates a comic opera out of the story of Thomas Inkle, a white Bristol merchant, who is shipwrecked on the shore of America.

Isaac Bickerstaffe's *The Padlock* (1768)

Mungo's song:

Dear heart, what a terrible life am I led!
A dog has a better, that's sheltered and fed;
Night and day, 'tis de same,
My pain is dere game:
Me wish to de Lord me was dead.
Whatevers to be done,
Poor blacky must run;
Mungo here, Mungo dere,
Mungo everywhere;
Above and below,
Sirrah, come; sirrah, go;
Do so, and do so.
Oh! Oh!
Me wish to de Lord me was dead.

Inkle is rescued from natives by Yarico, an Indian maiden, and they fall in love. But when they arrive in Barbados, an English colony, the cash-strapped Inkle tries to sell Yarico as a slave. When he discovers she is pregnant, he raises her price while plotting to marry Narcissa, a rich lady. This tear-jerker ends with Inkle finally discovering his own good heart, repenting and embracing the loyal Yarico. Sarah Siddons is sublime as Yarico, and the story is so popular that Elizabeth Inchbald writes a preface to the published version of the play, praising it for raising the subject of the abolition of slavery. Although the play is successful, it doesn't really question the institution of slavery, Gabriel tells us. Colman, he points out, is more of a populist than a liberal, and in fact he grows into an arch-conservative: when he works as the Lord Chamberlain's Examiner of Plays, he is an exceptionally severe censor.

In the gloom of the print shop, as the candles flicker in the draught, Gabriel warms to his subject. He says that Shakespeare's *Othello* is very popular at the time, which sends mixed signals about this black character: he's both a successful general (good) and a jealous homicidal maniac (bad). But what about black actors, we ask? 'For that,' says Gabriel, 'we must wait until 1825, when Ira Aldridge is the first to perform in Britain.' Born in New York, son of a church minister, Aldridge gets a classical education and debuts as Shakespeare's Romeo. But frustrated by the lack of opportunities to perform because of racial discrimination, he emigrates to London, which he believes to be more welcoming to people of colour. Here he enjoys some success as Mungo in *The Padlock* and as Gambia in *The Slave*, as well as some white roles. But he once again experiences prejudice — newspaper critics claim his thick lips make his voice indistinct — and he is forced to go touring around Britain. He returns to London to play Othello in 1833, at the age of twenty-six, taking over the role from star actor Edmund Kean, who has just died. But newspaper critics give him a hard time. Talking about the actress playing Desdemona, one writes: 'In the name of propriety and decency we protest against an interesting actress and a decent girl like Miss Ellen Tree being subjected to the indignity of being pawed about on the stage by a black man.' The reactions are so strong that Aldridge only lasts two nights. He is forced to tour again, this time to Europe, and his greatest triumphs are in Prussia and Russia, where heads of state shower him with honours. As Gabriel says, 'We are no longer slaves, but we are not yet completely free.'

As the night deepens, Gabriel outlines the other conflicts of Regency England: in the countryside, Captain Swing rioters are protesting against Enclosures (the privatisation of land by rich owners); in the north, the newly formed industrial working class is demanding recognition of trade unions and workers' rights; in some new manufacturing areas the Luddites are smashing machinery; everywhere there is agitation for electoral reform (most of the population doesn't have the vote). All the traditional institutions, which the radicals call Old Corruption, face pressure for change. The monarchy is not immune. In 1795, the unpopular Prince Regent agrees to marry Princess Caroline of Brunswick. His motive is to appease parliament, whose members know about his secret liaison with the Catholic Maria Fitzherbert and won't pay off his massive debts unless he marries a Protestant. He hates his new bride, and the couple soon live separate lives. When he inherits the throne as King George IV, Caroline becomes the figurehead of a popular movement against the spendthrift monarch. Everywhere there are cries for reform.

Patriots and rioters

In the 1790s, the French Revolution descends into the Reign of Terror, and Britain is soon at war against France. National heroes are the Tory prime minister William Pitt, admiral Horatio Nelson and the Duke of Wellington. Within a decade British soldiers and sailors are fighting to keep Britain free from the Emperor Napoleon. To show us the impact of this on theatres, Gabriel takes us to see a wall in the Strand which is plastered with posters for performances. He points out in a rather tight-lipped way that, as always, war produces an atmosphere of heady patriotism heightened by xenophobia.

Gabriel uses his cane to point out a poster for *Naval Triumph; or, The Tars of Old England*, put on at Sadler's Wells in 1794, which he says features brave British sailors pitted against cruel French revolutionaries. A large water tank is built at this venue for the purpose of staging aqua-dramas — large spectacles staged on water — such as *The Siege of Gibraltar* (1804), with its sensational sea battle. Up with Nelson; down with Napoleon! The poster makes thrilling reading. 'There is tremendous enthusiasm,' says our guide, 'for Nelson and Wellington, heroes of the battles of Trafalgar and Waterloo.' So at Astley's Amphitheatre you can witness re-enactments of *The Battle of the Nile* (Nelson) or *The Siege of Salamanca* (Wellington). At the Royalty Theatre, an epic account of the Battle of Waterloo, Napoleon's final defeat, is staged within six months of victory in 1815. Interest in the growing British Empire is also reflected in plays with names like *Tippoo Saib; or, British Valour in India*. Crowds of ordinary Londoners throng to see these shows, and we notice that other people have gathered to look at the newer posters.

Then Gabriel points to a large poster with the name *Pizarro* in large black letters. 'In 1799,' he says, 'Drury Lane manager Richard Brinsley Sheridan kisses the witty style of his *The School for Scandal* goodbye and goes populist.' His *Pizarro* is an adaptation of a play by August von Kotzebue, and it is an allegory of British opposition to Napoleon. Set in the exotic location of South American forests, it delights audiences with its spectacular stage image of the Inca Temple of the Sun. A key scene takes place on a bridge above a waterfall, where Rolla (the doomed Inca hero fighting the invading Spanish conquistadores led by Pizarro), is making his escape, with the child of his beloved Cora in his arms. John Philip Kemble plays Rolla as a noble savage, delivering a stirring patriotic speech: 'They follow an adventurer who they fear — and obey a power which they hate — we serve a monarch who we love — a god who we adore.' 'When King George III attends a performance on 5 June 1799,' says Gabriel, 'the dangerously over-crowded theatre erupts with loud exclamations of loyalty.' God save the King! But there are even more patriotic plays. George Colman the Younger does his bit for nation building with *John Bull; or, The Englishman's Fireside*, staged at the Little Theatre Haymarket in 1803, which features a hero called Job Thornberry, who warns despots at home and abroad to respect English liberties. But as well as serious plays, there are also comic romps. At Covent Garden in 1798, Thomas Morton's comedy *Speed the Plough* has a lasting effect in that it introduces an offstage character called Mrs Grundy, who becomes a symbol of priggish neo-Puritanism. At the same venue in 1791, another comedy, the Dublin-born John O'Keefe's *Wild Oats* features Sir George Thunder, a naval captain, and his bosun John Dory on a hunt for deserters, as well as telling the delightful tale of a young Quaker woman who disapproves of the theatre, and then not only becomes smitten by a touring actor but also develops a craze for Shakespeare.

'This is also an era of riots and fire,' says Gabriel, as we move away from the poster wall. When actor John Philip Kemble, now manager of Covent Garden, raises admission prices after rebuilding the venue following the fire of 1808, he gets his fingers badly burned. Kemble has been an impressive tragedian but —

THEATRE A&E: BURN BABY BURN!

1789: KING'S THEATRE IN LONDON BURNS DOWN.

1808: LONDON'S COVENT GARDEN BURNS DOWN.

1809: LONDON'S DRURY LANE BURNS DOWN.

1820: BIRMINGHAM THEATRE BURNS DOWN.

1826: ROYALTY THEATRE IN LONDON BURNS DOWN.

1834: LONDON'S LYCEUM BURNS DOWN.

like Richard Brinsley Sheridan before him — he's not a very good manager. The first show after Kemble raises prices is Shakespeare's *Macbeth*. Dressed in tartan and wearing a kilt, Kemble comes on stage in the lead role, but no one can hear what he says because the audience is so outraged at being charged more that it boos, hisses and wails. He carries on manfully, but to no avail. On subsequent nights, these Old Price (or OP) demonstrations spiral out of control: spectators wear protest badges, wave protest banners and sing protest songs. At one point, a coffin is carried in with the message 'Here lies the body of the new price'. The OP riots run for an amazing sixty-seven nights — and Kemble has to give in. Rejoice, the price rise is abolished. But disorder is not the only hazard. On 24 February 1809, Sheridan's theatre, Drury Lane, burns to the ground. While this is happening he sits in the Piazza Coffee House. When asked by a colleague to explain his cool demeanour, he says: 'A man may surely be allowed to take a glass of wine by his own fireside.'

Melodrama and romanticism

Fear of revolution reaches fever pitch. The Tory government brings in a list of repressive laws to quell the agitation for reform. In 1792, King George III issues a royal proclamation against seditious publications, which criminalises any pamphlet that advocates change. Three years later, the 'Two Acts' condemn meetings of reformers as treason, thus making this a capital crime. In 1819, the Peterloo Massacre exemplifies state brutality: a troop of cavalry charge a demonstration demanding the vote in St Peter's Fields in Manchester, killing fifteen people and injuring hundreds. But while political violence is on the rise, this is also a time of creativity. Jane Austen's novels are admired by the Prince Regent. It is the Age of Romanticism, with dashing young poets such as Lord Byron, Percy Bysshe Shelley and John Keats. Mary Shelley, daughter of William Godwin and wife of the poet, publishes her novel *Frankenstein* in 1818. Some of these youthful creatives try their hand at serious drama, but with little success. Their favourite genre is tragedy. Shelley writes *The Cenci* in 1819, but it is not performed until 1886. Poets William Wordsworth and Samuel

Mary Shelley

Taylor Coleridge also attempt noble tragedies. Byron writes plays with names such as *Sardanapalus*, which we have to tell Gabriel are quite forgotten today. What is not forgotten, however, is the work of theatre critics, essayists such as William Hazlitt and Charles Lamb, whose writing evokes the performances of the actors of the age. These critics are also politically acute: Hazlitt condemns the patent theatres as Old Corruption.

As the nineteenth century starts, the traditional theatre forms of tragedy and comedy — the staples of playwriting since Elizabethan times — are on their last legs, practically dead. In popular esteem, they are shoved aside by burletta and pantomime, and then by melodrama. The first play to call itself a melodrama is *A Tale of Mystery* by Thomas Holcroft, whose story he pinches from René Charles Guilbert de Pixérécourt's French original, and stages at Covent Garden in 1802. Previously, Holcroft's most successful work, *The Road to Ruin* (1792), explored a social issue — a run on a family bank. Its social conscience is not surprising, given that he is a political activist whose friends include Tom Paine and William Godwin. As a result of his radicalism, he is indicted for high treason in 1794 and held in Newgate Prison. The charge carries the death penalty, but the case is dropped at the eleventh hour. *A Tale of Mystery* is a full-on melodrama: it has a picturesque Alpine setting, with swirling music and storm-swept lofty mountains suggesting a sublime romantic feel. Here, the virtue of Selina, an innocent young heiress, is threatened by the aristocratic rake Romaldi. He

THEATRE THEORY: MELODRAMA

Melodrama is an import from France. It is invented by playwright and director René Charles Guilbert de Pixérécourt, who aims to create new entertainments for working-class audiences by staging plays with heightened emotions and clear moral storylines. He is an amazingly prolific theatre-maker who delights Parisian spectators with more than sixty plays during the first thirty years of the nineteenth century. These are performed in boulevard theatres, mainly attended by ordinary people, not cultural snobs. In Britain, melodrama is an updated version of tragedy, with noble heroes, evil villains and damsels in distress. Taking inspiration from French examples and German *sturm und drang* (storm and stress) plays, these stories deliver poetic justice in an unjust world: good always wins over evil. Their values are those of hearth, home and the moral virtue of ordinary folk. Melodrama breaks with the traditional structure of the five-act play, preferring a three-act formula: in part one, the hero is separated from the heroine; in part two, the heroine is threatened by the villain; in part three, the hero saves the heroine. Written in everyday language, melodrama specialises in the use of dramatic scenery, natural catastrophes and dramatic music to raise emotions. It also influences literature, especially the novels of Charles Dickens.

is defeated by Francisco, his own brother who is dumb because his tongue was once cut out on Romaldi's orders. A flavour of this breathless melodrama is best sampled by reading not its dialogues, but its stage directions. One begins: 'Music: terror, confusion, menace, command' — *sturm und drang* indeed.

Thomas Holcroft's *A Tale of Mystery* (1802)
Act I Scene 3 stage directions:
Thunder heard, while the scene changes. Music. Scene III: The wild mountainous country called the Nant of Arpennaz; with pines and massy rocks. A rude wooden bridge thrown from rock to rock; a rugged mill stream a little in the background; the miller's house on the right; a steep ascent by a narrow path to the bridge; a stone or bank to sit on. The increasing storm of lightning, thunder, hail and rain, becomes terrible. Suitable music.

As well as romantic wildness, there is a taste for the mysterious and the uncanny – in a word, the gothic. The pioneer is the pale, sickly looking Matthew Gregory Lewis, who has already written a handful of gothic novels, including a bestseller — *The Monk*. His 1779 Drury Lane play, *The Castle Spectre*, is full of dank dungeons, drear forests and ghostly apparitions, and is a hit both in London and New York. Seven editions of the play are published in its first year. The heroine, Angela, is in danger, tormented by the villainous Earl Osmond. Yet she is so pure that she forgives him in the end. Osmond has black servants, which makes the play more exotic and possibly more frightening. Both the patent theatres compete to electrify the public. When Covent Garden stages Lewis's grandly romantic melodrama, *Timour the Tartar*, in 1811, they use a troupe of horse from Astley's Amphitheatre. The scene in which the hero plunges with his horse into a torrent to save his drowning mother is so overwhelming that it becomes a media phenomenon, and is condemned in parliament for its excesses. Other plays also raise the hair on the back of the audience's neck — Charles Maturin's tragedy of 1816, *Bertram*, opens like this: 'Night. A gallery in a convent. A large Gothic window in the extremity, through which lightning is seen flashing. Distant thunder. Two monks enter in terror.' Likewise, gothic drama gives licence to stage designers to indulge their imaginations: Thomas Greenwood's designs for George Colman's *Bluebeard* feature the Blue Chamber, whose walls are streaked with bright-red blood. The taste for the gothic also leads to new stage innovations: for James Robinson Plancé's *The Vampire; or, The Bride of the Isles* a 'vampire trap' is invented. It is used to good effect at the end of the play when the terrifying character of Ruthven suddenly disappears through this concealed trapdoor with 'a terrific peal of thunder'.

Most shows pander to the audience — especially to their love of domestic animals: Frederick Reynolds's melodrama *The Caravan; or, The Driver and His Dog* at Drury Lane in 1803 features a dog which at the climax leaps into a roaring river to rescue a drowning child. In William Barrymore's *The Dog of Montargis; or, Murder in the Wood* (based on Pixérécourt's original) at Covent Garden in 1814, a faithful hound avenges the murder of its master. William Thomas Moncrieff's *The Cataract of the Ganges* causes a sensation in 1823 at the same venue when the heroine of the play rides a horse up a white-water cataract while fires rage all around. Production costs are £5000, a gobsmacking sum.

Drury Lane reborn

Gabriel now takes us through the familiar streets to Drury Lane, so that we can see a show at this venue. As usual, the roads are noisy with the sounds of carriage wheels on cobblestones, the cries of street vendors, dogs barking and a hubbub of voices. Then finally we are at the entrance of the Theatre Royal Drury Lane in Catherine Street. 'No other theatre in the world,' says Gabriel, his face illuminated by a broad smile, 'is so proud of its traditions, nor so large and so splendid.' The heavy classical-style portico and steps are recognisable: this is the sight that still welcomes twenty-first-century Londoners. As we pass under the royal coat of arms, Gabriel tells us that the colonnade at the side of theatre in Russell Street is added in 1831 to protect the richer patrons from the rain while they wait for their carriages.

We venture inside, climbing the magnificent staircase, noting the splendid rotunda and luxurious saloon, which convey the sense of a grand occasion. Gabriel takes us to a private box. We are all ears. This is an age of frantic rebuilding. In the 1770s, both Drury Lane and Covent Garden are reconstructed by Robert and James Adam. Then in the 1790s both venues are completely rebuilt yet again! 'This is because,' says Gabriel, 'they need to accommodate more people.' Henry Holland reconstructs both buildings, increasing their capacity, with each housing about 3000 people. When Drury Lane burns down in 1809, it is rebuilt in 1812, partly funded by a share issue, an early form of crowdfunding. Turning to a small table, Gabriel shows us a beautifully engraved share certificate. Under this scheme, subscribers rent some of the boxes, gaining entry by showing a token inscribed with their names. Among the accessories that Gabriel has assembled for us are fans decorated with pictures of the theatre. Then he shows us a small room, next to our box, 'Where you can have an intimate supper, or entertain someone in private,' says our guide with a wink. He quotes Richard Brinsley Sheridan's opinion, which he expresses only in private, that the theatre 'is the greatest nursery of vice and misery on the face of the Earth'. Well, he should know.

Since we were last inside a London theatre a great transformation has taken place. We notice two things: the huge size of the place and the blaze of light. Looking out over the auditorium, Gabriel points out that more than ever before the space is organised on class lines. The tiers of boxes are for richer patrons; the backless benches in the pit for the middle classes; and the upper gallery above the boxes for the working classes. He shows us the huge stage, with its decorated proscenium arch, and we note the fact that the platform that used to project into the stalls has disappeared. Most of the action now takes place behind the arch. After 1817 the theatre is lit by gas, which is much brighter than candles. Twenty years later, limelight (burning blocks of calcium oxide) arrives. The expression 'in the limelight' refers to the brilliantly illuminated front of the stage.

When the curtain rises, the lights remain full on and people still talk during the show, much as they always have done. The scenery, we notice, is much more realistic and the lighting effects brighter than in the past. Gabriel tells us that the quality of paints for scenery has improved and that they are better than the muddy colours of yesteryear. It's something to do with new discoveries of metallic pigments, but we're not really listening. We're too busy looking at the stage: the costumes are more historically accurate than before, and the actors wear white or rouge make-up. The show we are watching is a typical melodrama: we notice how the frenzied activity on the stage alternates with moments of great stillness, when the characters freeze while the music swells — just like living paintings. With the audience at a greater distance than ever before, actors have to strain to make themselves heard, and use bigger gestures to convey their feelings. Subtle acting is a no, no. During one of the intervals, Gabriel shows us *Practical Illustrations of Rhetorical Gesture and Action*, a 1807 book by Henry Siddons, Mrs Siddons's eldest son, which shows the meaning of typical thespian gestures. Armed with this, we practice 'defiance' by flinging one arm into the air and the other back while standing erect.

Gabriel's rich store of anecdotes includes one about the tempestuous relationship between King George III and the Prince Regent. One evening both father and son visit Drury Lane. When they meet, the Prince bows but King George, who thinks he's being insolent, boxes his ears. After this unseemly fracas, the management of the theatre creates a separate royal box for the Prince so that he does not have to share his father's. From now on, smiles Gabriel, this is the only theatre in Europe to have two royal boxes. The evening has been quite long and, by midnight, we are keen to leave the bright lights of the theatre behind.

Age of reform

We are now at the George Inn, a galleried coaching stop on Borough High Street in Southwark, and Gabriel is telling the story of the fall of Old Corruption and the triumph of reform. In the aptly named Parliament Bar, with its wooden beams and oak tables, all glowing in warm yellow gaslight, he tells us that in 1832 parliament finally passes the 'Great Reform Act', which makes general elections fairer, although, he notes, women still don't get the vote. Large numbers of solid middle-class men do, however, and the act sweeps away many corrupt practices. But, to liberal-minded reformers like our guide, Drury Lane and Covent Garden are just as bad as the unreformed parliament. By now, their finances are in a mess: their overheads are too high; their payroll is too long. In the economic depression of the 1820s, which follows the Napoleonic Wars, they face bankruptcy.

By the 1830s, some changes are on the way. The patent theatres manage to stage some plays that reflect social problems. For example, playwright Douglas William Jerrold uses melodrama to highlight current social conditions. *The Rent Day*, inspired by David Wilkie's painting of the same name, shows a respectable tenant farmer who is unable to pay his rent and thus faces eviction, a common occurrence in a rural jobs market flooded by returning soldiers from the Napoleonic Wars. At one point in the play, the actors freeze in exactly the same poses as the figures in Wilkie's painting. Although the story, staged early in 1832 at Drury Lane, is not a call to arms, it does feel provocative in the year of the Great Reform Bill.

But, nods Gabriel, the duopoly of Drury Lane and Covent Garden is being challenged by a host of minor theatres springing up on the outskirts of London. Using an Act of Parliament of 1752 that allows theatres to be built within twenty miles of London as long as they have a magistrate's licence, the minor theatres adopt various devices to avoid infringing the rights of the patent theatres. Since only the patent houses can play regular drama (that is, straight plays with fixed dialogue that has been approved by the Lord Chamberlain), the other theatres stage burlettas, which have music and are thus not classed as straight plays. So regular dramas, such as Shakespeare, are rewritten and performed as musicals. Dialogue is written on placards, or turned into rhyming songs. The centre of gravity in London theatre shifts decisively to the fringe, with crowds of poorer patrons buying cheap tickets from new outlets such as tobacconists and booksellers. In the eyes of hard-working people the new venues are gorgeous palaces of light, luxury and warmth — a better place to spend the evening than a cramped flat in a dirty tenement. For thousands of workers, sailors, shopkeepers and clerks theatre-going is now the leisure activity of choice.

Some two dozen new theatres appear. 'As well as established places such as Sadler's Wells, Astley's and the Little Theatre Haymarket,' says Gabriel, leaning across the table, 'new managers enter the fray.' In 1796, Charles Dibdin—the actor who created the role of Mungo—opens the Sans Souci Theatre in Leicester Square. In 1806, Jane Scott, a solo singer, runs the Sans Pareil, providing a diet of burletta and pantomime, and the venue is renamed the Adelphi on her retirement in 1819. Soon the name 'Adelphi drama' becomes a byword for vivid melodramas which specialize in showing women facing moral choices. Off the Tottenham Court Road, the Regency opens in 1814 and soon acquires the nickname of the Dusthole. South of the river are the Surrey (formerly Royal

Circus) and the Coburg. Comic actor Robert Elliston runs the Surrey and stages melodramatic versions of Walter Scott novels, such as *The Bride of Lammermoor*. He ends up making so much profit that he buys a share of Drury Lane. The Coburg (where black American actor Ira Aldridge appears as Oroonoko in *A Slave's Revenge* in 1825) is nicknamed the Blood Tub because of its sensational crime melodramas, with true stories pinched straight from the newspapers. It has an amazing mirror curtain. Made up of sixty-three sheets of glass it is so heavy it threatens to bring the roof down — literally. So it is replaced by a cloth curtain, and the venue is renamed the Old Vic, and as such is still standing today.

At the Olympic, another new venue, actor-manager Eliza Vestris, who after an early career in a series of slightly naughty breeches roles, stages elegantly costumed burlettas and classical extravaganzas, featuring mythological gods and goddesses in urban settings. 'Her legs are so shapely,' says Gabriel, 'that plaster casts of them are made and sold.' As well as having nice legs, she transforms this theatre from a disreputable rat hole into a fashionable venue. At the same time, she introduces the box set, which shows three walls of a room and puts the audience in the position of peering through the fourth wall. With this, she makes a radical break from the fake-looking backcloths normally used to depict indoor scenes. This is one innovation that will enjoy a great future.

But although the patent theatres, under the beady eye of the Lord Chamberlain, are not allowed to talk about the political reform of social conditions, the minor illegitimate theatres step into the gap. At the Surrey, John Walker's *The Factory Lad* (1832) is about the unfair working conditions of the Lancashire cotton factories, the 'dark satanic mills' of William Blake's poem, and is a forerunner of political theatre. At the Adelphi, William Thomas Moncrieff's adaptation of Pierce Egan's flash novel *Tom and Jerry; or, Life in London* (1821) — a tour of London from Burlington Arcade to the slums of St Giles — shows images of high life and low life: it's *The Beggar's Opera* of its day, drawing huge crowds to more than a hundred performances. But it is not universally popular: outside the theatre Evangelical protestors parade with placards denouncing the show's immorality. The same author's *Reform; or, John Bull Triumphant* appears at the Coburg in 1831 during the run up to the Great Reform Bill. Meanwhile, at the Surrey again, Douglas Jerrold's *Black-Eyed Susan; or, All in the Downs* is staged in 1829. Its story concerns a sailor, William, who returns to England after serving in the Napoleonic Wars to find his wife, Susan, being harassed first by her landlord uncle and then by William's captain. Much of the play's humour comes from the sailor's nautical dialect and the play glorifies the patriotic British tar while attacking the abuse of power by the mighty. It makes a star of Thomas Potter Cooke, a former sailor who plays William, and sets a new record of more than 150 performances. (Cooke, wearing green make-up for the ghastly hue of putrescent flesh, is also a memorable Monster in a stage version of Mary Shelley's *Frankenstein*). Other political plays look to the past. In 1832, amid mass agitation for parliamentary

INDUSTRIAL REVOLUTION

Britain is the workshop of the world. In the nineteenth century, the factory — as a system of production — has a dramatic impact on the lives of millions of labourers. As workers, they are subject to the relentless discipline of mechanisation in what the philosopher and essayist Thomas Carlyle calls 'the age of the machine'. This industrial discipline creates a working class that is not only dragooned into the new factories but also disciplined into being hard working, sober and respectable. The northern cotton mills have a huge impact because for the first time large numbers of workers, particularly women and children, are employed in one building. By 1830, Lancashire cotton spinning is entirely a steam-powered factory operation, and weaving follows suit. Soon Britain produces more than half of the total world production of cotton cloth. Coal is the fuel of industry and by 1848 Britain mines two-thirds of world output. But horrific working conditions provoke a series of reforming 'Factory Acts'.

reform, the Coburg revives Henry Fielding's satire on royalty, *Tom Thumb*, updated to mock King George IV and his consort.

Public image

Gabriel now takes us to Somerset House, on the north bank of the Thames, and home of the Royal Academy of Arts, set up by Joshua Reynolds under the patronage of King George III. There's an exhibition of paintings and it's quite crowded, with fashionable Regency society rubbing shoulders with middle-class professionals and

Edmund Kean

their wives. Our guide helps us squeeze past some of the crowds and shows us a painting of Edmund Kean, the star actor of the time. This depicts him in a dramatic pose as the rapacious Giles Overreach in Jacobean dramatist Philip Massinger's *A New Way To Pay Old Debts*. 'Apparently,' says Gabriel, 'his performance is so intense that it throws Lord Byron into a convulsive fit.' Born into a struggling theatre family and with lots of experience as a child performer, Kean makes his Drury Lane debut in 1814 with a dignified Shylock. He is a small man, with a chip on his shoulder about his impoverished background, but his energy is amazing. Fuelled by feelings of resentment, he is the quintessential Romantic actor — passionate, intense and wild. He has gusto; he has guts. The poet Coleridge describes his impact: 'like reading Shakespeare by flashes of lightning'. In *The Examiner*, William Hazlitt writes: 'We wish we had never seen Mr Kean. He has

THE CRITIC'S VIEW: HAZLITT ON KEAN

William Hazlitt describes Kean's 1814 debut as Shylock in the *Morning Chronicle*, 27 January 1814:

For voice, eye, action and expression, no actor has come out in many years at all equal to him. The applause, from the first scene to the last, was general, loud and uninterrupted. Indeed, the very first scene in which he comes on with Bassano and Antonio showed the master in his art, and at once decided the opinion of the audience. Perhaps it was the most perfect of any.

destroyed the Kemble religion and it is the religion in which we were brought up.' 'Backstage gossip,' says Gabriel, 'has it that Kean has sex with various women in between the acts of the plays he's performing in!' Despite his meteoric rise, Kean ruins his health by drinking too much, and his career by refusing to perform if the theatre is half full (a petulant attitude that spoils his tour of America). His reputation takes a nosedive when he is sued for adultery by a City alderman. He is fined £800 and when he appears on the Drury Lane stage the audience boos and pelts him with fruit. After making a comeback, he finally collapses and dies while playing Othello in 1833. Three years later, French novelist and dramatist Alexandre Dumas, père, produces *Kean*, which glamorizes the actor as a working-class rebel. So whereas Kemble's image is of the actor as a respectable professional, Kean is the actor as bad boy.

Moving us through the crowds, and trying to see the paintings despite the forest of top hats and women's bonnets, Gabriel brings us to a painting of William Charles Macready in the role of Virginius from the ancient-Roman tragedy of that name by Irish playwright James Sheridan Knowles. 'Macready,' says our guide, 'is more Kemble than Kean.' Making his debut at Covent Garden in 1816, Macready is destined to become one of greatest theatre managers of the Victorian era. Meanwhile, the Kean dynasty lives on with his son Charles Kean, who makes his debut in a revival

...s at Drury Lane in 1827, and the Kemble ...mble whose 1829 debut at Covent Garden ...t. Gabriel shows us several other portraits ...ean roles, saying that the bard continues to ...e of the two patent theatres. Yet, away from the stage, his work is also enjoyed as family reading matter. In 1818, the physician and philanthropist Thomas Bowdler publishes *The Family Shakespeare*, an expurgated edition which cuts out all the bawdy bits and is thus 'suitable for women and children'. Bowdler's name becomes synonymous with censorship of sexual content. Likewise, the essayist Charles Lamb and his sister Mary publish *Tales from Shakespeare*, which retells the stories of the plays for youngsters.

There are two more pictures that Gabriel wants us to see. One is that of the most popular entertainer of the Regency era — Joseph Grimaldi. Born into a family of entertainers — his grandfather John Baptist Grimaldi once played Pantaloon opposite John Rich's Harlequin — Joseph or Joey enjoys success as a child actor, first taking the stage at the age of three in 1780. Gradually, he elaborates the role of the clown in pantomimes, by adding various improvisations and impersonations. In his hands, the Clown is so successful that it becomes the main character in hit shows such as *Harlequin; or, Mother Goose*, using extraordinary physical comedy and inventive

William Charles Macready

visual tricks. With his large face, sparkling eyes and self-approving chuckle, he pokes fun at his audience, and creates the pantomime tradition of audience participation. His catchphrases include 'Here we are again!' and he teases spectators with 'Shall I?', to which the answer is a roar of 'Yes!' With his distinctive whiteface make-up, he becomes so famous that Charles Dickens writes his biography and other clowns become known as 'Joey'. Similarly popular is the infant prodigy known as Master Betty, whose portrait shows a child actor with an innocent pink face. 'When he tours England in 1804 at the age of thirteen,' says Gabriel, 'there's an explosion of Bettymania: at Covent Garden, guards are hired to control the crowds of fans who want to see him.'

As we leave Somerset House, Gabriel winds up the story of Regency theatre by saying that just before Queen Victoria becomes monarch in 1837, reform is knocking at the door of the patent theatres. In 1832, a parliamentary committee chaired by the youthful MP and playwright Edward Bulwer-Lytton takes evidence from a host of witnesses and concludes that the old duopoly is no longer relevant. It recommends that all theatres should be allowed to stage spoken drama. The committee's observations include the fact that 'political allusions appear to be much more popular than any licentiousness'; its members are more worried by subversion than by sex. One year later, the 'Copyright Act' gives playwrights some protection against theatres stealing their ideas and their scripts. As a smiling Gabriel bids us farewell, we note that the reign of Queen Victoria begins with the ringing in of changes.

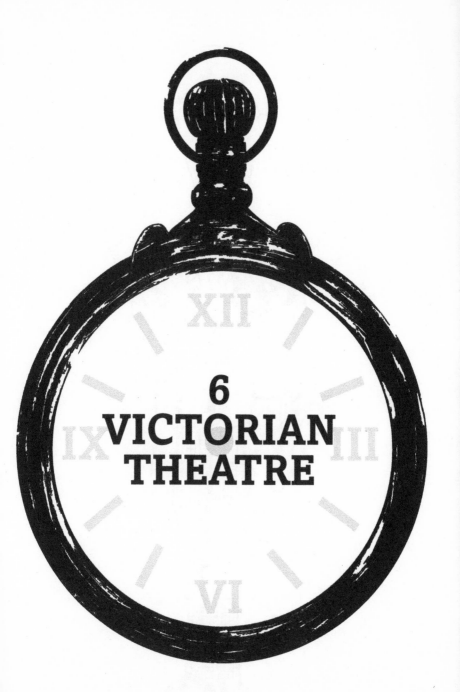

6
VICTORIAN THEATRE

6
Victorian Theatre

Meet our guide: Jack

Our new guide is Jack Goodheart, a Victorian teenager who has overcome a difficult background to become a responsible member of society. As a child, he lost his parents to cholera and was brought up at a union workhouse, where, although half starved, he did learn to read and write at one of the many London schools for pauper children. His was a 'monster school' with more than 1000 pupils, and he tells us that in his childhood his skin was perennially tormented by lice and scabies. However, this made him even more determined to succeed. He picked up knowledge wherever he could, at one point even doing a stint as a rat catcher. Then he became a class monitor, and finally a teacher. Now, Jack is a lively young gentleman of eighteen with sparkling eyes and a quizzical expression on his face. He is dressed in a dark frock coat, a bright green silk waistcoat and check trousers, with a white shirt and frilly cravat. After so many years of drabness, Jack loves colour. He has a silver pocket watch, and sports a fashionable walking stick. However, under this smart attire is a streetwise kid who, in the blink of an eye can spot any suspicious character. He takes us first to his lodgings in the south London suburb of Camberwell. When we are comfortable in the front parlour, Mrs H, his mature and maternal landlady, makes a rather flustered entrance, carrying a tray of tea along with Jack's favourite homemade jam sponge. As we settle down, he tells us that on this trip we will be looking at British theatre during the reign of Queen Victoria, from the 1840s to 1901.

Victoria and the Victorians

In Queen Victoria's reign, London's population explodes. From about two million it grows rapidly to more than six million. It is the first world city. This expansion creates new modes of transport: first horse buses, then railways, trams and underground trains. Roads have to be given a solid surface; streets are paved. On one of our first outings with Jack, we notice gas lights in the street: he says that it cuts crime. In the best districts, everything looks cleaner and safer than ever before. While in previous eras, rich and poor lived in close proximity, now the rich live in gated communities such as Belgravia, while the middle classes inhabit detached and semi-detached suburban villas in areas such as Clapham. Respectable workers live in terraced houses; the poor in slum tenements and then, after 1890, in council flats. At the centre of the mega metropolis is the heart of Empire, with its newly built Houses of Parliament gleaming in neo-Gothic splendour, its monumental Whitehall ministry buildings, West End department stores, solid office blocks, palatial railway hotels, and new places of education such as the Victoria and Albert Museum, British Museum and Tate Gallery. But pollution, poverty and overcrowding are the dark underbelly of this shining metropolis, nicknamed the Great Wen, a modern Babylon. When Jack takes us down the streets of central London we can barely breathe because millions of coal fires have created a thick pea-soup fog, a greasy, heavy swirl that hangs permanently over the city. And that's only half of it. In 1858, the Thames is so contaminated by sewage that the resulting Great Stink, as it is called, forces MPs at Westminster to have their curtains soaked in chloride of lime to combat the noxious stench. Plans have to be made for a whole new sewer system to be built.

For a glimpse of the monarch, the young Queen Victoria who marries her German cousin Prince Albert of Saxe-Coburg and Gotha in 1840, Jack dons a top hat and takes us to see the Crystal Palace, built temporarily in Hyde Park to house the Great Exhibition of 1851. Despite the wave of revolutions sweeping across Europe in 1848, Britain is relatively at peace. The Chartists, who want more political reforms, do not riot, but deliver petitions to parliament. The Great Exhibition is Prince Albert's idea: while the country is experiencing a manufacturing boom, he wants to showcase the wonders of industry from home and abroad. Watched by more than half a million spectators lining the streets, Queen Victoria and Prince Albert ride from Buckingham Palace to the Crystal Palace to open it. Jack takes us to the central hall of the gigantic glass construction and, over the heads of the gathered crowd, we can see the royal family standing on a carpeted platform, surrounded by dignitaries, foreign ambassadors and assorted royals. Prince Albert, in his German accent, reads a formal statement about industry and endeavour; the Archbishop of Canterbury calls for God's blessing; a six-hundred-strong choir sing the Hallelujah chorus from Handel's *Messiah*. Queen Victoria, small, plump and dressed in a formal pink gown suited to this official occasion, declares the Great Exhibition open. Jack says that this palace of marvels is packed full of wonders. For a start, it contains many of the park's trees, to which have been added palms, fountains, statues and 100,000 exhibits, from cotton-spinning machinery to steam hammers, from stuffed rabbits dressed as humans to an Indian elephant and howdah, emblem of the expanding Empire. Some twenty thousand people come on opening day alone; by the time the Exhibition closes five months later, more than six million have gone through the turnstiles.

To escape the crowds, we take a walk in Hyde Park, where Jack tells us that Queen Victoria is rather keen on the theatre. 'Her first experience,' he says, 'was a private performance of James Planché's history play, *Charles XII*, at Windsor Castle when she was not yet ten years old.' In the 1830s, she loves seeing circus shows, such as Isaac Van Amburgh's lions, which she saw seven times in six weeks at Drury Lane. As a young princess, she risks her reputation by visiting the Olympic Theatre, just off the Strand, to see Eliza Vestris and her husband, the eccentric light comedian Charles James Mathews. Her joy in seeing Vestris in the role of Beauty in Planché's charming extravaganza *Beauty and the Beast* is complete. As the St James Theatre is close to Buckingham Palace, she often visits it to sample its French farces. Later, she sees Dion Boucicault's hit play *The Corsican Brothers; or, The Fatal Duel* five times, noting in her diary that the duel scene, in which one of the brothers, Louis, is killed by Château-Renaud, a villainous womanizer, is 'beautifully grouped and quite touching'. Another favourite is novelist Wilkie Collins's *The Frozen Deep*, a contemporary melodrama co-written with his friend Charles Dickens. Queen Victoria also revives the ancient tradition of command performances by asking actor Charles Kean, son of Edmund Kean, to come to Windsor Castle to entertain her family. The Christmas pantos at Drury Lane are also a great joy for the royal family (by 1857 the couple have nine children). Queen Victoria is less keen on Shakespeare: she finds *Hamlet* and *King Lear* too turgid. Then in 1861 her theatre-going comes to a sudden end when Prince Albert dies from typhoid fever at the age of forty-two. Heartbroken, she goes into mourning, wearing black for the rest of her life and renouncing the pleasures of going out.

Free at last

After Edward Bulwer-Lytton's parliamentary committee of 1832 recommends reform of the age-old duopoly of Drury Lane and Covent Garden, with their exclusive rights to stage spoken drama, change is slow in coming. Eleven years go by. Then in 1843, parliament finally passes the 'Theatres Act', which abolishes the duopoly of the patent theatres. From now on, any theatre can put on straight plays: all they need is a licence from the Lord Chamberlain (the theatre censor). Now theatre is a free-for-all.

To tell us more, Jack takes us to the Garrick Club in what today is Garrick Street in Covent Garden. He gains admittance to this exclusive club through his friendship with a more mature actor, who is described by Jack as his mentor and companion. Understood! The club was, Jack explains, founded in 1831 by a group of literary gents under the patronage of the royal Duke of Sussex. Their mission was to create a place where 'actors and men of refinement and education might meet on equal terms'. As well as managers and actors, members include novelists Charles Dickens, William Makepeace Thackeray and Anthony Trollope. On the club's grand wooden staircase, Jack shows us some of the paintings of theatre subjects, part of a collection started by the actor Charles Mathews (father of Charles James Mathews), who acquired four hundred paintings and drawings. Later, when we are settled in leather armchairs in the elegant, slightly dimly lit members' room, Jack fills us in about the theatre system.

The key movers and shakers are the actor managers, who run the theatres and play the lead roles. Lord of the West End is William Charles Macready, who manages first Covent Garden and then Drury Lane. Although reluctant to embark on a stage career, he soon becomes an eminent tragedian and a pillar of Victorian respectability. He is the epitome of propriety. But behind the mask of the perfect gentleman lurks an unquiet spirit. He has a particular antipathy to Alfred Bunn, previous manager of Drury Lane. For some reason, which Jack can't fathom, in 1835 Macready punches Bunn in the face — and is fined £150 for assault. Even more violent is his New York tour in 1849, when he plays Macbeth at the Astor Opera House, and provokes a riot. This results from the rivalry between him and American star Edwin Forrest, who also plays Macbeth, this time at the Bowery Theatre, a hotbed of anti-British sentiment. So on the evening of 10 May 1849 the atmosphere is poisonous: Forrest is supported by the gangs of New York, who go into battle outside the Opera House with the slogan 'Down with the codfish aristocracy!', which refers to Macready's respectable Anglophile public. In the ensuing clash of thousands of rival fans in Astor Place thirty-one people are shot dead by police.

Back in London, Macready is hard at work. He strives to create a respectable theatre where the best of national drama can be staged. He excels as Macbeth, Hamlet and Lear. The keynote of his acting style is restraint: he has Victorian gravitas in spades. He also introduces a touch of domestic tenderness into his portraits of heroic grandeur. He likewise works hard to restore Shakespeare texts to their original form, for example by reinstating the tragic ending of *King Lear* (which had been changed by Nahum Tate to a happy marriage in 1681). As a director, he wants more authenticity in costumes and scenery: his production of *King Lear* is set in Saxon times with Druid stone circles, round-helmeted soldiers and flowing robes for the women. Macready is also the first to introduce the modern system of rehearsals, which now last a merciless five or six hours a day. Prior to this the lead actor almost never rehearsed with the rest of the cast. Macready is the first actor manager to be a modern director.

'To W. C. Macready' by Alfred Lord Tennyson (1851)
Farewell, Macready, since to-night we part;
Full-handed thunders often have confessed
Thy power, well-used to move the public breast.
We thank thee with our voice, and from the heart.
Farewell, Macready, since this night we part,
Go, take thine honours home; rank with the best,
Garrick and statelier Kemble, and the rest
Who made a nation purer through their art.
Thine is it that our drama did not die,
Nor flicker down to brainless pantomime,
And those gilt gauds men-children swarm to see.
Farewell, Macready; moral, grave, sublime;
Our Shakespeare's bland and universal eye
Dwells pleased, through twice a hundred years, on thee.

Although Drury Lane continues to be a premiere West End theatre, Covent Garden changes completely after a fire in 1856. It is rebuilt to look like a white neo-classical Greek temple, and becomes an opera house. Its place in London's theatre ecology is taken by the minor theatres. And the key trend is that actor managers now offer more comfortable surroundings for their respectable middle-class patrons. Jack tells us that there are many such managers, but only two names we have to remember: the Bancrofts and Kean. In 1855, actor managers Squire Bancroft and his wife, Marie Effie Wilton, get royal permission to name their theatre the Prince of Wales's. Although it is located in an unfashionable district north of Oxford Street, they turn it into a magnet for the carriages of the wealthy. The Bancrofts lay carpets in the stalls, where they replace the benches of Regency theatres with plush individual seats, covered with lace antimacassars, protecting them from staining by hair oil — just like any respectable Victorian home. Similarly, their taste in decoration is rosebud chintz. At the same time, they introduce lots of new ideas: for example, they show only one play each evening, which now starts at eight o'clock to allow the audience to eat dinner beforehand. They encourage ensemble acting. They pay well. They keep out the riff-raff and, by playing to an exclusive middle-class audience, they make a fortune.

In the 1850s, at the Princess's Theatre in Oxford Street, actor manager Charles Kean aims to change the way that Shakespeare is staged. His watchword is authenticity. He's obsessed with the past. As a Fellow of the Society of Antiquaries he's crazy about the historical accuracy of sets and costumes (in lengthy playbills he bores on about the scholarship behind his choices). His productions are like elaborate history lessons, with carefully crafted stage pictures that appeal to the desire of his audiences for self-improvement. You leave his productions, acknowledges Jack, feeling that you've learnt what the past was really like. Soon, this way of staging Shakespeare becomes fashionable. Queen Victoria and Prince Albert visit his playhouse, and so do writers such as Charles Dickens and Lewis Carroll, and top politicians such as Lord Palmerston and William Ewart Gladstone. But this kind of pictorial drama has a downside: scene changes become longer and longer because the whole set has to be changed.

Charles Kean

The great actor managers, explains Jack, do everything: they run the company and choose the plays. They casts actors and employ backstage staff: plus supervising rehearsals, keeping an eye on the box office and stage door, watching the business manager, making sure that the stage machinery works, cutting plays and interviewing actors, inspecting the auditorium, checking on safety, organizing publicity, making sure the accounts show a profit, networking with investors, planning tours, creating his Christmas pantomime. Sometimes the manager is the lead actor too, so lines have to be learnt, rehearsals fitted in. Because stage machinery, especially the lighting, is more complicated than ever, more backstage technicians are needed. The same goes for scene painters, costume designers and dressers. A conductor and musicians are required for music, especially for the pantomime, which also needs a dancing master. Huge numbers of supernumeraries, or extras, are employed on the big shows. For the actor manager there is no rest — it's a busy life. And, just like engineers and entrepreneurs, actor managers embody the Victorian idea of the heroic individual. 'Their role,' says Jack, quoting from Alfred Lord Tennyson's poem 'Ulysses', 'is "To strive, to seek, to find, and not to yield."'

On the right track

Jack now takes us to a newly opened art gallery at number 7 Haymarket. He explains that this is run by a dealer, Louis Victor Flatou, and we can see that it is full of smartly dressed men and women — who are crowding around one painting in particular: *The Railway Station* by the popular artist William Powell Frith. The monumental picture shows Paddington station filled with dozens of people: we can see a family hurry to the train behind a porter; a woman pleading with a railway official to be allowed to bring her lapdog; two Scotland Yard detectives arresting a fugitive; two boys going off to boarding school; army recruits embracing loved ones; a wedding party. Like a play, the spectacular canvas tells several stories. 'It is 1862,' says Jack, who mingles easily with the gentlemen and ladies here, 'and Frith has annoyed the art establishment by exhibiting his work at a private gallery rather than at the Royal Academy, located around the corner at the National Gallery in Trafalgar Square.' *The Railway Station* is an immense commercial success, attracting widespread press coverage and some 80,000 spectators. Jack says that Frith has been paid more than £8000 for it, a new record. It has cost us one shilling each to enter the gallery, and other visitors have ordered prints of the picture. But Frith is not the only one to benefit from the age of steam.

Since the railway boom of the 1840s, London networks have expanded, with Euston, Paddington and Waterloo stations followed by King's Cross and St Pancras in the 1860s. The railways allow the growth of middle-class suburbs, whose inhabitants can also pop into town to see more shows. On stage, trains and railways become increasingly topical. Dion Boucicault's sensational *After Dark*, staged at Drury Lane in 1868, features a hero who is tied to the rails while a train approaches. You can almost hear the flutter of nervous hearts in the audience. In 1882, the same venue stages a double train crash in Augustus Harris and Henry Pettitt's *Pluck: A Story of 50,000*, while the Princess's Theatre features a scene of *The Silver King*, by Henry Arthur Jones and Henry Herman, set in Euston station with passengers of all classes crossing the stage. By the 1900s, the innovative scenic artist Bruce 'Sensation' Smith is putting a full-size train engine on stage in *The Whip* at Drury Lane. This spectacularly crashes into a horsebox (the real-life horse is saved in the nick of time). More audience palpitations! Using ropes, flats, bridges, treadmills and revolves, and from 1894 hydraulic machinery, Smith can produce realistic depictions of anything from a chariot race in *Ben Hur* to an underwater scene with real fish.

To experience the full drama of Victorian railways, Jack suggests a train trip to Manchester, one of the booming northern towns that make up the industrial base of Victorian Britain, a place that's big on cotton and big on civic pride. Armed with *Bradshaw's Railway Guide*, a must for any intrepid traveller, we catch the steam train from Euston on the London and North Western Railway ('One of the largest joint stock companies in the world,' says Jack with a hint of pride). In the first-class restaurant car, lunch is a five-course affair, and we choose from the menu of grilled turbot, roast sirloin, salmon with hollandaise sauce, bread-and-butter pudding, apple tart and crème caramel. 'The waiters,' says Jack, 'learn to balance by walking along a white line wearing a blindfold while the train speeds along.' Then, deep in the padded blue velvet-covered seats of our compartment, we watch our arrival at Manchester Piccadilly station, a cathedral of steam and noise.

From the station, Jack takes us by horse-drawn omnibus to see the Prince's Theatre in Oxford Street, a 1800-seat venue built at

Calvert's Henry V

a cost of £20,000 in 1864. It's a large white-stone building that looks both imposing and somehow imperial. At the entrance, people queuing for tickets are protected by decorated awnings. We walk into the lobby, where Jack finds us a quiet corner to tell us about Charles Calvert, its manager. Like other provincial managers, such as Edward Saker at the Alexandra Theatre in Liverpool, Calvert has been inspired by Charles Kean's authentic Shakespearean productions. In Kean's footsteps, Calvert travels to Venice to prepare designs for his production of *The Merchant of Venice*. He even brings back a real gondola. When he stages *Henry V* he follows Kean's lead by adding a new scene: the triumphal entry of the king into London after his victory over the French at Agincourt. This allows him to create a massive spectacle on stage, with dozens of extras — citizens, youths, maidens and nobles — and stirring victory music, followed by ecstatic hurrahs and hymns of praise. On a set loaded with gnarled medieval buildings, bells ring out, and thousands of red roses, symbol of the house of Lancaster to which Henry V belongs, are strewn on the pavements. It's unforgettable. In the past, Jack tells us, provincial theatres were nurseries of acting talent, whose best graduates moved to London. Now they are places with a reputation for fine productions. 'It is also worth noting,' says Jack, 'that the most popular Shakespeare plays are the big tragedies and the history plays, or plays such *A Midsummer Night's Dream*, which work well as visual spectacle.'

Real comedies for real people

On the train back from Manchester to London a couple of days after our visit to the Prince's Theatre, Jack is in a relaxed and chatty mood. While puffing on a cigarette, an increasingly popular habit, he talks about two of the mid-century's most important playwrights — Dion Boucicault and Tom Robertson. Boucicault dominates the West End in the 1860s and 1870s. Originally christened Dionysius Lardner Boursiquot, this Dublin-born actor was sent to London to complete his education at the age of ten. Now elegantly dressed, proud of his fine moustache and goatie, he is extravagant, generous and larger than life. An all-rounder, he works as a comic actor, manager, producer and even advocate of theatre safety. As a playwright, he is the ace copyist — stealing ideas from here, there and everywhere.

Dion Boucicault

Boucicault's prodigious output of some 150 plays includes the best comedies since Richard Brinsley Sheridan, another Irish playwright, and before Oscar Wilde, ditto. His debut, written in 1841 at the age of twenty-one, is *London Assurance*, which owes a lot to the play doctoring of Eliza Vestris and her husband, Charles James Mathews, the golden couple of London theatre management. The plot of this story of love and marriage, which involves Dazzle (played by Mathews) and his friend Charles Courtly, dissolute son of Sir Harcourt Courtly, is an imitation of Georgian comedy, with characters having names such as Lady Gay Spanker, a horse-riding virago, and a lawyer called Meddle. Sir Harcourt Courtly is an ageing dandy in the tradition of George Etherege's Sir Fopling Flutter, and there's a lot of fun to be had in seeing this townie out of his depth in the countryside, where he plans to marry eighteen-year-old Grace Harkaway who — inevitably — his son also falls for. The play is a massive hit.

Boucicault regularly visits Paris, seeing the latest comedies and writing English versions of them (his cape-and-sword melodrama *The Corsican Brothers* is copied from an original by Alexander Dumas père). Other hits include *Jessie Brown; or, The Relief of Lucknow* (1858), a patriotic melodrama about the siege of the British residency at Lucknow during the Indian Mutiny of 1857, and *The Octoroon* (1859), about slavery in the American south. But his gift for fresh dialogue really comes into its own when he invents the classic Irish play, with its smart-talking heroes, a new kind of stage Irishman: 'Instead of a blundering blockhead,' says Boucicault, 'he is the true son of the sod, bold and courageous even to recklessness, with all his virtues and virtuous errors.' As an actor, he excels in playing lovable Irish rogues in his own plays, which travel between New York and London thanks to the new steams ships.

The Colleen Bawn; or, The Brides of Garryowen is a good example of this new kind of Irish play. While in New York, Boucicault pops into Brentano's Bookshop to shelter from a downpour and buys Gerald Griffin's novel, *The Collegians*. He is so excited by the story that he starts writing a play version and begins rehearsals for it within a week, with only the first act finished. It is completed during the rest of rehearsals. Set near Lake Killarney, it's about an impoverished gentry family led by Mrs Cregan, who encourages her son Hardress to wed his cousin, the wealthy heiress Anne Chute. She says: 'By this marriage with Anne Chute we redeem every acre of our barony.' But Hardress is already secretly married to Eily O'Connor, a peasant known as the Colleen Bawn (fair-haired girl). So Danny Mann, Hardress's crippled servant, decides to save his master by murdering Eily. But as he tries to drown her in Lake Killarney, he is shot by Myles-na-Coppaleen, one of her former sweethearts. Myles rescues Eily and, at the end of the play, she is welcomed into the family by Mrs Cregan as Hardress's wife, while Anne saves the Cregan estate by paying off its debts.

Dion Boucicault's *The Colleen Bawn* (1860)

Myles rescues Eily from a watery grave:

(Music changes.)

DANNY Then you've lived too long. Take your marriage lines wid ye to the bottom of the lake. *(He throws her from rock backwards into the water with a cry; she reappears, clinging to rock.)*

EILY No! Save me. Don't kill me. Don't Danny, I'll do anything, only let me live.

DANNY He wants ye dead. *(Pushes her off.)*

EILY Oh! Heaven help me. Danny – Danny – Dan – *(Sinks.)*

DANNY *(Looking down.)* I've done it. She's gone. *(Shot is fired; he falls — rolls from the rock into the water.)*

(Myles appears with gun on rock.)

MYLES I hit one of them bastes that time. I could see well, though it was so dark. But there was somethin' moving on that stone. *(Swings across.)* Divil a sign of him. Stop! *(Looks down.)* What's this? It's a woman — there's something white there. *(Figure rises near rock. He kneels down; tries to take the hand of figure.)* Ah! that dress; it's Eily. My own darlin' Eily. *(Pulls off waistcoat — jumps off rock. Eily rises — then Myles and Eily rise up – he turns, and seizes rock, Eily across left arm.)*

The first production is at the Laura Keene Theatre in New York on 27 March 1860, with Boucicault playing Myles as both a rascal, an illicit poteen distiller, and the most charming person on the stage. Dressed in an oversized coat and battered hat, he exudes a warmhearted appeal. In the story's most spectacular moment he makes a dive into Lake Killarney, saving the Colleen Bawn. As well as writing such trademark sensation scenes, Boucicault also wants to make his fortune. Having once been sacked from the cast of *The Octaroon*, his own play, for demanding more money, he is determined not to make the same mistake. So he has a contract drawn up that allows him to control all aspects of the production. And when he brings *The Colleen Bawn* to London later in 1860 he stipulates that he must be paid a royalty as author for each performance, an innovation in an industry in which managers usually just buy plays from playwrights for a small fee. *The Colleen Bawn* runs for ten months at the Adelphi Theatre, with Queen Victoria seeing it three times, and makes the playwright £23,000, a fortune! As our train rattles along, Jack shows us a copy of the satirical magazine *Punch*, which declares: 'I can't believe the

Strand would ever have been blocked up with Colleen cabs as it has been, or that by wish of the police the doors need have been opened sooner than their wont, merely on account of this one aquatic feat.'

Jack now shows us a copy of *The Illustrated London News*, which has a report of *The Shaughraun*, another of Boucicault's hit Irish melodramas. The story concerns Robert Ffolliott, fiancé of Arte O'Neil, who returns to Ireland after escaping Australia, where he has been a transported convict. He is innocent, but is hunted and escapes various suspenseful situations with the help of Conn the Shaughraun (meaning a wanderer), the 'fiddlin' poaching vagabond' played by Boucicault. At one point, Conn seems to give his life for his master, and falls dead, hit by the bullets meant for the escaping Robert. For added pathos, he expires as the rays of moonlight fall on a statute of St Bridget, whose extended arms stretch over his prostrate body. But Conn survives and, in the next scene, attends his own wake. As he says, 'Would you have me spile a wake? After invitin' all the neighbours!' All works out happily in the end. The original production is at Wallack's Theatre in New York in 1874, and the play makes Boucicault a millionaire. In Edith Wharton's 1920 novel, *The Age of Innocence*, Newland Archer reports on the original production: 'In the galleries the enthusiasm was unreserved; in the stalls and boxes, people smiled a little at the hackneyed sentiments and claptrap situations, and enjoyed the play as much as the galleries did.' When the play comes to Drury Lane in 1875, all fashionable London turns out. Boucicault reprises the role of Conn, but before he makes his first appearance on stage, his voice is heard from the wings, saying 'There's somebody talking about me.' The audience immediately cheers, welcoming him back to London. He is theatre's first truly transatlantic superstar.

'Meanwhile,' says Jack, puffing on another cigarette in our first-class compartment, as he shuffles some more newspapers, 'it's time to talk about the Bancrofts, the other power couple of London theatre.' At the Prince of Wales's, these impresarios introduce a new playwright: Thomas William Robertson, a dour-looking man, with heavy black beard and thick wavy hair. Jack shows us a photograph of him in *The Illustrated London News*. His success, he notes, is a long time coming. After years of dogged attempts, during which this son of a provincial actor manager, and fifth generation of a theatrical family, tours up and down the country, trying unsuccessfully to adapt the novels of Charles Dickens for the stage, he finally shrugs off failure at the age of thirty-six in 1865, with his play *Society*. The Bancrofts see his potential and produce a string of his 1860s plays, usually with one-word titles: *Ours*, *Caste* and *School*. In doing so, they invent a new kind of play which becomes known as Cup and Saucer Drama.

Robertson writes dialogue that is conversational and quietly understated, thus breaking with the conventions of broad farce and barnstorming melodrama. His settings are domestic, his characters are recognizable individuals, and his plots are skillfully worked out. As a director, he aims to create a realistic and coherent performance. So he insists on adequate rehearsals, attention to detail in design, and ensemble acting, with no one actor upstaging the others. Robertson pioneers naturalism, and his characters behave like ordinary people; the atmosphere on stage is that of normal family life. His actors don't 'act' so much as 'behave'; they speak, they don't declaim. Robertson does the job of the modern director, who not only rehearses the cast, but also makes sure that all the meticulously specified props are ready to hand for each performance. Instead of painted flats, the sets have real doors with real door handles, and the actors wear well-made clothes, not just items from a dusty theatre wardrobe. For the audience, eavesdropping on the action by looking through the fourth wall, theatre has never been more real.

Robertson's masterpiece is *Caste*, a comedy about the Victorian class system first produced at the Prince of Wales's in 1867. The Honourable George D'Alroy, an aristocratic officer, falls in love with a lower-class woman, Esther Eccles, whose father is an unemployed drunk. At the same time, Esther's sister Polly pairs off with Sam Gerridge, an ordinary gas-fitter who knows his place. Disregarding the advice of his friend, Captain Hawtree, George insists on marrying Esther, quoting a couple of lines from Alfred Lord Tennyson: 'Kind hearts are more than coronets, and simple faith than Norman blood!' But when he is ordered to rejoin his regiment in India to help quell the Indian Mutiny, his mother, the

Marquise de St Maur, is horrified to discover who he's married. 'There is blood, and blood, my son,' she says. 'Let radicals say what they will.'

Tom Robertson's *Caste* (1867)

Hawtree remonstrates with his friend George D'Alroy:

HAWTREE Now, look here, D'Alroy! Of course you are not so soft as to think of marriage? You know what your mother is — and what she would think of it. You will behave properly — with a proper regard for the world and all that sort of thing — or do the other thing. The, ah, girl is nice enough, no doubt, for her station, but you can't dream of making her Mrs D'Alroy!

D'ALROY Why not? What's to prevent me?

HAWTREE The social laws — so good — of caste! The inexorable laws of caste!

D'ALROY My dear Art!

HAWTREE My dear D'Al! The other sort of thing — the marriages with common people — is all very well in novels, and plays on the stage, where the people don't exist. There's no harm done, and it's sometimes interesting. But real people, real mothers, real relations, real connections, in real life, it's quite another matter. It's utter social and personal annihilation!

D'Alroy's mother rejects Esther, who plainly belongs to the wrong class. As Hawtree exclaims: 'Caste! The inexorable law of caste! The social law, so becoming and so good, that commands like to mate with like, and forbids a giraffe to fall in love with a squirrel.' A year later, everyone thinks that George has been killed in India, and Esther is living in poverty with their son, her father having drunk away all their money. Now the Marquise wants to take possession of the baby. At the moment of greatest danger, George returns, and Esther and his mother are reconciled: 'Caste is a good thing,' concludes George, 'if it's not carried too far.' His return is a classic Robertson understatement. Instead of arriving home with a melodramatic flourish of cape and sabre, he quietly enters his wife's cheap Lambeth lodgings, puts his hat on the battered upright piano, and places a milk can on the table, saying, 'A fella hung this on the railings, so I bought it in.' This deliberately understated approach characterizes Robertson's writing, but he is not averse to spelling out his message: at one point, Sam Gerridge says, 'Life's a railway journey, and mankind's a passenger — first class, second class, third class. Any person found riding in a superior class to that for which he has taken his ticket will be removed at the first station stopped at, according to the bye-laws of the company.' Seeing that our Jack is accustomed to travelling first-class, we deduce that caste was no hindrance to his upward mobility.

As our train approaches the London suburbs, Jack hurriedly finishes off his account. The plays of Boucicault and Robertson typically run for more than 100 consecutive nights, he informs us, and their audience includes visitors to the capital from the provinces and tourists from overseas. Other hit plays are Edward Bulwer-Lytton's *Money*, which satirizes greed and applauds romance at Theatre Royal Haymarket in 1840, and Henry James Byron's *Our Boys*, whose theme is class and which runs for more than 1000 nights after opening at the Vaudeville in 1875. This shows the relationship of the young Talbot (rich but weak) and Charles (poor but strong-willed), and how both are disowned for refusing to marry women chosen by their parents. Likewise, Tom Taylor's *The Ticket-of-Leave Man*, first performed at the Olympic in 1863, is a huge success, partly because of its recognizable London settings: the Bellevue Tea Gardens, the Bridgewater Arms pub, the churchyard of St Nicholas, as well as modest rented rooms and an office in the City. Similarly, its central characters, Bob Brierly, a Lancashire felon on parole, and Hawkshaw, the police detective, are bursting with life in this portrayal of the criminal underworld. But there is another connection between crime and Taylor. It is at a performance of his play *Our American Cousin*, at Ford's Theatre in Washington DC in 1865, that the disgruntled actor and Confederate fanatic John Wilkes Booth assassinates President Abraham Lincoln.

Crime and punishment

Back in London, Jack suggests that we take a trip to the north of the smoky metropolis, to see the new cemetery in the village of Highgate. He can't afford to travel first-class in London — by Brougham, Phaeton or Landau carriage — so we take a hail-and-ride horse-drawn omnibus up Highgate Hill. In this crowded conveyance, Jack has to raise his voice above the babble of the passengers, saying that Highgate Cemetery is owned by a private enterprise, the London Cemetery Company. 'It is the most fashionable place to be buried and there is plenty of room,' says our guide. When we arrive, he shows us Egyptian Avenue, which has a massive Pharaonic arch and sixteen vaults, each holding a dozen coffins on stone shelves. The cemetery is very exclusive: a vault costs £136 (average income is £40 a year). 'So burying people is a serious business,' says Jack, throwing us a cheeky wink.

Jack shows us the graves of some personalities such as Tom Sayers, the last bare-knuckle boxer, F W Lillywhite, the cricketer, and then the final resting place of Lizzie Siddal, the wife of the Pre-Raphaelite painter and poet Gabriel Dante Rossetti. As we stand around this slightly overgrown plot, our Jack shows his relish for gossip by telling us that Rossetti was so distraught by Siddal's death that he buried a manuscript of his own poems in her coffin. Seven years later, however, he changed his mind and had her body exhumed so he could reclaim the poems. What a grisly thought! Then, as we stroll away in the good clean air, among the trees, a funeral procession passes in the distance, all the mourners elaborately decked out in black, with black top hats and black ribbons: we wonder whose last journey this is and contemplate the Victorian way of death. Then Jack — perhaps to distract us from gloomy thoughts — offers to take us to jollier locations, such as Wyld's Monster Globe in Leicester Square, or the new Zoological Society collection at Regent's Park, or even the Blind School in St George's Fields, where Victorians apparently go to watch its inmates working as a tourist attraction.

Talking of death, the craze for blood-curling stories of murder on stage reaches its mid-Victorian heights. As we cross Highgate Cemetery, Jack — swinging his cane with an insouciant air — tells us more, and a chill runs down our spines. Among the most popular is *Maria Marten; or, The Murder in the Red Barn*, which dramatizes the 1827 killing of a young woman by her lover, William Corder. Performed in dozens of stage versions this is one of the most frequently revisited plays of the century. Although in real life the couple were of a similar age and Maria had had two illegitimate children with other men, on the stage the fictional

Maria is represented as the stock character of the young innocent and Corder as the older predatory monster. High points of the drama include the dream of Maria's stepmother that leads the authorities to discover her body in the barn, and the public execution of her killer. Equally compelling is the 1849 case of Marie Manning, a Swiss domestic servant who is publicly hanged along with her husband Frederick George Manning for the murder of her lover, Patrick O'Connor, in a case called the Bermondsey Horror. Known as Black Marie on account of the colour of the silk dress she wore at her trial, her story is staged at numerous East End theatres. Charles Dickens, Jack tells us, witnesses their execution and writes a letter to *The Times* to express his disgust at the callousness of the crowd. But that doesn't stop

Charles Dickens

him basing one of his characters — Mademoiselle Hortense, Lady Dedlock's maid, in *Bleak House* — on Black Marie.

Talking of Dickens, Jack has a treat in store for us. In the evening, he takes us to St James's Hall in Piccadilly, which is the capital's main venue for orchestral music concerts. As we enter, he points out that the hall has some decorations which imitate the great Moorish Palace of the Alhambra. We take our seats on the uncomfortable narrow, green-upholstered benches, which have seat numbers fastened to their backs with bright pink tape, like office files. On the stage is a single lectern with screens forming a black background for the reader, none other than Dickens himself, who arrives to tumultuous applause. In evening dress, with a bright buttonhole, purple waistcoat and gold watch chain, he radiates charisma. 'Ladies and gentlemen,' he begins, pausing briefly, 'I am to have the pleasure of reading tonight: *A Christmas Carol*.' Pause. Then he says: 'Marley was dead — to begin with...' And he's off. The greatest storyteller of the age grabs the audience and the applause that greets the finale is like thunder. After all the excitement is over, Jack escorts us out and says that Dickens is a real theatre man, and his novels are packed with references to the stage. In *Great Expectations*, for example, Wopsle — the church clerk with absurd pretentions to be an actor — insists that young Pip must listen and learn from his reading of the entirety of George Lillo's play, *The London Merchant; or, The History of George Barnwell*. Many of Dickens's novels are soon turned into stage melodramas, one of the most popular being *Oliver Twist*. In such versions, when Bill Sykes kills Nancy he usually drags her screaming across the stage by her hair, and then provocatively looks defiantly at the audience. 'Very effective,' says Jack. 'But Dickens also has a more intimate connection to the theatre,' he whispers. It is rumoured that he is the lover of actress Ellen Ternan, who first appeared on stage at the age of three as an infant phenomenon and is some twenty-seven years his junior. When we tell him that we know about this affair already, he's visibly surprised.

To wind up the evening, Jack says some more about crime and punishment. At the Britannia, George Dibdin Pitt's *The String of Pearls; or, The Fiend of Fleet Street* opens in 1847, and tells the story of Sweeney Todd, the demon barber who first appeared the year before in *The People's Periodical*, a 'penny dreadful' pulp fiction magazine. Dibdin Pitt is an actor and prolific playwright, and he turns a minor character from the original story into the razor-wielding Sweeney Todd, a legendary monster. In 1883, the play is finally published as *Sweeney Todd: The Demon Barber of Fleet Street*. Another Victorian legend is Sherlock Holmes, the superlative sleuth. In 1901, the American actor William Gillette's *Sherlock Holmes*, which first premiered at the Star Theatre in Buffalo, comes to the Lyceum in London. With his austere and cold stage persona, and his use of long pauses to screw up the tension, Gillette creates the popular image of the great detective. His props include the curved brair pipe, which allows audiences to see his face more easily than a straight-stemmed pipe would, as well as the magnifying glass and syringe. He also invents the phrase 'Oh, this is elementary, my dear fellow', which soon mutates into 'Elementary my dear Watson', one of the most famous expressions in the language. Our young Jack is impressed by the intense friendship between Sherlock and Watson — doubtless it reminds him of his own relationship with his mentor.

Before we retire, Jack is happy to talk some more about the vitality of London theatre, whose must-see shows are often retellings of popular novels. *East Lynne*, a stage version by T A Palmer of Ellen Wood's tear-jerking sensation novel of 1861, is a national favourite. It tells the story of the refined Lady Isabel, who leaves her lawyer husband and infant children to elope with an aristocratic suitor. After he deserts her, she is caught up in a railway accident and left for dead. Then, in disguise, she returns to East Lynne, becoming a governess in the household of her former husband and his new wife. Okay, it strains credibility, but most melodramas do. Her son dies without knowing who she really is, a cue for her classic lines: 'Oh, Willie, my child dead — dead — dead! And he never knew me, never called me mother!' (Words much parodied long after.) For the next forty years, some fifteen different stage versions of the novel enthral audiences in both Britain and North America. Similarly popular is *Lady Audley's Secret*, a novel by Mary Elizabeth Braddon adapted for the stage by Colin Henry Hazelwood at the Victoria Theatre 1863, in which the title character appears to be a perfect domestic doll, but is actually a violent criminal who attempts to murder her husband, commits bigamy and abandons her child; sensational. Other popular melodramas include Harriet Beecher Stowe's *Uncle Tom's Cabin*, the most famous abolitionist work of fiction, which becomes a stage play in 1852. After its American success, the play opens at London's Adelphi. The scene in which the slave Eliza escapes with her baby from her pursuers by crossing the frozen Ohio river is truly memorable.

The music hall

The music hall is the quintessential Victorian entertainment. From their origins in all-male drinking clubs, music bars and supper rooms where performers sang songs while the audience ate, drank and joined in, music halls proliferate in the 1850s, including Wilton's in Whitechapel (still there today). The first purpose-built music hall is the Canterbury Hall in Lambeth, the creation of Charles Morton, publican of the Canterbury Tavern. Nicknamed the Father of the Halls, he builds the venue, a drinking house for 1500 people with entertainment thrown in, next to his pub. Morton is a real cultural entrepreneur: he not only provides popular music, but also opens a picture gallery and reading room next to the hall in order to attract a respectable clientele. His main auditorium is a huge hall brightly lit by chandeliers of gas lights, with elegant decorations, classical in style, and a balcony — it's more like a refectory than a theatre. In the main hall are long tables and chairs. The stage, at one end, is like a concert platform raised above the heads of the seated diners and the backdrop is a wall decoration of a mythological scene. Admission is six pence to the floor and nine pence to the balcony. Food, charged separately, is served by waiters. The atmosphere is lower-middle class and predominantly male, attracted by the chance to smoke or drink, with the lure of uncensored entertainment. At the Canterbury, however, Morton encourages women to come because he believes they have a civilizing influence on men. This is why he introduces Ladies Thursdays, when women can bring a gentleman with them. However, gents do not always bring their wives, which sometimes gives rise to gossip.

Songs are the heart of the music hall. Many are sentimental, about true love, a mother's love, the moon in June; many are about working-class life, rent arrears, the bailiffs coming; others are about wives and husbands, mothers-in-law and lodgers. If a song is a hit, people come back time and again to hear it. Some singers only need a handful of songs to fill their slot — they are asked to sing the same songs every evening. As the music hall grows in popularity, the main attraction is the entertainers rather than the food and drink. The big stars perform in numerous halls each night, crossing London at speed in their carriages. This way, they earn big money. By the end of the century, there are as many as twenty acts per show and performances can last four hours. In between the singers and comedians are the speciality acts, which include ventriloquists, jugglers, magicians, sword swallowers, aerial acts, animal acts, one-legged dancers, slapstick sketches and illusionists.

Stars of the London music hall include Hoxton-born-and-bred Marie Lloyd, who begins her career at the local Eagle Tavern, with cockney hits such as 'My Old Man (Said Follow the Van)', 'The Boy I Love Is up in the Gallery' and 'Oh Mr Porter What Shall I Do'. She uses saucy innuendo and double meanings — with knowing looks, smiles and winks to the audience. And she has an endearingly goofy smile. Her song 'She Sits Among the Cabbages and Peas' has to be re-titled after protests from the Social Purity Alliance to 'I Sits Amongst the Cabbages and Leeks'. One of the other big names is George Robey, known as the Prime Minister of Mirth. He wears a black coat, a vicar's collar, a bald-headed wig, plus red nose and arched black eyebrows. Robey is famous for the song 'The Simple Pimple', with its refrain 'They knew her by the pimple, the pimple on her nose'. He sings this for his first ever tryout at a matinee performance at the Oxford Music Hall when he is twenty-two, and it brings the house down. In the 1890s, Dan Leno

Marie Lloyd

becomes one of the highest-paid comedians in the world, with his comic songs and surreal observations. When he performs his Huntsman's sketch in front of the new monarch, King Edward VII in 1910 he gets the title of the King's Jester. But — like many other music hall artists — he suffers from alcoholism. The star of the Canterbury is Sam Cowell, a former child actor who has been poached from Evans's Supper Rooms and whose best songs include 'The Ratcatcher's Daughter' and 'Villikins and his Dinah'. He is such a draw that profits from his singing enable Morton to expand his hall.

The music-hall heartthrobs are the Lions Comiques. Known as 'swells' these character singers dress as fashionable, swaggering men and sing laddish cockney songs about the high life. George Leybourne is the most famous, with his song 'Champagne Charlie' and 'The Flying Trapeze', based on the amazing success of the circus performer Jules Léotard, who lends his name to a common item of gym wear.

> George Leybourne's 'The Flying Trapeze' (1867)
> Once I was happy, but now I'm forlorn
> Like an old coat that is tattered and torn;
> Left on this world to fret and to mourn,
> Betrayed by a maid in her teens.
> The girl that I loved she was handsome;
> I tried all I knew her to please
> But I could not please her one quarter so well
> As the man upon the trapeze.
> He'd fly through the air with the greatest of ease,
> That daring young man on the flying trapeze.
> His movements were graceful, all girls he could please
> And my love he purloined away.

Leybourne's rival is Arthur Lloyd, whose song 'Walking in the Zoo' popularises the word zoo. Alfred Vance is known for his 'coster' songs, written in a Cockney dialect and celebrating East End fruit and veg vendors. As more women begin to feature in music hall programmes, male impersonation grows in vogue. One of the best paid is Vesta Tilley, who is so successful at doing this that rumours spread that she really *is* a man. Men in the audience like the cut of her clothes so much that they rush to their tailors to get the same design.

By 1875 there are 375 music halls in Greater London. These include the Oxford on the corner of Oxford Street and Tottenham Court Road, which pioneers a promenade space in the main hall, moving the tables to the balcony so that crowds can walk and talk while the entertainments are on. Also there's the Bedford in Camden Town and the Metropolitan in Edgware Road. The major West End music halls, like the Palace and the Coliseum, begin to attract a higher social class, often wearing evening dress. Managers like Oswald Stoll and Edward Moss combine their efforts to make music hall respectable. In the second part of the century come the classy West End venues, The Alhambra (formerly the Panopticon of Science and Art) and its rival the Empire, both in Leicester Square. Such venues spread all over the country: Birmingham, Manchester, Leeds, Sheffield, Plymouth and Aberdeen.

Despite the respectability of a handful of West End halls, the music hall — especially in London's East End — is still associated with unpredictable audiences, made up of both aristocratic swells and working-class blokes; the God-fearing middle classes regard most of the halls as vulgar places, too risqué for comfort. In some of them, audiences can be a bit unruly, throwing bottles, old boots, even dead cats, at unpopular performers. In some halls, bottles carried by waiters have to be chained to the trays to prevent audience members from snatching them, and the orchestra is protected from the missiles by steel grilles stretched over the pit.

Other places for popular entertainment are the penny gaffs, the cheapest form of theatre, which appeal to the poorest audiences. Charging a penny, and usually in a back room of a pub, with a capacity of some two hundred people, these crude rooms stage what Henry Mayhew, who is a playwright as well as a reforming social researcher, denounces as 'filthy songs, clumsy dancing and filthy dances by men and women'. These are patronized mainly by poor juveniles, not unlike our guide in his early youth, who are usually drunk on gin. The most popular plays are gory murder stories, or popular standards such as the adventures of Jack

Sheppard the eighteenth-century highwayman. A piano provides the music.

A proper night out

In need of a change of scene, and a more genteel atmosphere, Jack takes us to the newly opened tea room at the Fortnum and Mason department store in Piccadilly. This is Jack's favourite haunt for celebrity spotting. But today we are here because he has to pick up a hamper, which are now all the rage. When Dickens reports on his visit to the Epsom race course in *Household Words*, he writes: 'Look where I will I see Fortnum & Mason. And now, heavens! All the hampers fly wide open and the green Downs burst into a blossom of lobster salad!' At events in the social calendar, such as Ascot, Henley, Wimbledon, Lord's and Twickenham, Fortnum's hampers make the store a household name. Once we're in the tea room, enjoying a lovely slice of sponge cake, washed down with a warm pot of darjeeling tea, Jack brings us up to speed with the latest theatre news.

Henry Irving

A new generation of movers and shakers dominates the century's end. These big men with big ideas are led by actor-manager Henry Irving, who like Charles Kean before him is the star of his own shows. He rules the London theatre scene for a quarter of a century, with his career coming to a climax in 1895 when he is knighted, the first time an actor gets this honour. Born John Henry Brodribb, he takes his stage name while slaving as an apprentice touring the regions. In 1871, at the age of thirty-three, he becomes an overnight star at

London's Lyceum Theatre due to his magnetic performance as Mathias in *The Bells*, a play by the alcoholic and erratic playwright Leopold Lewis based on *Le Juif Polonais* by French playwrights Émile Erckmann and Alexandre Chatrian. The play is a study of guilt: Alsace burgomaster Mathias is a family man who, fifteen years previously, has murdered a wealthy Polish Jew and now becomes obsessed with guilt, hallucinating the ghost of his victim and hearing the bells of his sledge. Hence the lines, soon to be parodied by comedians in other theatres: 'The bells! The bells! Sleigh bells on the road!' 'When he hears them, Irving's Mathias shivers' — says Jack, raising his eyebrows — 'his jaw chatters and his hair writhes like a nest of snakes.' During that first exquisite performance, Irving is intensity itself. Mesmerism is involved: some fainthearted members of the audience pass out. Irving's

THE CRITIC'S VIEW: IRVING'S DEBUT

Critic George R Sims describes Henry Irving's performance as Mathias in *The Bells* for *The Evening News* (1871):

The play left the first-nighters a little dazed. Old-fashioned playgoers did not know what to make of it as a form of entertainment. But when the final curtain fell the audience, after a gasp or two, realized that they had witnessed the most masterly form of tragic acting that the British stage had seen for many a long day, and there was a storm of cheers. Then, still pale, still haggard, still haunted, as it were, by the terror he had so perfectly counterfeited, the actor came forward with the sort of smile that did not destroy the character of the Burgomaster or dispel the illusion of the stage.

stunning interpretation runs for 151 performances. Later on, he revives the play throughout his career, performing it 800 times. *The Bells* is also one of the first melodramas to be made into a full-length silent film in 1913, and then remade starring Boris Karloff in 1926. 'But Irving's professional life takes precedence over his personal life,' Jack says. Apparently, on the way home after the opening night of *The Bells*, his wife Florence, pregnant with their second child, asks him if he intends to carry on acting: 'Are you going on making a fool of yourself like this all your life?' He stops the carriage, jumps out and never sees her again.

In 1878 Irving and his leading lady Ellen Terry take over the Lyceum, with its gleaming white façade and portico (which still stands today). She had been a child actor, and then wife at the age of sixteen to George Frederic Watts, a painter and neurotic almost three times her age. But this lasted only a year and by the time she joins Irving at the Lyceum she is thirty-one and an experienced Shakespearean. Together Irving and Terry create a repertory of romantic melodrama. The couple, Jack tells us, are as close in private life as they are in public, but on stage they are complete opposites. She is all speed and instinct, while Irving is slow and pedantic. His forte is playing aloof characters, who are secretly tormented by guilt. 'But although he can be hypnotic, he is never fast enough for Terry who,' says Jack, 'has been known to whisper on stage: "Oh come on, get a move on."' Terry, of course, is statuesque and plays many of Shakespeare's leading roles. The society painter John Singer Sargent memorably depicts her in the role of Lady Macbeth as a haunting figure, dressed in the richest emerald green with long plaits of red hair cascading down to her waist.

Irving has a fanatical dedication to the theatre, calling the Lyceum his Temple of Art. His business manager is none other than Bram Stoker — the bearded Irish author who in his spare time pens the gothic classic *Dracula*. But whoever he employs, Irving is a control freak: he is meticulous about every aspect of the production, design, music and acting. He commissions the top artists of the time, such as the Pre-Raphaelite painters Ford Madox Brown and Edward Burne-Jones to design productions of *King Lear* (1892) and *King Arthur* (1895), while artist Lawrence Alma-Tadema designs *Cymbeline* (1896). He is also quick to grasp the possibilities of new technology: in his 1885 production of Johan Wolfgang von Goethe's *Faust*, in which he plays Mephistopheles, electricity is used to create real sparks during a sword fight. Hero-worshipped by respectable audiences, Irving makes Lyceum first nights a must in the social, literary and artistic calendar. By the time he dies in 1905, he is given a quasi-state funeral and buried in Westminster Abbey. King Edward VII and the President of the United States send their condolences. Jack says, 'That's celebrity for you!'

Another theatrical knight is Herbert Beerbohm Tree, an outstanding character actor and manager of Her Majesty's Theatre, which is built for him in French Second Empire style by Charles J Phipps in the Haymarket (still there today). It is on the site of the old Georgian Queen's Theatre, and named in honour of Queen Victoria, opening in 1897, the year of her Diamond Jubilee. Under Tree's management, the ushers are dressed in wigs and frock coats, and an atmosphere of respectable elegance is cultivated. It is here that in 1904 he establishes the Royal Academy of the Dramatic Arts (RADA), which is still the most prestigious drama school in Britain today. As an actor, Tree loves make-up, plastering his face with Leichner greasepaint, and adding crepe hair and wigs. One commentator writes: 'Even when he was hopelessly miscast, Tree's acting is so clever, so inventive, so varied, so intensely interesting, that for unalloyed entertainment one would rather see him in a bad play than anyone else in a good one.' His roles include the flamboyantly over-the-top mesmerist Svengali in Paul Potter's stage adaptation of George du Maurier's novel *Trilby* (1895). As an impresario, he presents Shakespeare in spectacular stagings. 'In *A Midsummer Night's Dream*,' says Jack, 'real rabbits run around the enchanted wood.' (We suspect that this might just be the fruit of Jack's imagination.) George Bernard Shaw, who is a theatre critic at the time, says acidly: 'You can't see the Shakespeare woods for the Beerbohm Trees!'; in *Twelfth Night* there is real grass growing onstage; in *The Tempest*, the shipwreck has real water washing over the deck. Tree's *Antony and Cleopatra* includes processions of priests, soldiers, dancing women, strewn flowers and clashing cymbals. He also uses amazing stage effects. In *Nero*, Rome burns so realistically that some audience members almost flee; in *Joseph and His Brethren*, the onstage Palestine is inhabited by camels, oxen, asses, sheep and goats. 'What a smelly menagerie,' says Jack, wrinkling his nose. But there is a downside to spectacle: audiences have to sit through grindingly long intervals while the massive sets are changed.

The building boom of the last part of the century creates the West End theatres that we still love today. After the 1870s, when new theatres such as the Vaudeville and the Imperial arrive, some fourteen new theatres are built, including the Comedy, the Savoy, the Novelty, the Shaftesbury, the Garrick, the Duke of York's and, in west London, the Court in Sloane Square and the Lyric Hammersmith. Most seat between 700 and 1000. They are smaller but with better acoustics and more comfort than the massive older barns of yesteryear. In 1879, Charles Wyndham gets control of the Criterion Theatre, a tiled basement playhouse next to Piccadilly Circus (still there today). With Mary Moore, his leading lady and second wife, he creates a nice and respectable venue, serving coffee at the interval and selling programmes in the foyer. His staging of French farces is so profitable that in 1898 he achieves his dream of having a venue named after him by opening the new Wyndham's Theatre (still there today). Now the stress is on safety as well as comfort: in the final thirty years of the Victorian period there are some ninety major theatre fires (at Exeter Theatre Royal 180 die in one conflagration in 1887). So the new theatres come with safety curtains and fire exits.

Night has fallen. As we sip our tea in the soft-carpeted hush and golden light of Fortnum's, with the discrete clinking of china all around us, Jack draws his chair closer to us and lowers his voice. He wants to tell us theatrical ghost stories that may chill our blood. We overcome our nerves and lean forward. He begins. During the 1880s, one couple at the Lyceum glance over the balcony and see a severed head grinning up at them from the lap of a woman in the stalls below. After the show, they look for her but fail to find her. Years later, the same couple visit a house in Yorkshire and find a portrait of a man whose face is identical to that of the severed head they had seen at the Lyceum. The owner explains that the mysterious man in the picture is a distant ancestor who once owned the land the Lyceum stands on. He'd been beheaded for treason. Our hearts skip a beat. 'Old wooden staircases seem to be popular with spirits,' says Jack. The Old Crimson Staircase to the Palladium's Royal Circle is rumoured to be a remnant of Argyll House, and the lady sometimes spotted ascending the stairs in a crinoline dress is thought to be Mrs

Shireburn, mistress of the eighteenth-century Duke of Argyll. What will she discover when she gets upstairs? Then there's the case of William Terriss, a matinee idol who starred in melodramas at the Adelphi Theatre and was murdered at the stage door by Richard Arthur Price, a deranged unemployed actor who blamed him for his lack of success. His ghost still haunts the nearby Covent Garden Underground station. 'Some theatres,' says Jack with a nervous laugh, 'are very popular with ghosts': Drury Lane is said to have quite a community of them, including the Grey Man who crosses the upper circle dressed in Queen-Anne-era clothes and disappears through a wall. During renovations in the 1870s, builders find a bricked-up room behind the same wall: in it is a skeleton with a dagger through its ribcage. He is believed to be an actress's lover, murdered by a jealous actor. More jam sponge, Jack? Two Victorian prostitutes, meanwhile, are said to roam the upper gallery of the Royal Albert Hall on All Souls Night, a memory of the brothel that previously occupied the site. Then, at the Old Vic, a spectral woman is sometimes seen clutching bloodstained hands to her breast — although some sceptics say that the blood is just make-up, and that she is an unconvincing Lady Macbeth.

Respect and respectability

It is a windy, rainy day and Jack is struggling with his umbrella as we cross Westminster bridge. Two young ruffians approach and as he tries to shoo them away, a policeman appears — and they promptly vanish. Jack thanks the 'bobby' and comments that this new police force is a symbol of how orderly London life has become. Well, he corrects himself, just as long as you stay out of the East End. 'In the West End,' he says, gesturing over the bridge, 'theatres increasingly cater for the middle-class audiences.' Even their architecture reflects class society: entrance to the expensive seats in the stalls, dress circle or boxes are via the grand staircase at the front; entrance to the cheap seats in the upper galleries is by a different side entrance, which is much less plush. The unruly world of the Regency period has been replaced by a new order of good behaviour — personified by the censorious figure of the priggish, if fictional, Mrs Grundy. The typical Victorian audience is quieter and more attentive than those of previous ages. It forms a solid block of respectable middle-class folk. By now, most new dramas follow the model of the French well-made play and all the stage action takes place behind the gilded and gleaming proscenium arch, a four-sided frame that means that the stage is like a live picture. A great example is the Theatre Royal Haymarket (still there today), which pioneers matinee performances and is refurbished in 1879 by its new managers, the Bancrofts.

DRAMA THEORY: THE WELL-MADE PLAY

The influence of French culture on British theatre continues with the popularity of the skillfully crafted well-made play (a translation of the French drama genre *la pièce bien faite*). The well-made play is tightly plotted, with an initial exposition which introduces the characters and their aims, followed by complications in which their wishes are blocked, and suspense generated, followed finally by a climax and then a resolution in which all loose ends are neatly tied up in a happy ending. Suspense can involve misunderstandings between characters, mistaken identities, lost or stolen documents, often letters, and similar contrivances. It is developed in the early nineteenth century by popular French playwrights Eugène Scribe and Victorien Sardou. In Britain, novelist and playwright Wilkie Collins sums up the formula of the well-made play as 'Make 'em laugh; make 'em weep; make 'em wait.' This works well also as a formula for the influential French farces of Georges Feydeau. Although this kind of playwriting dominates the nineteenth century it is criticized because its neatness of plot and theatrical effectiveness often results in mechanical and stereotypical plays.

As we pass the old Theatre Royal Drury Lane, we shelter from the rain and Jack says that this is home to that most popular of

VICTORIAN THEATRE

English genres, the pantomime. Augustus Harris, nicknamed
Druriolanus, is the Father of Pantomime and his seasonal shows
at Drury Lane are the market leader — they are so popular that
they run not just at Christmas but for months after. Bearded,
stocky, intense yet good-humoured in a heavy Victorian way, he
stuffs his entertainments with music hall stars. His productions
— new stories about Dick Whittington, Cinderella and Jack and
the Beanstalk, with puns and cross-dressed Principal Boys and
Pantomime Dames — are pure spectacle. And sometimes very
long. *The Forty Thieves*, which opens in December 1886, begins at
7.30pm and ends at 1am. There are five hundred people on stage
and two enormous processions, one of which takes forty minutes
to march out of a cave at the back of the stage. The highpoint is
a grand progress, on the theme of the British Empire, now at its
zenith, with richly dressed performers representing different
countries. The cost is huge; Harris regularly spends ten thousand
pounds on a show. At the time, *The Forty Thieves* costs £65,000
to stage. But his pantomimes always sell out and each year the
theatre makes massive profits.

Now we brave the rain again to go to the Savoy Theatre,
where in the lobby Jack tells us about satirical penman William
Schwenck Gilbert, who with composer Arthur Sullivan creates a
series of light operas. Beginning with *Trial by Jury* at the Royalty in
1875, these develop into a wonderfully humorous and charmingly
addictive form of musical which gently mock the big authorities
and the big issues of the day: the army in *Patience*, the navy in
HMS Pinafore and the peerage in *Iolanthe*. *The Pirates of Penzance*
pokes fun at Grand Opera and the Victorian cult of duty, while
The Mikado makes fun of bureaucracy and the craze for all things
Eastern. *Princess Ida* is a spoof on women's education and the war
of the sexes. Other favourites include *Ruddigore*, about the genre
of melodrama, and *The Yeomen of the Guard*, about Shakespearean
England. Their tunes soon become a familiar part of popular
culture. You can hear them being whistled in the street, although
Jack resists the urge to demonstrate, claiming that he's tone deaf.

The new Savoy Theatre, built by impresario Richard D'Oyly Carte, provides a great venue for Gilbert and Sullivan. In 1881 he introduces electricity here, making this the first public building in the world to be lit entirely by electricity (using 1,200 Swan lamp bulbs). D'Oyly Carte is a great innovator: he introduces numbered seating, free programmes, whisky in the bars, queuing for seats in the gallery and a policy of no tipping for cloakroom services. And, of course, electricity hastens a revolution in spectatorship across the West End: now the house lights can be dimmed and the audience watches plays quietly in the dark, concentrating on the stage picture. Instead of several pieces of theatre per night, gradually offerings shrink to one main play, occasionally with a short play called a 'curtain raiser' (20–30 minute light entertainment a bit like the afterpiece). The start time is now after 8pm. Programmes tell audiences who is in the cast, and give information about the running time of the show, with a note such as 'Carriages at eleven', which, says Jack, 'Tells you everything you need to know about the upper-class nature of fashionable West End audiences.' By the end of the century, the long run of a single play rather than the repertory of several different plays becomes the norm.

Jack reminds us that while Drury Lane is famous for its spectacular melodramas and Henry Irving's Lyceum is producing lavish Shakespearean productions, some other new plays are worth a mention. In 1892 Brandon Thomas's farce *Charley's Aunt* is produced by former D'Oyly Carte actor William Sydney Penley, a friend of the author who appears in the lead role of Lord Fancourt Babberley, an undergraduate whose friends Jack and Charley persuade him to impersonate the latter's aunt. At the Royalty, the play sets a record of 1500 performances. Within a year, it tours in four versions around Britain and then around North America in nine. One of the offshoots of the railway and steam ships is the touring of West End shows to all parts of Britain, and also to New York, which means big profits. At about the same time, over at the Prince of Wales Theatre, *A Gaiety Girl* — by Owen Hall, Harry Greenbank and Sidney Jones — is a brilliantly successful musical comedy which gives this form of entertainment an international boost, playing well in both London and New York. And as well as exports there are imports too. When legendary French actress Sarah Bernhardt comes to London, she appears in the role of Cleopatra, in a drama by Parisian dramatist Victorien Sardou, during which in one scene she smashes her palace to pieces. 'As she collapses with a shriek,' Jack says, 'an old lady in the stalls is heard to say: "How different, how very different from the home life of our own dear queen."'

Oscar Wilde

Wilde times

Another day, another location. Jack takes us to Savile Row, an elegant street in Mayfair celebrated across the Empire for its bespoke tailoring for men. Here every house has a workshop with master tailors working on the best textiles from all corners of the world, and we are impressed by the way central London looks more orderly, quiet and clean than in past centuries. Noting that our guide is wearing a new yellow waistcoat, we stroll past the premises of Henry Poole, who Jack tells us is the creator of the dinner jacket or tuxedo. He earns the title of Founder of Savile Row when he creates a grand Palladian entrance to his tailoring workshops. Another tailor, James Lock, invents the bowler hat. This is commissioned by William Coke to be worn by his gamekeepers as protection against attacks from poachers — and, during the shooting season, falling pheasants. Jack, strutting manfully and swinging his cane, tells us that Queen Victoria and her family, especially Edward the Prince of Wales, patronize the best of these tailors, and that the Irish playwright and dandy Oscar Wilde is a customer of James Lock.

It's the 1890s, the so-called Naughty Nineties, a time of fun-loving laxity, especially in sexual morals. The brilliant but short career of Oscar Wilde exemplifies the spirit of the times. Known as the Apostle of Aestheticism, an advocate of decadence, this Dublin-born writer is one of the first global literary celebrities. His flamboyance and eccentricity starts at Oxford, where he becomes known for his wit, his epigrams and his outrageous dress; and his long hair. When asked to explain reports that he parades down London's Piccadilly wearing knee-breeches, a velvet jacket and carrying a lily, Wilde replies, 'It's not whether I did it or not that's important, but whether people believed I did it.' The image of him with a lily becomes iconic, and is lampooned by Gilbert and Sullivan's *Patience* and caricatured in *Punch* by George du Maurier. Once, when he leaves his house in Tite Street, Chelsea, with his wife, a number of boys follow them. One calls out: ''Amlet and Ophelia out for a walk, I suppose!' To which he replies, 'My little fellow, you are quite right. We are!' 'He's constantly seeking attention,' says Jack, with a knowing smile. But there is a serious side to this posing. Wilde has a theory of art, arguing that beauty for its own sake is more important than politics.

Although Wilde poses as an idler, in reality he works hard. His rise to fame takes ten years of graft: he publishes his first book of poems in 1881, then undertakes a gruelling series of lecture tours in England, Ireland and the United States. Next comes *The Picture of Dorian Gray*, which to some is scandalous because its central character, Lord Henry — Dorian's mentor — advocates hedonistic inversions of moral norms ('The only way to get rid of a temptation is to yield to it'). Jack dismisses this judgment with a sweep of his hand, and says that actually it's a very moral work,

OSCAR WILDE

Born: 16 October 1854, Dublin.

Family: Anglo-Irish intellectuals, William Wilde, acclaimed doctor who founded St Mark's Ophthalmic Hospital, and Jane Elgee, eccentric, poet (pseudonym Speranza) and supporter of Young Ireland Rebellion in 1848.

Education: Portora Royal School at Enniskillen; Trinity College, Dublin; Magdalen College, Oxford (outstanding scholar with a First in Classics).

Private life: Marries wealthy Englishwoman Constance Lloyd in 1884. Two sons: Cyril and Vyvyan. Ten years later, Wilde has affair with Lord Alfred Douglas.

Career: Edits *Lady's World*. Beginning in 1888, writes *The Happy Prince and Other Tales*, *The Picture of Dorian Gray*, art criticism and plays.

Scandal: Imprisoned for homosexuality; after two years' hard labour at Reading Prison, where he writes a letter 'De Profundis', goes into exile in France; writes poem 'Ballad of Reading Gaol'.

Greatest hit: *The Importance of Being Earnest* (1895).

Death: 30 November 1900, Paris.

Epitaph: 'We are all in the gutter, but some of us are looking at the stars.' (*Lady Windermere's Fan*)

but the bigots don't get it. Wilde's first play, *Lady Windermere's Fan*, opens in February 1892 and is an overnight hit, but *Salome*, written at the same time in French for Parisian actress Sarah Bernhardt, is banned outright by the Lord Chamberlain because at the time stories from the Bible are not allowed on stage. They are seen as a form of blasphemy. His other plays include two more social comedies, *A Woman of No Importance* and *An Ideal Husband*. But they are all trumped by his masterpiece, *The Importance of Being Earnest*.

Wilde's theatrical success depends on yet another actor-manager — the shrewd George Alexander. In 1891, he takes on the St James Theatre, and turns it into an elegant West End boutique venue. He decorates it, using prints and fresh flowers, hanging fetching photographs of the cast in the lobby. He insists on good manners in his theatre, making the box office manager wear a top hat while on duty and insisting that his actors wear high-society costume even during their free time. Everything about him justifies the idea that although he's an actor-manager he is 'one of us'. By contrast to the contemporary fashion for staging adaptations of French playwrights, Alexander encourages home-grown talent. Most of his choices are new plays, usually comedies of manners, which reflect the world of the audience, set in fashionable drawing rooms, at dinner parties and country-house weekends. Alexander also acts, for example taking the role of Lord Windermere in *Lady Windermere's Fan*.

The Importance of Being Earnest premieres at the St James on St Valentine's Day in 1895. At this time Wilde is at the height of his celebrity and this is his fourth West End hit in three years. *The Importance of Being Earnest*, subtitled 'a trivial comedy for serious people', is one of the most perfectly plotted plays in British history. It opens in Algernon Moncrieff's London flat, with this idle rich youngster being visited by his friend, Jack Worthing. It emerges that both men use false identities to evade social conventions. Jack goes by the name of Ernest in the city and Jack in the country, where he pretends that he has a naughty brother, named Ernest, who he has to rescue from trouble. Algernon admits that, when he wishes to escape society, he pretends to have a sick friend named Bunbury, whom he must visit. Jack wants to marry Algernon's cousin Gwendolen, while Algernon is interested in Jack's pretty young ward, Cecily. Both young women say that their ideal husband should bear the name of Ernest. The main obstacle is Lady Bracknell, Gwendolen's mother, who — when she discovers that Jack was adopted after being found in a handbag at Victoria station ('You see, another mention of the railways,' says Jack) — will not consent to the marriage.

Act Two shifts to Jack's house in the country. Jack and Algernon tell Gwendolen and Cecily that they will change their names to Ernest. After a subplot concerning Cecily's governess Miss Prism and the local cleric Dr Chasuble results in the revelation that Jack is the elder son of Lady Bracknell's late sister and not an orphan with no family, Lady Bracknell withdraws her objections. Likewise, his original name turns out to have been Ernest all along. Jack is now able to marry Gwendolen and Algernon Cecily. All ends well, with the last line being Jack's 'I've now realised for the first time in my life the vital importance of being earnest'.

Oscar Wilde's *The Importance of Being Earnest* (1895)
Lady Bracknell questions Jack Worthing's suitability to marry Gwendolen:

LADY BRACKNELL Now to minor matters. Are your parents living?

JACK I have lost both my parents.

LADY BRACKNELL To lose one parent, Mr Worthing, may be regarded as a misfortune; to lose both looks like carelessness. Who was your father? He was evidently a man of some wealth. Was he born in what the Radical papers call the purple of commerce, or did he rise from the ranks of the aristocracy?

JACK I'm afraid I really don't know. The fact is, Lady Bracknell, I said I had lost my parents. It would be nearer the truth to say that my parents seem to have lost me... I don't actually know who I am by birth. I was... well, I was found.

LADY BRACKNELL Found!

JACK The late Mr Thomas Cardew, an old gentleman of a very charitable and kindly disposition, found me, and gave me the name of Worthing, because he happened to have a first-class ticket for Worthing in his pocket at the time. Worthing is a place in Sussex. It is a seaside resort.

LADY BRACKNELL Where did this charitable gentleman who had a first-class ticket for this seaside resort find you?

JACK *(Gravely.)* In a handbag.

LADY BRACKNELL A handbag?

The first night is a glittering occasion, as jewels flash and dazzle on the steps of St James. In the road, there is a traffic jam of hansom cabs, private carriages and pedestrians avoiding muddy puddles. The noise is terrific. Jack, who was there, recalls bumping into Wilde, who wears a coat with a black velvet collar, a green scarab ring and carries white gloves. As Wilde waits for the performance to start, a man from the Savile Row tailor James Lock delivers a hat to him. While he tries it on, he is asked whether his

George Bernard Shaw reviews *The Importance of Being Earnest* in the *Saturday Review* (1895):
I cannot say that I greatly cared for *The Importance of Being Earnest*. It amused me, of course; but unless comedy touches me as well as amuses me, it leaves me with a sense of having wasted my evening.

play will be a success, and he replies, 'The play *is* a success. The only question is whether the first night's audience will be one!' Actor-manager George Alexander plays Jack, and our guide, who makes some jokes about sharing his name with this character, shows us a photograph of the original production in *The Sketch* magazine. The evening is a big success, and Allan Aynesworth, who plays Algernon, says, 'I never remembered a greater triumph; the audience rose from their seats and cheered and cheered again.'

The epigram is Wilde's trademark. His masterpiece is bursting with witty sayings, exemplified by Algernon's 'All women become like their mothers. That is their tragedy. No man does. That's his.' This creates a charmingly artificial world of words that represents a break with, and a great improvement on, the melodramatic aspects of his other plays. Although Wilde stole the plot of the play from a French farce, *The Foundling*, by William Lestocq and E M Robson, he injected his source material with a big dose of his very own cleverness and joy. *The Importance of Being Earnest* is full of surprising verbal twists, and plot reversals, and these unexpected turns are a major part of the piece's fun. It is also littered with social and moral observations that hide their profundity under a veneer of lightness. Although not everyone is impressed — George Bernard Shaw remains a dissenting voice — the play delights its audience. And has continued to do so ever since.

At the final curtain, Wilde is called for but doesn't take a bow. Jack lowers his voice almost conspiratorially. He knows why. Wilde is avoiding the Marquess of Queensberry, the father of Lord Alfred Douglas (aka Bosie), who is Wilde's by now not so secret lover. When Queensberry (who Jack reminds us was responsible for formulating boxing's Queensberry Rules) finds out about this relationship, he goes mad. And starts stalking Wilde, eventually leaving an insulting message at his club: 'For Oscar Wilde: Posing Somdomite', a misspelling of sodomite. Wilde sues for libel, loses the case, is arrested for gross indecency and on 25 May 1895 sent to Reading Prison. Perhaps conscious of his own relationship with his mentor, Jack talks a little awkwardly about 'the love that dare not speak its name' (a phrase from Bosie's poem 'Two Loves'), and says that at this time homosexuality is a serious criminal offence. After the arrest, Alexander removes Wilde's name from the programme and posters. But audiences take fright, the box office collapses and the play closes, having run for only 83 performances. So sudden is Wilde's fall that he forgets to pay the bill for his hat from James Lock (we tell Jack that it remains unpaid until the year 2000, the centenary of Wilde's death, when a cheque clearing the debt is sent anonymously to Lock). With the playwright in prison Alexander buys the rights to his plays. Life is really strange, Jack tells us with a bitter smile, for while Wilde dies in poverty, Alexander is knighted in 1911 and makes a mint from Wilde's work.

Before we take our leave, Jack sums up the state of British theatre at the end of the Victorian era. 'Long runs of shows have transformed the lives of actors,' he says. 'They no longer have to know some thirty roles word perfect, and be ready to go on stage with little notice to play any one of them.' Now they can enjoy regular employment, acting the same part night after night as long as customers are willing to fill the theatre. But there are other changes: now formal auditions become the norm, hand in hand with casting agents and actors agents. With auditions stimulating competition among actors, thesps now need to advertise and respond to adverts, usually in the weekly trade newspapers *Era* (from 1838) or *The Stage* (from 1880). This is a time when acting editions of the plays, which include details of staging and props to be used for revivals, are printed by publishers such as French's.

By the end of the century a more restrained and natural style of acting is the norm.

It's time for Jack to say cheerio, but he has one more piece of information to impart. On 21 February 1896, a small audience at the Great Hall of the Polytechnic Institution in Regent's Street watches the first film show in London. Created by the French brothers August and Louis Lumière, these short documentaries show people boating, bathing and a train arriving in a station. The event lasts just seventeen minutes, but it heralds a change: the new age of mass entertainment starts here.

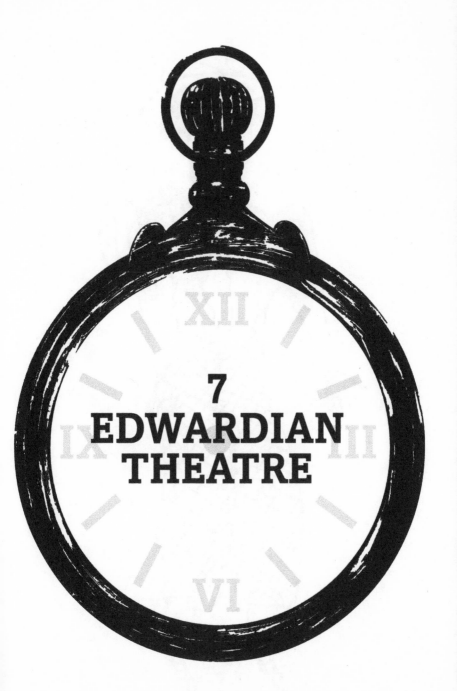

7
EDWARDIAN
THEATRE

7
Edwardian Theatre

Meet our guide: Constance

Our new guide, Constance Wright, comes pedalling towards us on her tricycle, a metal contraption that looks impressively modern. As she dismounts to introduce herself, slightly breathlessly, we notice that she's wearing a bicycle suit which consists of bloomers which show off her ankles, and a smart top. On her head is a neat boater with a ribbon; she wears her dark hair short and wavy. Her face, which has a touch of make-up, has a bright expression. Her appearance exudes confidence and vitality — yes, she is a New Woman. We are outside Selfridge's — the grandest new West End department store — and as we approach its monumental entrance we are dazzled by the plate-glass window displays. Inside, the floors are carpeted in bright green and the hustle and bustle makes the place feel like a luxurious miniature town. One of nine lifts take us to the fourth floor where the tea garden welcomes us. Constance says that Mr Selfridge is an American whose mission is to attend to every woman's whim. As we take tea, she tells us more about her background. Her father is a retired banker, her mother dabbles in poetry, and the family home is a Hertfordshire mansion. She has recently moved to a rented flat in London and works as an interior designer, having helped decorate some of the latest crop of West End theatres. She is a supporter of the suffragettes and she's taken part in some of their demonstrations, once sailing up the Thames and shouting abuse through loud hailers at what she calls the 'pompous toads' sitting in Parliament. Constance says that on our trip she will take us through British theatre from 1901 until the end of the First World War in 1918, the Edwardian age.

The Edwardians

In January 1901, Britain and her Empire, on which the sun never sets, mourn the passing of Queen Victoria, and the end of an era. For more than six decades she has ruled with a sober authority, but her decision to remain secluded in mourning after Prince Albert dies in 1861 means that a generation has never seen her in person. Her son, whom she despised, is now King Edward VII. By now, we are following Constance along Oxford Street, jostled by the crowds, and we get the idea that although she doesn't care much for royalty she is amused by this bad boy. Overweight, cigar-smoking and bearded, he spends his time eating, drinking, gambling, whoring, shooting, sailing and watching horse racing. He loves the theatre, and meeting pretty young actresses. He has many affairs, some with stars such as Lily Langtry, a close friend of playwright Oscar Wilde and later manager of the Imperial Theatre. However, once he is king, Edward shakes off his playboy lifestyle, devoting himself instead to attending great occasions, opening municipal buildings and launching battle ships. He gradually becomes a point of stability in a nation beset with new problems: trade union militancy, suffragette direct action and a growing crisis in Ireland as the movement for Home Rule clashes with the desire of Protestants in the North to remain part of Britain. In general, the country is conspicuously divided by class, symbolized by the formation of the Labour Party in 1900, which gives a voice to the workers.

We walk with Constance to Hyde Park, where she says, 'We can observe the new rituals of the rich.' Here, she points out that members of high society can be seen riding daily on horseback between 8am and 12pm, then between 5pm and 7pm driving in their open-top motor cars, and on Sundays taking part in church parade between 1pm and 2pm. 'This is an era,' she says, 'when the high life of champagne and diamonds is punctuated not only by the syncopated rhythm of American Ragtime music, but also by new inventions: the rumbling motorcar, the buzzing airplane, the luxurious ocean liner.' By 1910 London extends for ten miles in every direction from Charing Cross. It's the heart of Empire, a place where bankers, financiers, administrators and politicians rub shoulders with manual workers, clerks, artists and jobless migrants. 'The City to the east,' says Constance, 'is the commercial quarter (Bank, Stock Exchange, insurance) which makes the money, while the West End is the quarter that spends it (in department stores, luxury boutiques, music halls, cinemas, museums, galleries).' Due to the fact that the majority of the working population enjoys a rise in real income of around forty per cent, particularly among the expanding white-collar professional and clerical middle class, there is a consumer boom. The big new thing is electricity: this power source brings changes in transportation, with the electrification of the Underground. It lights up the streets, starting with Electric Avenue in south London's Brixton, and with regular patrols by bobbies they are safer than ever, but also noisier. Motor buses, trams, lorries, carts and bicycles all fight for space in the streets. The downside of electricity is that it makes it easier to work at night thus lengthening working hours. This means more exploitation of the workers, adds Constance earnestly, which leads to strikes and demands for better conditions. We get the sense that her slogan is: 'Up the workers!'

Henrik Ibsen

From Ibsen to suffrage

Constance begins her account of Edwardian theatre by looking back at the influence of Henrik Ibsen, the Norwegian playwright and a key figure in modern theatre. She takes us to Bedford Street in Covent Garden, location of the offices of William Heinemann, the English publisher of Ibsen. As we climb the stairs of this rather gloomy building, Constance leads the way and, having settled us into some chairs in a meeting room, lights a cigarette — a gesture typical of the New Woman — and fills us in about the Norwegian. Pictures of the playwright show a man with eccentrically extravagant side-whiskers, and there is something of the stern father about this giant of European drama. His plays are the biggest influence on progressive playwrights because he dares to write about realistic sexual and social subjects at a time, the last quarter of the nineteenth century, when these are taboo on the respectable British stage. In his play, *A Doll's House*, a young wife walks out on her husband and her children — and is not punished. In *Hedda Gabler*, a young wife shoots herself to avoid scandal. In *Ghosts*, there is hereditary syphilis. These are shocking topics for

ENEMIES OF THEATRE:
THE LORD CHAMBERLAIN

By the twentieth century, the Lord Chamberlain is an increasingly archaic figure. A royal official — usually a retired military man — whose authority to censor play scripts comes from the 'Theatre Acts' of 1737 and 1843, his duties are strengthened by parliamentary guidelines laid down in 1909. Plays can only get licenses if they are not indecent, offensive, blasphemous, violent, or represent royalty or other living people. Political plays, especially if they are too left wing or might impair relations with a foreign power, are also refused a licence. So, until the outbreak of the First World War in 1914, this means 'hands off Germany'. In keeping with Victorian prudery, all references to genitals, intercourse, STDs or birth control are prohibited. The word pregnant is rarely used, seen as too 'indelicate', most playwrights preferring to use the French *enceinte*. Homosexuality must never be mentioned — not until 1958 are serious plays about gay people even considered for a licence. Nudity is only permitted if the actress is motionless and 'artistic'. Foreign playwrights are viewed with particular suspicion. As a result, the long list of plays banned in Britain includes work by Henrik Ibsen, August Strindberg and Luigi Pirandello.

the middle-class audiences of British theatre and they are hard to stage because the Lord Chamberlain is determined to censor them. 'This is why more people read them than see them on stage,' says our guide, stubbing out her cigarette.

From a shelf, Constance produces some copies of Ibsen in English. We look at the title page of one and see that *A Doll's House* has been translated, back in 1889, by William Archer, a Scottish intellectual and theatre critic. He's bilingual in English and Norwegian because his grandfather emigrated from Scotland to Norway, and the Perth-born William grew up in Larvik, only thirty miles from Ibsen's birthplace in the port town of Skien. 'Archer,' explains Constance, 'is one of a small group of erratic young men, often foreigners or outsiders, who change British theatre forever.' But although her eyes shine as she says this, she quickly adds that this is not achieved without setbacks. In 1884, the first London production of *A Doll's House* — scandalous because it criticizes the traditional roles of men and women in marriage — is not a straight translation but an adaptation by Henry Arthur Jones and Henry Herman called *Breaking a Butterfly*. They completely rewrite the play by changing the name of Ibsen's Nora to Flora (or Flossie) and giving it a happy ending in which Flora repents and stays with her husband! The true version, with Nora walking out on her marriage and slamming the door, is finally staged on 7 June 1889 at the Novelty Theatre in Kingsway, with Janet Achurch — who specializes in New Woman roles — as Nora. Clement Scott, theatre critic of the *Daily Telegraph*, jokes that the play is 'ibscene' but acknowledges that 'the interest was so intense last night that a pin might have been heard to drop'. But when the Lord Chamberlain refuses to licence any performance of another Ibsen play, *Ghosts*, two cultural radicals, Jacob Thomas Grein, a Dutch-born impresario and critic, and George Moore, an Anglo-Irish novelist, take matters into their own hands. They set up the Independent Theatre Society, which exploits a loophole in the 'Theatres Act' of 1843. Their society is classed as a theatre club with a limited membership and this means that it is not under the jurisdiction of the Lord Chamberlain. This allows them to stage *Ghosts* to a small audience of members only, which they do in 1891. This time Clement Scott goes wild: in an editorial, he

DRAMA THEORY: NATURALISM AND THE PROBLEM PLAY

At the end of the nineteenth century, the genre of naturalism emerges in European drama, pioneered by French novelist Émile Zola, who uses detailed realism to describe the social condition of his characters. As a result of scientific advances during the Industrial Revolution, the idea is that just as the natural world determines the shape and actions of animals (according to Charles Darwin) so the social environment determines the situation and actions of humans. European plays attempt to create an illusion of observed reality — including a new frankness about sex — and to criticise unjust social conditions. More and more plays are set among the working classes. Henrik Ibsen is highly influential and his example stimulates British playwrights to create the new genre of the serious Problem Play, exemplified by Arthur Wing Pinero's *The Second Mrs Tanqueray*. Such dramas typically pose a question: *The Second Mrs Tanqueray* asks, Can a marriage between a woman with a past and a respectable upper-middle-class gentleman work? Often the playwright includes a *raisonneur* character — usually an urbane gentleman — who guides the audience into the right way of thinking about the issues raised by the play, providing advice and explicating morality. The greatest practitioner of the Problem Play is George Bernard Shaw, whose dramas are plays of ideas, which engage audiences intellectually by staging debates between characters who have opposing views.

denounces *Ghosts* as 'an open drain, a loathsome sore unbandaged, a dirty act done publicly'. 'Although most middle-class audiences would not wish to see these plays,' says Constance, 'there is an important minority who appreciates their realistic view of life.'

Before long, British playwrights are inspired by the spirit of Ibsen to produce the new genre of the problem play. Enter Arthur Wing Pinero, the playwright as consummate craftsman. His achievement is to unite the clockwork plotting of the Victorian well-made play with new concerns about the relations between the sexes. Pinero is an impressively sharp-featured figure whose head combines a bald dome with a thatch of black eyebrows. After working as an actor in Edinburgh and then with Sir Henry Irving, the foremost actor of his generation, he takes up writing. He makes his name with laugh-out-loud farces, such as *The Magistrate* (1885), and gently humorous plays, such as *Sweet Lavender* (1888), which runs successfully for 683 performances and contains what Constance thinks is a nice line: 'While there is tea, there is hope.' But Pinero wants to be taken seriously as a dramatist so he turns to serious subjects. He attempts, with little success, to write tragedy in *The Profligate* (1889), where a man takes poison after he realizes that his marriage has failed. Then he writes *The Second Mrs Tanqueray*, a box-office hit which brings its author the recognition he desires as a serious dramatist.

The key date is 27 May 1893, when *The Second Mrs Tanqueray* opens at the St James Theatre, a venue which also hosts the work of Oscar Wilde. The play's story starts at the Albany — an exclusive apartment complex in Piccadilly — home of the forty-two-year-old widower Mr Aubrey Tanqueray, who is dining with male friends. They are surprised that he intends to marry a woman called Paula Ray, and when he tells them that 'My marriage is not the conventional sort of marriage likely to satisfy society' they understand that she is a lower-class woman with a questionable past. After they leave, Paula appears, and gives Aubrey a letter containing details of her past, which he chivalrously burns without reading. The next three acts are set in Highercoombe, Tanqueray's country house. Two months after their marriage, the couple are not happy. Paula is bored with inactivity, while Tanqueray is apprehensive about her poor relationship with Ellean, his pious daughter from his first marriage. Eventually, Ellean asks her father's permission for her engagement to Captain Ardale. Paula then has to confess to her husband that the man who now intends to marry his daughter was once her lover. Ellean instinctively understands the situation but the sexual double standard applies: it is okay for Ardale to have a past, but not for Paula. When Ellean is finally struck with pity for her stepmother, it is too late. Paula has killed herself. 'Killed — herself? Yes, yes,' says Ellean. 'So everybody will say. But I know — I helped to kill her. If I had only been merciful!'

Arthur Wing Pinero

Constance says that this is the first serious attempt on stage to examine the woman question, which she explains is a public debate about the role of women in society and covers everything from issues of suffrage and legal rights to marriage and sexual freedom. Most plays about this subject, she points out, have been satires on the New Woman. But Pinero is different. She praises him for raising the subject of the Woman with a Past and the question of the sexual double standard. The key line in the play is Paula's despairing realization that 'The future is only the past again, entered through another gate.' However, Constance also points out that Pinero's conclusion is a very conventional one: Paula commits suicide. Pinero doesn't let her live. Constance explains that the epithet 'fallen woman' is still given to any woman that has sex outside of marriage, or who commits adultery. Although these situations are common in real life, and on the stage in Paris for example, most British plays either avoid the subject or punish the woman with an early demise. In West End melodrama, you can find plenty of seduced innocents, wicked seductresses and penitent Magdalens. But they always die untimely deaths, she tells us with a hint of exasperation. She quotes a satire by Jerome K Jerome, whose 1889 book *Three Men in a Boat* is a bestseller. In the satire, he writes: 'Never repent. If you value your life, don't repent. It always means sudden death!'

The Second Mrs Tanqueray is the play in which Mrs Patrick Campbell, who plays Paula, first makes her name. Born Beatrice Stella Tanner, Mrs Pat (as she is known; her husband died in the Boer War) is dark, beguiling, and fascinating. She plays opposite the

St James actor-manager George Alexander as Tanqueray, and enjoys her success so much that she begins to favour New Woman roles, such as Mrs Alving in Ibsen's *Ghosts* and the lead in *Hedda Gabler*. 'She is also,' Constance says, 'very successful as Mélisande in Maurice Maeterlinck's *Pelléas and Mélisande*.' Constance doesn't really gossip, but she can't resist telling us that among the many admirers of Mrs Pat is one George Bernard Shaw, writer, critic and budding playwright. Constance says that apparently they exchange passionate letters, and is quite surprised

Mrs Patrick Campbell

when we tell her that these have now been published. Mrs Pat is also known as a wit. She defines marriage as 'the deep, deep peace of the double-bed after the hurly-burly of the chaise-longue', and her best-known remark, spoken when a young actress complains that an actor shows too much affection for a leading man, is 'My dear, I don't care what they do, so long as they don't do it in the street and frighten the horses.'

Pinero also examines the fallen woman again in his play *The Notorious Mrs Ebbsmith* (1895). Constance likes the scene in which the exasperated Agnes Ebbsmith throws a bible into a stove. But she also comments on Pinero's cowardice: he makes Agnes pull the bible out of the fire. 'He's always balancing the desire to make a radical point with the fear of offending his audience,' says our guide. His reward for his timidity and his crowd-pleasing craftsmanship is that he is knighted by King Edward VII in 1909! Another playwright, Henry Arthur Jones, pens a number of plays on the same subject, the best being *The Case of Rebellious Susan* (1894), a play which poses the question: Can a woman repay her husband's adultery by doing the same — and survive in society? It concludes that: 'What is sauce for the goose will never be sauce for the gander. In fact, there is no gander sauce.' Jones's heroine, Lady Susan Harabin, is advised to renounce her new lover and return to her husband although the main motive for her affair is his unfaithfulness. The play, Constance tells us, is staged by actor-manager Charles Wyndham, who also acts in it. But he has cold feet about one line which confirms that Susan has committed adultery: 'Oh, I should kill myself if anyone knew! You have never spoken of me, boasted to any of your men friends?' This is spoken by actress Mary Moore, who plays Susan. Constance thinks that Wyndham is particularly sensitive about secret affairs because he himself is having a discreet liaison with Moore. And Moore is not alone, Constance tells us, lowering her voice. Many actresses are unwilling to say lines which might be seen as applying to their private lives. So the unmarried Evelyn Millard withdraws from Jones's The Lackey's Carnival (1900) because the role requires her to say 'I swear to you by my unborn child', which she thinks is indelicate. As Constance points out, the role of women in society remains problematic. We tell her that the same is still true today.

Some plays do overturn the conventional image of the fallen woman. Not surprisingly, they are by women. Elizabeth Robins does this in her Votes for Women!, a play that Constance clearly likes. She is also keen to tell us about its author. Robins is an American actress who comes to London after her actor husband commits suicide by jumping into Boston's Charles River wearing a full suit of heavy armour. When George Bernard Shaw makes a pass at her, she pulls a gun on him. Great stuff, laughs Constance. When writer and critic Max Beerbohm lunches with Robins, he cannot resist peeping under the table to see if she's really wearing a skirt. Robins plays the first British Hedda Gabler in 1891, and is vilified for having 'glorified an unwomanly woman', as the critics say. But she remains clear-eyed, remarking acidly that what mainstream audiences want of 'women of the stage is, first and mainly, what is wanted offstage — a knack of pleasing men.' Her eventual response is to write Votes for Women!, first staged at the Court Theatre in 1907. In the play, the classy heroine Vida Levering, a women's suffrage campaigner, is shown to be the former lover of an MP.

But this time the woman shows no sign of penitence, doesn't kill herself, or retire to a convent. Instead she campaigns for women's rights and for better conditions for destitute females. She ends by insisting that only collective political action can change and improve the condition of women. The middle act is particularly memorable: it stages a rally in Trafalgar Square with a cast of forty actors, a plaster-cast base of Nelson's Column and two large 'Votes for Women!' banners. Robins gives a quarter of her royalties to the suffragette movement, and in 1909 her play is staged in New York, taking its feminist message with it. Edith Wynne-Matthison, who plays Vida, is converted to the cause; she and Robins set up the Actresses Franchise League in 1908 to support women's suffrage. Constance is all for it.

The Sloane Court

It's time to go in search of a more avant-garde venue. And since Constance is in the know about who is in and who is not, she takes us to the Court Theatre (today called the Royal Court), which is in Sloane Square next to the Underground station. We travel there by tube train, on the District Railway line, which has been newly electrified by an American entrepreneur called Charles Tyson Yerkes, a speculator and art collector whose business life has been marred by a series of bribes, defaults and dodgy deals. 'That's entrepreneurship for you,' sniffs Constance. The carriages rattle along nicely, and we soon emerge into the spring sunlight, turn right and find ourselves on the steps of the Court. Designed by Walter Emden and Bertie Crewe, the theatre boasts a lovely frontage of warm red brick and a stone façade in an Italianate style. Constance ushers us in with a brisk gesture. Although she doesn't think much of the interior design of the place, which we suspect is because it was designed by one of her rivals, she knows the manager who lets us all in for a quick morning tour.

Inside, the Court looks like a classic medium-sized late-Victorian theatre, decorated in velvety red wallpaper, and as we take a seat in the stalls Constance is keen to give us the details about the venue's central role in the promotion of new drama. 'Its location,' she says, 'is its USP.' Away from the West End the Court attracts a new, more open-minded audience than the respectable middle-class patrons of the mainstream. Still, some of the plays put on here are quite safe. For example, in 1898, Arthur Wing Pinero's *Trelawney of the Wells* — a nostalgic love letter to the theatre of the mid-Victorian times — is a lighthearted story about an actress, Rose Trelawney, who gives up the theatre to marry her sweetheart. It's also a hit in New York.

Constance stresses the fact that the new theatre depends mainly on the good work of alternative theatre groups. These courageous producers are led by the Independent Theatre Society, which introduces Ibsen to Britain, and the Stage Society, set up in 1899 with the aim of giving drama a shot in the arm by promoting new plays about new subjects. These new play-producing societies do not depend on box office, but on the subscriptions of their members. The biggest advantage of this system is that they are classed in legal terms as private clubs and so they don't have to submit their plays to the censor. According to the rules, tickets can only be bought by members, two weeks in advance, but they can stage any play, however taboo its subject. These are usually put on at the Court as Sunday matinees, a time when actors engaged in professional runs are available. Examples of Stage Society productions with adult themes that offend the Lord Chamberlain include Shaw's *Mrs Warren's Profession* (about prostitution) and Harley Granville Barker's *Waste* (about an affair which leads to an abortion). Constance really likes Barker so she fills us in on his career.

Barker is a key figure in modern British theatre. Having made his stage debut at the age of fourteen in 1891, he works as an actor — including touring in the same company as Mrs Pat — until he becomes dissatisfied with the triteness of the commercial West End. With his striking good looks, enormous charm, expressive voice and total dedication, he soon becomes a vital advocate of the new drama. In 1900 he joins other progressive polemicists such as William Archer and George Bernard Shaw, along with feminists such as Janet Achurch and Elizabeth Robins, in the Stage Society, which produces his first play, *The Marrying of Ann Leete*, a story set in the eighteenth century about a devious politician who marries off his daughters to advance his

Harley Granville Barker

own political ends. With the Stage Society, Barker develops his acting, writing and directing skills, becoming a complete man of the theatre. 'In 1904 he teams up with John Eugene Vedrenne, an experienced producer, and they stage three seasons of new plays at the Court,' says Constance, giving the back of her seat a smart tap.

The mission of the Stage Society is to search for new playwrights, especially those that are not afraid of writing about social problems. 'The Barker—Vedrenne 1904–07 seasons at the Court are a remarkable achievement,' says Constance, 'notching up a grand total of 988 performances of thirty-two new plays by seventeen playwrights.' Although these include the Professor of Greek Gilbert Murray's new translations of three plays by Euripides, the majority are contemporary works. These seasons introduce the work of Continental playwrights such as Gerhart Hauptmann and Arthur Schnitzler, and of British playwrights such as John Galsworthy and St John Hankin. The seasons are dominated by the plays of Shaw, 701 performances of eleven plays (about which more later, promises Constance). Barker also directs and acts in ten of them. The whole enterprise is part of Barker and Archer's vision of a future national theatre. These Court plays are staged in a repertory system, first during afternoon matinees and then in the evenings too, with short runs (which would not be possible in the commercial sector, requiring long runs of sure-fire hits). Barker and Vedrenne agree to spend no more than £200 on each production. Expenses are pared down to a minimum so production values are pretty basic and actors' fees kept low. The whole enterprise is a financial success, but only just.

'Let me tell you a bit more about the plays of Barker,' says Constance, lighting a cigarette. When we say we are surprised that she smokes inside a theatre — isn't it a fire risk? — she says not to worry: no one will know. At which point, we give an embarrassed cough. *The Voysey Inheritance*, Granville Barker's 1905 play for the Court, is a five-act well-made Problem Play. It shows what happens when the wealthy Edward Voysey discovers that his solidly respectable solicitor father has been speculating with his clients' capital; and that his father himself was the inheritor of a fraudulent business: 'You must either be the master of money or its servant,' he says. After revealing the fraud to the family, Edward exclaims, 'Oh, they're all shocked enough at the disgrace but will they open their purses to lessen the disgrace?' Edward knows that his family is unwilling to help right the financial wrongdoing of his father. After his father's death, Edward tries to restore money to the clients, but this proves to be harder than he thinks. Barker's play is both a portrait of a single family and an attack on the immorality of capitalism: a point of view expressed by Edward's artist brother Hugh, an impecunious artist who regards all unearned income as tainted. Hugh is the author's mouthpiece, but Barker also illustrates the fundamental hypocrisy of Edwardian life. 'You must realise,' says Voysey senior, 'that money making is one thing, religion another, and family life a third.'

Constance now moves on to *Waste*, which after having been refused a licence by the Lord Chamberlain is privately performed by the Stage Society in 1907. At its centre is a maverick independent politician, Henry Trebell, who has ambitious plans for an Act of Parliament to reform relations between church and state. But his career is ruined because of his affair with Amy O'Connell, the estranged wife of an Irish Republican. 'Amy,' says Constance, 'it doesn't take much to guess, gets pregnant.' She doesn't want the child; Henry doesn't help her; she has an abortion, and dies.

NATIONAL THEATRE

The late-Victorian advocates of a progressive drama are also supporters of the idea of a national theatre, a flagship venue where the best of national and international drama would be staged. For although most European countries have state-subsidised national theatres which symbolise their cultural aspirations, Britain does not. Instead it has Shakespeare, a symbol of national greatness, and a thriving commercial West End. Actor-manager David Garrick first advocates a national theatre in the eighteenth century, and then radical publisher Effingham Wilson publishes a plan in 1848, followed by poet and critic Matthew Arnold, who in 1880 writes an impassioned plea for a subsidised theatre in London, ending with the call: 'The theatre is irresistible; organize the theatre!' But nothing is done. So in 1904 the critic William Archer and the playwright and director Harley Granville Barker launch a campaign by writing a fully costed plan for a national theatre, along with details of its repertoire of classics and new plays. It is published in 1907 as *A National Theatre: Scheme and Estimates*. The campaign gathers pace and is supported by people such as actor-manager William Poel, who is interested in reviving Elizabethan stagecraft, and those who want to set up a lasting memorial to William Shakespeare. In 1908 they form the Shakespeare Memorial National Theatre Committee, launch an appeal and raise £100,000 in five years. They lobby parliament for state funding, but the outbreak of war in 1914 results in the postponement of these plans until the 1960s.

Now the scandal threatens both Henry's career and the success of his reform of the church. Can the wily cabal of politicians save the situation — and what price will Amy's husband, Sinn Feiner Justin O'Connell, extract from them? 'What provokes the Lord

Chamberlain to ban it,' says Constance, 'is not only the mention of an abortion (illegal at the time), and its sexual frankness, but also its unflattering depiction of politicians.' Despite Barker's satire on how political deals are made, the play's aphorisms ('scandals weaken confidence in the governing classes') are few and far between. When they talk about affairs of state, it's clear that Barker's interest is more in power than sex. But the smugness of the men in the play, Constance points out, is almost unbearable. 'Yet Barker,' she says, 'also has a real compassion for women: he shows how Henry manipulates Amy, being as calculating a seducer as he is manipulative as a politician.' In the end, Henry concludes, 'Emotion has been killed in me unborn before I had learned to understand it — and that's killing me.' His ruthless logic leads him to commit suicide. The resulting disgrace illustrates the waste of life and talent due to the unforgiving moral codes of society.

At the end of the 1907 Court season, Barker moves to the much larger Savoy Theatre, where he hopes to repeat his success. He fails. In 1909, another opportunity comes his way. The American impresario Charles Frohman takes over the Duke of York's Theatre and aims to stage mainstream plays in the evening and new plays during matinées. Barker is asked to direct the new plays, one of which is his own *The Madras House* (1910). 'This is,' says Constance, 'his most important exploration of the position of women in society.' The play opens in the comfortable middle-class home of Henry Huxtable, a wealthy draper whose six unmarried adult daughters live with him. 'Their allowances are small and they have no economic independence,' adds Constance, 'and thus no real freedom.' One of them, Emma, spells out their trivial, unambitious activities: 'We're always busy. I mean there's lots to be done about the house and there's calling and classes and things.' The repetitiveness of their dialogue represents the tedium of their lives, and their repressed sexuality — the family has never approved of any suitor. The second act exposes the inequity of the 'living-in system' that chains the firm's drapery workers to their employers. It's as oppressive as the middle-class home, and despite the chance of economic independence, the women workers are strictly controlled by Miss Chancellor, the housekeeper. 'No suitors for them either,' says Constance.

> Harley Granville Barker's *The Madras House* (1910)
> *Emma Huxtable explains why none of the sisters are married:*
> **EMMA** It isn't exactly that one wants to get married. I daresay mother is right about that.
> **PHILIP** About what?
> **EMMA** Well, some time ago a gentleman proposed to Jane. And mother said it would have been more honourable if he had spoken to father first, and that Jane was the youngest and too young anyhow to know her own mind. Well, you know, she's twenty-six. And they heard of something he'd once done and it was put a stop to. And Jane was very rebellious and mother cried.

The exception, and key figure in the play, is Marion Yates, a shop assistant who gets pregnant but refuses to get married. Good on her. 'She has guts,' says Constance, 'but her future is not a bed of roses.' The third act is set in the Madras House, a fashion emporium designed with an oriental flavour. Here Barker's aesthetic is more symbolic, and there is a fashion parade of mannequins rather than models, which, explains Constance, represent the objectification of women. Mannequins are paraded like cattle. Men construct women's sexuality. The play ends with Philip Madras and his wife Jessica discussing the position of women. There is no resolution and the play breaks off in mid-sentence as Jessica replies 'Yes...' to Philip's point that 'men and women are a long time in the making'. Barker's last stage direction is: 'She doesn't finish, for really there is no end to the subject.' The play is too long, and Constance tells us that even Barker's friend William Archer suggests that it would

George Bernard Shaw

benefit from cutting because, by the last act, audiences are exhausted. *The Madras House* only has ten performances; Frohman is delighted to be able to use the death of King Edward VII (when many theatres close for a period of mourning) as his excuse for bringing the experiment to an end.

Time to leave the Court. 'Oh, I almost forgot,' says Constance. Anxious not to appear as a Little Englander, she tells us that the minority theatre draws its inspiration not only from Ibsen, but also from the avant-garde theatres of Europe. So they are galvanized by the visits to London of André Antoine's Théâtre Libre, a Parisian theatre which puts on plays by Ibsen and Émile Zola, and of the companies of the Duke of Saxe-Meiningen and the state-funded Comédie-Française, whose wealth allows them to enjoy longer rehearsals than in Britain, which result in amazingly well worked out stage pictures, with the actors looking like real people and not stuffed dummies. 'The *mise-en-scène*,' adds Constance, deliberately using the French word for the visual impact of a play's staging, 'is breathtaking.' Yes, there's a real thrill about the new, the modern, the contemporary.

Shaw's corner

The next day the British Museum looms ahead of us, its massive portico and columns stained with soot from millions of coal fires, looking particularly gloomy in the thin morning drizzle as Constance, in her raincoat and having provided us with umbrellas, leads us toward it. She gathers her skirts and moves purposely up the grand steps at the entrance, and heads straight for the Reading Room, in the centre of the building's Great Court. Once inside this domed library, with its green lamp shades and hushed atmosphere, she gives the wardens a nod and ushers us to seat number O7, where Karl Marx sat while writing *Das Kapital* during the middle of the previous century. She then tells us that the critic and translator of Ibsen William Archer met George Bernard Shaw — or GBS as Constance calls him — in this room in 1883. Apparently, Archer told her that one day while he was visiting the library to do some research he noticed that Shaw was sitting next to him, fiddling with his reddish untrimmed beard and balancing a French translation of *Das Kapital* against the orchestral score of Richard Wagner's opera *Tristan und Isolde*. Marx's book hadn't been translated into English yet, but the twin themes of politics and love were already weighing on his mind. The two men become friends, and in 1892, they stage their debut, *Widowers' Houses*, a collaboration written several years previously and featuring both a love story and an attack on slum landlords.

Since we can't talk in the hushed atmosphere of this august library Constance takes us to one of the museum's galleries to discuss the work of Shaw, who is the foremost critic and playwright of the age, one of very few dramatists (Shakespeare is another) to have an adjective (Shavian) named after him. Like the bard, GBS is a theatrical superman and his huge output has a massive influence on twentieth-century drama. But whereas most Irish playwrights had previously brought the gift of charm to British theatre, GBS arrives with something much more astringent: the desire to provoke. After rummaging in her capacious bag, Constance shows us a photograph of the great man: he's tall, thin, broad-chested with a long, bony face and a scraggy beard. He's partial to wearing tweed rather than formal Edwardian dress, and when he enters a room he's instantly noticeable because he moves in a jerky way, gesticulating, bright, mercurial. 'He is charismatic and awkward at the same time,' says Constance. This Irishman is a brilliant talker. He's a full-on radical, which means that he's also a committed vegetarian, causing a stir whenever he is invited to dinner because he prefers parsnips to roasts. He is also energetic and industrious,

GEORGE BERNARD SHAW

Born: 26 July 1856, Dublin.

Family: Protestant George Carr Shaw, corn miller and heavy drinker, and Lucinda Gurly, amateur singer.

Education: Lower-middle-class Protestant and Catholic schools until age fifteen. Then self-educated.

Private life: Moves to London in 1876.
In July 1897 he meets wealthy Irish activist and feminist Charlotte Payne-Townshend, and they marry the next year. She abstains from sex completely so Shaw has several affairs.

Career: Journalist, failed novelist, music critic and then theatre critic in the late 1880s and 1890s for *The Fortnightly Review* and *The Saturday Review*. Famous as a political orator; becomes member of the Social Democratic Federation (the first Marxist group in Britain) and in 1884 helps set up the Fabian Society. In 1893 attends the Bradford conference that sets up the Independent Labour Party (later Labour Party). Fervent advocate of the new theatre of Henrik Ibsen (*The Quintessence of Ibsenism*, 1891) and the music of Richard Wagner (*The Perfect Wagnerite*, 1898). Writes controversial plays, often censored, but also history plays such as *Caesar and Cleopatra* (1901) and *Androcles and the Lion* (1912). His unique voice is a combination of the dramatic, the comic and the socially corrective. Writes fifty-three plays.

Greatest hits: *Arms and the Man* (1894), *Candida* (1900), *Mrs Warren's Profession* (1902), *John Bull's Other Island* (1904), *Major Barbara* (1905), *Man and Superman* (1905), *Doctor's Dilemma* (1906), *Pygmalion* (1914), *Heartbreak House* (1920), *Saint Joan* (1923).

Awards: Nobel Prize for Literature, 1925; Oscar for screenplay of *Pygmalion* in 1938.

Death: 2 November 1950.

Afterlife: *Pygmalion* is the source of the hit American musical *My Fair Lady* (1956).

a busybody whose interests range widely from reforming the spelling of English to founding educational establishments such as the London School of Economics.

With a knowing look, Constance says that GBS is a bit of a late developer: he is already thirty-six years old when his first play is staged. For most of the 1890s, he is better known for being a critic than a playwright — with his outspoken socialist views, he's also a media celebrity. His motto is: 'If you do not say a thing in an irritating way, you may just as well not say it at all.' As a critic, he is an attack dog: he savages the insipid drama of the West End and Constance quotes from memory his put-down of a typical commercial play: 'a tailor's advertisement making sentimental remarks to a milliner's advertisement in the middle of an upholsterer's and a decorator's advertisement.' He has nothing but contempt for 'nice plays, with nice dresses, nice drawing rooms and nice people'. British theatre, according to him, is all style over substance. This he vows to change. What he wants is a drama that makes you think. So he single-handedly invents the drama of ideas. The fact that today we have a contemporary theatre that deals with social and ethical questions is due to GBS.

Shaw owes his playwriting career to the Independent Theatre Society, the theatre club which produces *Widowers' Houses* in 1892 after it has been refused a licence by the Lord Chamberlain. But things do not go smoothly. By 1898, GBS is demoralized because only two of his seven plays have been performed on stage — managements are too timid to risk upsetting their patrons. What does he do? He publishes his plays in a reading edition, with long stage directions that set the scene and help readers to visualize the play in their mind's eye. Copyright laws of the 1880s have finally outlawed the pirating of playwrights' work so he's onto a winner, and a good earner too. GBS groups his plays into collections — *Plays Unpleasant, Plays Pleasant* and *Plays for Puritans* — which makes his work look like an ambitious programme of change. He also includes long Prefaces and other explanatory notes which elucidate the politics of the plays. Typically, in the published version of *Man and Superman* there's a tract called *The Revolutionist's Handbook,* one of whose maxims reads: 'He who can does. He who can't teaches.' This is theatre as literature, something to be read and discussed rather than just watched.

Shaw's work finally reaches a wider public when he teams up with Barker, who — as Constance reminds us — is the biggest mover and shaker of new drama. During the Barker—Vedrenne seasons at the Court, eleven of GBS's plays are produced. Barker also acts in several of them, playing, for example, Marchbanks in *Candida* in 1900. Constance likes this play because it shows a woman facing a choice. Candida is married to the Christian Socialist clergyman James Morrell but is courted by a youthful poet called Eugene Marchbanks. In the end, she has to choose between the two men and she chooses the rather sententious Morrell over the bright Marchbanks. 'But the thing is,' says Constance, her eyes sparkling, 'she does the conventional thing for unconventional reasons.' She stays with her husband because she has decided to pair up with the man that needs her most. And in her opinion Morrell is weaker than Marchbanks. According to GBS, the provocation of the play is that it is 'a counterblast to Ibsen's *Doll's House*, showing how in a typical doll's house it is the man who is the doll'. Constance says that GBS is arguing that it is best to follow one's innate impulses, and she agrees with that. She also loves some of the lines from the play: 'We have no more right to consume happiness without producing it than to consume wealth without producing it.' Or 'Wicked people means people who have no love: therefore, they have no shame. They have the power to ask love because they don't need it: they have the power to offer it because they have none to give.'

For Constance, GBS's early masterpiece is *Mrs Warren's Profession*. The play is refused a licence by the Lord Chamberlain because it talks about prostitution and is finally staged in 1902 by the Stage Society. 'If you think that British censorship laws are bad,' says Constance, 'you should know that a public performance of the play in New York some five years later is raided by the police, who arrest the entire cast!' After a pause, while we smile, she adds, 'It's an amazing play because it completely subverts the conventional image of the fallen woman.' Mrs Kitty Warren is a successful businesswoman who runs a chain of brothels around Europe. The core of the play is the relationship between her and Vivie, her independent-minded daughter, who is romantically involved with Frank, a rather impoverished but charming young man. 'In the first production,' says Constance, 'Barker plays Frank.' When Vivie discovers how her mother earned her money, she is at first horrified and then gradually accepts the fact. But when she finds out that Mrs Warren still maintains the business, despite having enough money to live on, she is disgusted not so much by her unconventionality as by her conventionality: her use of money to buy respectability and social position. In the end, she rejects both her mother and Frank and vows to work to keep her independence. She is a New Woman and she needs neither men nor mother.

According to Constance, the play shows how social codes of decency are a sham and how money can only be accumulated through the exploitation of the labour of others, in this case the girls who work in the brothels. But as well as upending the Victorian image of the fallen woman, Shaw also plays with audience expectations: his audiences would have expected Mrs Warren to be reconciled with Vivie, perhaps with a clichéd deathbed scene. Instead, Shaw offers his spectators a New Woman who makes a rational choice not to accept social conventions. The villain of the piece is not Mrs Warren but the hypocritical Victorian social system that created her. The audience is thus invited to examine its own conscience about how it has acquired its own wealth and is deprived of the chance to indulge in mawkish sympathy for the victims of prostitution. 'That would be too easy,' says Constance.

But much as Constance likes some of GBS's many plays, there are things she finds odd. Like his inconsistent attitudes to women. For example, *Man and Superman*, which is part of the Court season in 1905, stars Barker and Lillah McCarthy (soon to married to each other), as the central couple, Jack Tanner and Ann Whitefield. Constance shows us a photograph of the first production and we have to laugh: Barker is wearing a scrawny beard just like GBS's.

THE CRITIC'S VIEW: MRS WARREN'S PROFESSION

George Slythe Street reviews *Mrs Warren's Profession*, *Blackwood's Magazine*, June 1900:

Mr Shaw has ideas. It might be thought from this remark that I propose to charge in his favour, but regretfully I am forced back upon criticism. Sheridan's weakness is his lack of ideas; Mr Shaw's weakness is his superabundance of them.

Constance says that although Shaw writes some good strong parts for women, he also has some questionable ideas: he thinks it is men's role to be thinkers while women's role is to be mothers; he believes that sex is for procreation not pleasure; he believes in eugenics. 'Yes,' says Constance dryly, 'there's something a bit sinister in his utopian ideas.' Little does she know that in the 1920s and 1930s, GBS turns out to be both a fan of Benito Mussolini, the Italian fascist, and of Joseph Stalin, the Russian dictator!

Shaw's plays are dismissed by some as not being plays at all, but merely an excuse to debate various issues of the day. Constance brings our attention to his unique tone of voice, both frivolous and serious. In his plays, which are like verbal fencing matches, he's scrupulous in giving both sides of the argument a fair crack of the whip. So in *Major Barbara* (1905), there's a lively debate between the arms dealer, Andrew Undershaft, and Barbara, the Salvation Army major who is also his daughter. Here GBS the iconoclastic thinker argues that if you make men richer they will be less brutish and that war can only be avoided by developing more advanced weapons. GBS also invents the modern state-of-the-nation play: *John Bull's Other Island* (1904) is about the Irish Question, but its serious points are enlivened by comedy. When King Edward VII sees it, he laughs so much that he breaks the chair he's sitting on. 'What's really clever about GBS,' says Constance, 'is that he always uses the form of a typical middle-class play to cunningly subvert middle-class values.' So *The Devil's Disciple* takes the form of an Adelphi melodrama, *Arms and the Man* a romantic comedy and *You Never Can Tell* a farce.

But Constance's favourite is *Pygmalion*, which tells the story of the pompous Professor Higgins, who makes a bet with his friend Colonel Pickering that he can turn Eliza Doolittle, an impoverished Covent Garden flower girl, into a lady. At first he gets mixed results from teaching her perfect elocution, but then, at an ambassador's reception, she is mistaken for a princess. And this creates a few problems because she has no money to back her new social status. As she says, 'I sold flowers. I didn't sell myself. Now you've made a lady of me I'm not fit to sell anything else.' At the same time, her father, Alfred Doolittle, who is a dustman and an example of what the Edwardians call the 'undeserving poor', gets a sudden legacy which means he has to abandon his feckless lifestyle and has to pretend to be a member of the respectable middle class. So it's a story about that quintessentially English subject: class. 'Higgins,' reckons Constance, 'is a brilliant larger-than-life character, who is so convinced of his own superiority that he happily insults anyone, including Eliza, whom he sees as inferior. He's a great stage creation, but just imagine what he would be like in real life — totally unbearable!' He's also — like GBS himself — strangely sexless. His behaviour to Eliza is at best ambiguous. Her love interest is the penniless gent, Freddy Eynsford-Hill. Of course, one of the great things about the play, argues Constance, is that GBS leaves the ending open — we don't really know who Eliza will marry.

By 1912, when the play is ready, GBS is enough of a star writer to anticipate a glamorous West End production of his masterpiece. He is also besotted by Mrs Pat, London theatre's star actress, and they exchange passionate letters although rumour has it that the affair is Platonic. As a result of his infatuation with Mrs Pat, Shaw offers her the role of Eliza — despite the fact that at almost fifty she is thirty years too old for the part. He also offers the part of Higgins to actor-manager Sir George Alexander, who refuses it because he can't bear the thought of acting opposite Mrs Pat, a notoriously difficult personality. In fact, he won't even speak to her! Instead, the part of Higgins goes to Sir Herbert Beerbohm Tree, a bit long in the tooth at sixty-two. Apparently, Constance has been told that rehearsals are rather fraught. Mrs Pat shows such scant attention to the dialogue that GBS goes down on his knees in front of her, begging her to just say the lines. Her response is typical: 'That's where I like to see my authors, on their knees at my feet.' Likewise, the ageing Tree is hard to control. His memory is not what it was and he has to write key words and key lines on pieces of paper and fix them on various parts of the set. He is desperate to embellish the part, asking GBS if he can play Higgins with a Scottish accent. 'No, just say the lines,' is the answer. Then, five days before the opening night, Mrs Pat disappears. Three days later, she reappears in time for the dress rehearsal. Where has she been? Oh, she just got married — and has been on her honeymoon.

Despite all this, the opening night on 11 April 1914 at His Majesty's Theatre is a triumph.

George Bernard Shaw's Pygmalion (1914)

Eliza causes a sensation:

HIGGINS *(Rising and looking at his watch.)* Ahem!

LIZA *(Looking round at him; taking the hint; and rising.)* Well, I must go. *(They all rise. Freddy goes to the door.)* So pleased to have met you. Goodbye. *(She shakes hands with Mrs Higgins.)*

MRS HIGGINS Goodbye.

LIZA Goodbye, Colonel Pickering.

PICKERING Goodbye, Miss Doolittle. *(They shake hands.)*

LIZA *(Nodding to the others.)* Goodbye, all.

FREDDY *(Opening the door for her.)* Are you walking across the Park, Miss Doolittle? If so —

LIZA *(Perfectly elegant diction.)* Walk! Not bloody likely. *(Sensation.)* I am going in a taxi. *(She goes out.)*

One scene especially causes uproar. When Higgins first introduces Eliza in her new guise as a lady to a group of high-class friends and family at a tea party, the flower girl manages to speak in a perfect accent but the things she speaks about — poverty, disease and crime — show that she hasn't managed to shake off her origins. At the climax of the scene, when she leaves and Freddie, her admirer, offers to walk her home, her instant response electrifies the audience: 'Walk! Not bloody likely. I'm going in a taxi.' The shock of hearing the swear word 'bloody' is such that the audience gasps — then explodes with laugher. Apparently, adds Constance, the laughter continues for so long that it is doubtful that the performance can continue. In the end, it does. At other performances, she has heard, Tree changes the ending of the play by throwing a rose to Mrs Pat, suggesting that Higgins will marry Eliza. When GBS objects to this, Tree says: 'My ending makes money, you ought to be grateful.'

Shaw is a prolific playwright, and he goes on writing well into the 1920s and beyond, with late masterpieces such as *Heartbreak House* and *Saint Joan*, but we've had enough of him and Constance looks pretty worn out so we adjourn for the day. Outside the British Museum it's still drizzling.

Radical currents

The following day, when we meet Constance, we notice that she's wearing a new hat, but before we can compliment her on it, she says, 'Right, it's time to talk about workers' rights.' This is an age of great social struggles, not only the campaign for votes for women, but also unprecedented industrial militancy, as, from 1910 to 1914, workers all over the country struggle for better pay and conditions. Miners, railway workers and factory workers all fight for their rights. These are years of strikes and demonstrations. It's called the Great Unrest and confrontations are many: the Liberal government dispatches two warships to the river Mersey to combat the seamen's strike; the young Home Secretary Winston Churchill sends troops to tackle miners in Tonypandy; during a railwaymen's strike, the entire town of Llanelli in Wales is put under siege by the military, who shoot two striking workers. One of the biggest strikes is that of 11,000 workers, led by women, against pay cuts at the Singer Sewing Machine factory in Clydebank, Scotland. Working days lost to strike activity in these four years are four times higher than in the previous decade. Constance takes us to London's Trafalgar Square, which is the site of frequent demonstrations, where people gather with their banners and speeches. But today things are quiet, with only a few pigeons squabbling over crumbs.

Theatre is not immune to these struggles. Constance takes out a leaflet about the Music Hall strike of 1907. It has a banner headline, announcing 'Music Hall War!' We're surprised that performers are as militant as other workers so she explains that the strike is due to the exclusivity clause in the contracts of most music-hall performers which forbids them from working at more than one venue thus limiting the amount of money they can earn in one night. Some unscrupulous managers also force their performers to work several matinees for no extra money. 'Eventually,' says Constance, 'things come to boiling point.' On 22 January 1907, the performers, musicians and stagehands of the Holborn Empire go on strike. Similar actions follow in other London halls, organized by the Variety Artistes Federation, formed the previous year. Artists picket the halls, distribute leaflets like the one Constance is showing us, and demand more pay for extra performances. It is Music Hall War!

Even big stars such as Marie Lloyd support the action. Constance has lots of stories to tell us about her. One time Lloyd sends a telegram to the Tivoli theatre, where she is due on stage, saying that she is too busy sewing her dress to appear. Apparently, Little Tich, Lloyd's co-star, also sends a telegram. His says: 'Learning a new cornet solo. Cannot tear myself away.' Angry managers try to keep the halls open by booking second-rate acts: one example is Belle Elmore (born Kunigunde Mackamotski, aka Cora). When Lloyd hears that strikers plan to picket a theatre to prevent Elmore performing, she tells them: 'Don't be daft. Let her in and she'll empty the theatre.' (Jokes apart, Elmore's life ends tragically. She marries American homeopath Dr Crippen, and is murdered by him in 1910.) Anyway, concludes Constance, the music hall strike is so successful that managers give in to the strikers' demands. During these turbulent times, even mainstream actors become unionised. After the setting up of RADA in 1904, new drama schools begin to appear and the acting profession becomes more organized. In the following year, as standards of training rise so does the self-esteem of the performers and the Actors' Union is formed to secure better pay and conditions.

While we are on the subject of militancy, Constance tells us that theatre is developing a social conscience. One reformer, the redoubtable Emma Cons, is an artist who wants to use the arts to improve the quality of life for the poor. Back in 1880, she had become manager of the Old Vic, which she renamed the Royal Victoria Coffee and Music Hall, and as well as putting on various entertainments, she also gives improving lectures on the perils of drink. Cons is the first female alderman to sit on the London County Council. Her niece, who helps her run the theatre, is Lilian Baylis, who takes over the Old Vic after her aunt's death in 1912, and soon becomes one of British theatre's most fearless pioneers.

Constance tells us about the two key political plays of the time: *Strife* and *Rutherford and Son*. *Strife*, first performed in 1909, is written by John Galsworthy, a middle-class privately educated writer who trained for the bar, but abandoned the law for a more independent lifestyle. What remains of his legal training is a sense of fair play. In *Strife*, he shows the two sides — bosses and workers — of a bitter strike in a tin works. Both the aged company chairman John Anthony and the workers' leader David Roberts are intransigent, while everyone else wants a compromise. After both of them are outmanoeuvred, the resulting agreement between bosses and workers is exactly the same as had been suggested four months previously — all the bitter strife has been for nothing. 'The best scene,' says Constance, 'is when the orator Roberts charismatically denounces capitalism, attacking "the thing that buys the sweat o' men's brows, the tortures of their brains, at its own price — capital!"' As she says that, she nearly punches the air. 'By the way,' she adds, 'another of Galsworthy's plays actually led to a change in the law': *Justice*, staged in 1910, features a wordless scene in which a man is shown losing his mind in a cell, pounding on the door, and this is credited with leading to the abolition of the practice of putting newly convicted prisoners into solitary confinement.

Rutherford and Son is first staged as a matinee at the Court in 1912. 'It is another sharp attack on the unacceptable face of capitalism,' says Constance, 'and taps into all of the social anxieties of the Great Unrest.' In the play, John Rutherford inherits a glassworks from his father, and puts his life into the business, which he intends to pass onto his sons John and Richard. But he treats them so tyrannically that they, along with their sister, leave home. With his children gone, Rutherford is left — for all sorts of complicated reasons — with Mary, the working-class wife of John, a person he has previously ignored. She now offers him a bargain: if he will keep her and her son (his grandson) for ten years, she will then hand the boy over to him ready to take on the business. Rutherford accepts, saying, 'I'm known as a hard man. But I don't know that I could have stood there and spoken as you have.' At the Court, with the playwright's name given as K G Sowerby, the story gets rave reviews. 'But, guess what,' says Constance with a mischievous grin: 'when the news gets out that Sowerby is a woman — Githa Sowerby — there is an outcry. How dare a woman write a serious play!' But Sowerby knows what she's talking about:

she is the daughter of the industrial dynasty that owns the massive Sowerby-Ellison glassworks in Gateshead. Anyway, whatever men think, no one can deny her success: *Rutherford and Son* transfers to the Vaudeville, where it is performed 133 times, then opens in New York, and is translated into German, French, Italian and Russian. Githa Sowerby becomes an instant celebrity and feminist hero.

Constance now introduces us to the feminist Pioneer Players, a group founded by Edith Craig, daughter of actress Ellen Terry. This company performs at the Little Theatre, which operates as a club to avoid censorship by the Lord Chamberlain. 'Like other such ventures, its purpose,' says Constance, 'is to instruct rather than just entertain.' But Edith is not the only radical in her family. Her brother is Edward Gordon Craig, the most modern stage artist of the Edwardian age. He is a lonely, crabbed figure who conceives of the director as a God-like being, believing strongly that the design of a play is its most important element — actors are just marionettes. For him scenography comes first. He is a notoriously difficult and demanding personality. So, after finding little success in Britain, in 1904 he goes to Europe to seek his fortune. There he writes an influential essay, *The Art of the Theatre*, in which he argues that audiences go to the theatre to see, rather than to hear, plays. According to him, they long to see exciting new stage pictures, designs that are modern and symbolic, rather than naturalistic. Just like Wagner, he strives to create a total work

Githa Sowerby

of art, conjuring up atmosphere by means of colour and abstract shapes. 'Almost like music,' says Constance. But Craig doesn't care about the social issues, she points out, and some of his ideas are 'a bit beyond me'. Too intellectual! So he remains a stranger to these shores. Although he designs *Hamlet* for Konstantin Stanislavski at the Moscow Art Theatre in 1911, he avoids practical theatre-making and concentrates on writing about the spiritual in art. Yet today any production that uses bold abstract designs owes him a debt.

West End opulence

Meanwhile, as these radical currents flow through British theatre, the West End flourishes in the old Victorian way, enjoying a golden age. There's an enormous range of offerings: striking spectacles at Drury Lane, Shakespeare at the Lyceum, musical comedy at the Gaiety, blackface minstrels at St James's Hall, pierrots at the Palace. Anywhere you can see drawing-room comedies, costume dramas, hilarious farces and light musicals. Audiences seek a relief from worry: worries about a German invasion, worries about Home Rule for Ireland, worries about rebellious workers and militant suffragettes. They flock to some forty gleaming West End venues, which are run by larger-than-life actor-managers: Herbert Beerbohm Tree, George Alexander and Charles Wyndham. These self-confident movers and shakers join together to form the Society of West End Theatre in 1909. In their hands, theatre is big business, and every evening (except Sunday) some 100,000 spectators out of a London population of more than seven million come into town to enjoy a show. Such an industrial scale entertainment is stratified on class lines: aristocratic and upper-middle-class patrons arrive from their large Belgravia mansions and pay about ten shillings to sit in boxes, stalls and the royal circle; lower-middle-class spectators from the suburbs pay less than half of this to sit in the so-called family circle, while ordinary folk pay a shilling to sit up in the Gods (gallery). This is the world of *Upstairs Downstairs*, and its settings are spectacular new theatres. The pre-eminent architect is Frank Matcham, who builds some hundred and fifty theatres across Britain, including

London venues such as the Coliseum, the Palladium, the Victoria Palace, the Hackney Empire and Shepherd's Bush Empire (all still in use). Matcham's theatres have notably exuberant interiors, using an eclectic mixture of styles, anything from mock Tudor to rococo stucco, and decorations ranging from military insignia to classical statues.

Typical West End fare for the respectable middle classes is a playwright such as James Matthew Barrie, the Scottish-born writer whose life was scarred when his older brother David, his mother's favourite, was killed in an ice-skating accident at the age of thirteen. Barrie was six years old and for him time stopped. As a child he wears his brother's clothes, trying to attract his mother's attention, thus telling her that he will be forever her little boy. In his best-known play, *Peter Pan; or, The Boy Who Wouldn't Grow Up*, which opens at the Duke of York's Theatre in 1904, the children of the Darling family are whisked off by Peter Pan to Never Land, where they have adventures with Lost Boys, Red Indians, lovely mermaids and pesky pirates led by the unforgettable Captain Hook. Flying around is Tinker Bell, Peter's sprite. The whimsical tone of the play — typical lines include 'To die would be an awfully big adventure' and 'when every new baby is born its first laugh becomes a fairy' — is quintessentially English. Peter, with his celebration of eternal boyhood, and the pirates, who want Wendy Darling to be their mother, are typical figments of Barrie's damaged psyche. In the first production, Captain Hook is played by Gerald du Maurier, who has a rather terrifying stage presence. Although Barrie wants a little boy to play Peter, the law says that children cannot go on stage after nine o'clock at night so Peter is played by Nina Boucicault, Victorian playwright Dion Boucicault's daughter, which establishes a tradition that actresses play the part as a breeches role. Very soon, *Peter Pan* becomes an annual pantomime, a fate that Barrie finds appalling.

Two years before *Peter Pan*, Barrie's greatest hit is *The Admirable Crichton*, also at the Duke of York's, which is managed by the astute American producer Charles Frohman. A big hit, it runs for 828 performances, and its theme is the quintessentially English one of class. Set in the household of Lord Loam, whose butler is the eponymous Crichton, it shows what happens when the family is shipwrecked on a desert island. Here the social system is turned on its head: the aristocrats are at a loss, Crichton is boss, and eventually proposes to Lady Mary, Loam's daughter. Before they can marry, however, the family is rescued and the social order is restored, with Crichton resuming his previously subordinate position. The message is clear: at home, the English upper classes are expiring from laziness; on a desert island, they can be turned into useful citizens by their so-called inferiors. But Crichton is no revolutionary: he remains as conservative as everyone else. When at the end Lady Mary, who has now returned to her previous aristocratic engagement, says, 'You are the best man among us.' Crichton replies, 'On an island, my lady, perhaps; but in England, no.' 'Then there is something wrong with England,' she says. 'My lady, not even for you can I listen to a word against England.' Max Beerbohm, brother of actor-manager Herbert Beerbohm Tree and a noted caricaturist and theatre critic for the *Saturday Review*, writes about the play: 'Our slaves are still servile enough, superficially, but we know that many of them are in all respects our superiors.' Which is a fine sentiment as long as the audience doesn't take it too seriously.

But such West End comedies are less important than the new blood being pumped into revivals of Shakespeare. On the one hand, there are traditional productions of the bard, full of fussy detail, with fussy sets, and fussy acting from great Shakespeareans such as Johnston Forbes-Robertson, one of the age's most refined Hamlets. These appeal to nostalgic audiences. On the other hand, are the reinventors of Shakespeare. Two key figures in this camp are Frank Benson and William Poel. Benson, who looks like a noble Roman, is a dedicated Shakespearean: he has spent thirty years touring around Britain, and since 1886 has been organising annual festivals at the Shakespeare Memorial Theatre, which opened in 1879 in Stratford-upon-Avon. As an actor, Benson is vigorous and his performances are often athletic. As a director, he takes the radical step of performing the full text: his *Hamlet* lasts six hours, plus, happily, a break for dinner! During a long career, he stages all but two of Shakespeare's plays, many of which had not been revived for generations. Equally important is William Poel, who was born into the Pole family but changed his name after it was misspelt on a theatre poster. Tall, thin, aquiline, he's a long-haired zealot who might be seen nibbling a dry biscuit and drinking a glass of milk in rehearsal breaks. He founds the Elizabethan Stage Society in 1894 with a mission to recreate the original feel of Shakespeare's theatre by using a simple platform stage with almost no scenery. His claim to authenticity in productions must be taken with a pinch of salt, but he does manage to publicize the plays of the bard's contemporaries, such as Jonson and Webster. Poel believes that fussy sets distract from the poetry of Shakespeare's words, and instead of the laboured verse-speaking style, his aim is 'to keep the exquisite rhythm and cadence of the verse even whilst the drama is hurtling along its swift tempestuous course'.

Our modern idea of Shakespeare is formed by Benson and Poel, along with the ever-present Harley Granville Barker. At the Savoy between 1912 and 1914, Barker and his wife Lillah McCarthy present three Shakespeare plays — *The Winter's Tale*, *Twelfth Night* and *A Midsummer Night's Dream* — which are influenced by both Benson and Poel. They create a bare platform stage, with draped curtains painted with symbolic designs. In *A Midsummer Night's Dream*, the wood is represented by a green velvet mound sprinkled with white flowers topped by a gauze canopy flickering with fireflies. Background curtains are illuminated with green, violet and purple lighting. The gilded fairies are painted with gold leaf (until some actors experience bad skin reactions). Puck has red berries in his yellow hair. Adhering closely to the original text, the lines are delivered with rapid, lightly stressed speech, rather than the drawn-out oratory that is the norm. Today, these performances are remembered for their simplicity and poetic beauty.

Beyond the West End

Constance takes us to Forest Hill, south London, for a visit to the Horniman Museum, built by the super-rich Frederick John Horniman, who made a fortune from importing tea in the Victorian era. Believing that knowledge is the key to improvement, he opens a museum to display the 3000 ethnographic objects, specimens and artefacts that he has collected from around the world, and, what's more, he donates the building to the London County

Council. Designed in the Arts and Crafts style by the Liverpudlian Charles Harrison Townsend — whose other work includes the Whitechapel Art Gallery — the building is striking in its eccentric look. On one outside wall is a mosaic mural, with three figures representing Art, Poetry and Music; inside, the galleries are full of archaic musical instruments, African masks and stuffed animals. Constance selects a quiet spot, and tells us that the connection with theatre is Horniman's daughter, Annie, who is a driving force behind theatre outside London at the turn of the century.

Constance calls Horniman a totally admirable woman. Starting out as a lonely little rich girl, she goes to the Slade School of Art, discovers that she is no artist, but develops instead an enthusiasm for the plays of Ibsen and for the theatre (to the horror of her father who is very religious and thinks that theatre is sinful). As a sign of independence, she wears trousers, smokes, cycles solo around Europe and supports female suffrage — 'Just like me,' says Constance. With her strict Quaker upbringing, she's a deeply principled woman, but also a bit of an eccentric: before making any decision, she consults tarot cards. Then, using a legacy from her grandfather, she funds a season of new plays at the Avenue Theatre (today called the Playhouse), which includes the first West End production of Shaw's *Arms and the Man* and Irish poet William Butler Yeats's first play in London, *The Land of Heart's Desire*. In fact, she becomes a devotee of Yeats and works as his unpaid secretary for several years.

Horniman's friendship with Yeats leads her to put up the money to open the Abbey Theatre in Dublin, where the poet — along with Lady Gregory and other intellectuals — has been keeping alive the Irish Literary Theatre project since 1899. Opening in 1904, this venue promotes the Irish literary revival and gradually becomes the national theatre of Ireland. But while Yeats's plays are full of obscure mythical Irishness, the work of the Anglo-Irish playwright John Millington Synge is more down to earth, and is the Abbey's foremost contribution to modern drama. *The Playboy of the Western World*, staged in January 1907, is his masterpiece. Set in a shebeen, an illicit bar, in County Mayo, a remote part of rural west Ireland, the story shows the effect on the local community of the arrival of Christy Mahon, a young man who claims to have killed his father.

But rather than repelling the locals, his boast gives him a heroic stature, especially with Pegeen Mike, the publican's daughter. At the end of the first act, Christy is so pleased with himself that he says, 'I'm thinking this night, wasn't I a foolish fellow not to kill my father in the years gone by.' Yet, during the first performance, the audience laughter becomes increasingly uneasy as Christy's father arrives on the scene, exposing his son as a liar and scoundrel. The public is starting to find the violent conflict between the two men a bit disrespectful to their notions of the proper relations between fathers and sons. Then Christy attacks his father offstage with a shovel; he returns and offers to marry Pegeen — boasting that he would choose her even if he was offered 'a drift of Mayo girls standing in their shifts itself'. At which point, a bystander pulls off her petticoat to provide him with a disguise to hide from his father. In the audience, bedlam breaks out. References to undergarments are simply too indecent. Each subsequent performance of the play is disrupted by hissing, booing, yelling and stamping of feet. Fist fights break out.

THE PLAYBOY RIOTS

W B Yeats describes the reception of J M Synge's
The Playboy of the Western World (1907):

Picturesque, poetical, fantastical, a masterpiece of style and of music, the supreme work of our dialect theatre, his Playboy roused the populace to fury. We played it under police protection, seventy police in the theatre the last night, and five hundred, some newspaper said, keeping order in the streets outside. It is never played before any Irish audience for the first time without something or another being flung at the players. In New York a currant cake and a watch were flung, the owner of the watch claiming it at the stage door afterwards.

These *Playboy* riots, explains Constance, are an expression of wounded pride by an audience which feels offended by the playwright's provocative portrait of country folk. But she feels sorry for Synge: two years later, he dies of Hodgkin's disease at the age of thirty-seven. Such talent cut short.

Horniman's mission, on the other hand, is by no means finished. As we sit in a gallery under the gaze of masks and totems from all around the globe, Constance continues her tale. After Dublin, Horniman moves to Manchester, where in 1907 she buys the Gaiety Theatre. Here, along with director Lewis Casson and his wife, the actress Sybil Thorndike, they develop a new way of putting on a wide variety of plays to their local audience. They call it the repertory system, although it is different from the *true* repertory system where different plays are put on for a handful of days at a time depending on demand. Instead, at the Gaiety one play is acted twice nightly for a week. Horniman charges affordable prices — she's an early advocate of subsidy, which she believes can raise

Harold Brighouse

standards and make plays more accessible. On their own, she argues, box office takings are not enough to ensure quality. In one decade, the Gaiety produces more than two hundred plays. Horniman especially promotes the work of the Manchester School of playwrights, notably Harold Brighouse and Stanley Houghton.

'Harold Brighouse's *Hobson's Choice* (1916) and Stanley Houghton's *Hindle Wakes* (1912) both feature strong women characters,' says Constance earnestly. *Hobson's Choice* is set in Salford, and takes its title from a popular expression which means 'no choice at all'. The key figure is Maggie, who runs Hobson's shoe shop while her father prefers to spend his time getting drunk with his cronies. In the course of this comic masterpiece, she gets the business's chief craftsman, the boot-maker Willie Mossop, to marry her, arranges dowries for her lazy sisters, Alice and Vicky, and manages to run the household while fooling old Hobson into believing that he is still in charge. He drinks so much he has no choice but to let her do it. 'Although it's a very funny play,' says Constance, 'it also shows how the balance of power in England has shifted from the old to the young, and from men to women.' Maggie proves that a woman can be as good at business as any man. And it predicts that the best workers will be more successful than the idle upper classes. 'In fact,' says Constance, 'there's a similar message in Houghton's play', which is set in Hindle, Lancashire, and centres on Fanny Hawthorn, who gets into trouble with her parents when her secret tryst with Alan Jeffcote, during the local wakes holiday, is discovered. She is an ordinary worker, in the cloth-weaving industry, while he is the son of the local mill owner. But although both sets of parents pressure the youngsters to marry, in the end Fanny rejects Alan because, smiles Constance, 'He is simply not good enough for her.' Her defiance leads her to strike out on her own, saying 'I'm a Lancashire lass, and so long as there's weaving sheds in Lancashire I shall earn enough brass to keep me going.' Hindle might be a sleepy place, but Fanny has woken into a strong, almost Ibsenite sense of her own self-worth. And she doesn't need any man.

Yes, Horniman is a pioneer of the repertory movement, but she is not alone. In Birmingham, Barry Jackson opens the Birmingham Repertory Theatre (usually shortened to Birmingham Rep) with a production of Shakespeare's *Twelfth Night*. Born into a wealthy merchant grocer's family in 1879, Jackson founds the amateur Pilgrim Players in 1907, staging shows in local halls, and goes on to build the elegant 460-seat Rep in 1913 (the company is still there today). Like Horniman, he is passionate about offering the people of Birmingham a wide variety of theatrical experience, and personally subsidises the new building. His venue rapidly becomes home to one of the most exciting theatre companies in the country, reinventing the idea of Shakespeare by playing the bard in modern dress. Jackson is also a great fan of Shaw. Following these examples, other reps are established in Glasgow, Liverpool and Bristol.

As the day darkens, Constance brings our minds back to London, and to the outbreak of the First World War in August 1914. This event means a surge in the number of plays aimed at pleasing the Khaki audience. So militaristic melodramas, full of heroic soldiers and spies with guttural German accents proliferate like an epidemic. But patriotic realism has a short shelf life. Escapist dramas, such as Walter W Ellis's long-running, and aptly named, *A Little Bit of Fluff* at the Criterion in Piccadilly Circus, emerge as the most popular entertainment of the time. Constance doesn't think much of it. However, the most successful show of the war is *Chu Chin Chow*, a kaleidoscopic oriental musical with a huge cast and sumptuous sets. Created by the Australian theatre-maker Oscar Asche and based on *Ali Baba and the Forty Thieves*, this extravaganza stars Asche as Abu Hasan, the robber chief, and his wife Lily Brayton as his captive Zahrat Al-Kulub. Constance rolls her eyes. 'Still, Asche is no fool,' she says. He makes a deal with Henry Dana, manager of His Majesty's Theatre, where the show opens on 31 August 1916, to take a percentage fee. When *Chu Chin Chow* runs for nearly five years, smashing all box office records (more than 2200 performances), everyone gets rich, especially Asche.

As the museum staff turn out the lamps, Constance indicates that it is time to leave. Her parting shot is to tell us that, by 1924, *Chu Chin Chow* had earned Asche £120,000. What does he do with this massive sum? He gambles it away during the Roaring Twenties. 'But that decade,' says our guide as she takes her leave, once again on her tricycle, 'is another story for another day.'

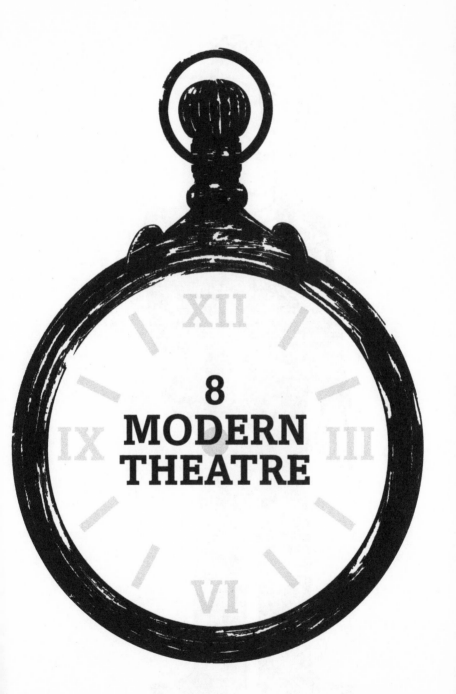

8
MODERN
THEATRE

8
Modern Theatre

Meet our guide: Roberts

The immaculately turned out Sidney Roberts, our new guide, meets us at the cenotaph in London's Whitehall. This familiar Portland stone monument by Edwin Lutyens commemorates the fallen of the First World War. As he introduces himself — 'Please call me Roberts' — he tells us that the cenotaph was built in 1920 to replace a previous version, hurriedly made in wood-and-plaster for the Victory Parade of 19 July 1919, which marked the formal end of hostilities. Roberts is in his fifties, and didn't fight in the war, but he lost a younger brother in the trenches. He is tall, thin, with grey slicked-back hair, and dressed in a black lounge suit topped by a cravat. His deportment matches the elegant cut of his suit, although we notice he has a slight stoop. He is the valet, gentleman's gentleman, of an aristocrat whose name he discreetly avoids mentioning and to whom he refers as 'his lordship'. As he glides over to the other side of the road, he indicates a car, so we have time to get a better look at him, noting his controlled demeanour. The navy-blue car, Roberts tells us, is a new Crossley 9T. As we climb in, we think we can detect a mild expression of disdain as he notices our trainers, and, oh, is that a hint of disapproval of our casual dress? In the car, we catch a whiff of vetiver. Could that be Floris No 89 perfume? We are too embarrassed to ask. As he turns his rather earnest face to us, Roberts explains that his lordship has granted him the use of his motor and, 'If I might make a suggestion...', proposes to drive us down to the family's country home in Hampshire. It sounds like a good idea, a perfect location to start a trip which will immerse us in modern British theatre during the first half of the twentieth century, from 1918 to about 1955.

Postwar Britain

As we drive out of London, past picturesque churches and newly built memorials to the fallen, we hit the south-west London suburbs, noticing how many modern homes are replacing the old decaying slums. As clouds scud across the sky, Roberts says that he was brought up in Brentford, and that he remembers when the town was polluted by industry, a grimy concentration of unhealthy hovels. Now it is a lively small town with a bustling market place. We drive down the new Great West Road, opened by King George V in 1925, and our guide tells us that his father was a salesman while his mother stayed at home, bringing up the children. 'Genteel poverty sums up my childhood, but my mother held the family together,' he says. One of the big changes, since the end of the war, he points out, has been in the status of women. Women over the age of thirty win the vote in 1918 and the franchise is extended to all women ten years later. We might expect Roberts, who is a confirmed bachelor, to be a bit scathing about women's rights, especially when it concerns staff below stairs, but if so he hides his feelings well.

Crossing into Surrey, we are surprised by the lack of vehicles on the road, and delighted by the huge tracts of green fields. Roberts is now talking about his lordship, a widower and landowner, who has surprisingly liberal views, although he's not happy about the rising taxes imposed by postwar governments. Nor is he as enthusiastic as some of the servants below stairs about the first Labour government, a short-lived coalition led by Ramsay Macdonald, which takes office in 1924. Then, after the Conservatives return — under the avuncular Stanley Baldwin — the General Strike of 1926 represents a test of strength in the struggle between capital and labour. After a week, the unions are defeated. 'His lordship is worried by these conflicts,' says Roberts, 'and of even greater concern is the 1929 Wall Street Crash.' These serious matters are of little interest, apparently, to his lordship's daughter, Annabel, who is one of the new postwar generation of Bright Young Things, a flapper more interested in sipping extravagant cocktails, smoking cigarettes and hosting fancy-dress parties. To the exasperation of his lordship, she prefers the cinema and the radio to the theatre

— and claims airily that she's never seen a single Shakespeare play in her life. She prefers American jazz music and the new dance crazes. Metropolitan dives are her church and chapel.

We finally arrive at his lordship's country house, a typical family pile originally built centuries ago, and now made a bit more bearable with some mod cons. Roberts parks the car and takes us through the main wood-panelled hall into the library, which has a warm atmosphere with its soft carpet, open fire and ranks of brown leather volumes. There are some battered, but comfortable armchairs. John the butler serves tea, complete with cucumber sandwiches and scones. As we take refreshment, Roberts tells us about his frequent visits to the London stage. He is a reader of *The Stage* and *Era*, publications about what's going on in the theatre, and his lordship's younger brother is an enthusiastic supporter of amateur dramatics. At their Belgravia town house, they stage their own Christmas panto, with Roberts sometimes playing an ugly sister role. We try hard to suppress a smile.

West End overview

Roberts gives us a quick survey of London's West End after the war. During the great influenza epidemic of 1918–19, which killed more people that the war, some audience members arrive at the theatre with their noses and mouths bandaged to prevent them catching the infection. There's an air of panic, and buses, theatres and cinemas are sprayed with disinfectant. Any sneeze causes concern. 'But,' says Roberts, 'some people respond with grim humour: at the Savoy, there's a new cocktail called the Corpse Reviver.' After the epidemic abates, commercial theatre in the 1920s thrives once more, but the larger-than-life actor managers of the halcyon Edwardian era are dying out, and by the mid-1920s, Gerald du Maurier is the only surviving actor-manager. 'Instead of being run by actor-managers,' Roberts says, 'theatres are being passed down to other family members who have little interest in producing plays.' These owners lease theatres to middle men who re-let them at a profit to managements which run the venues. Theatre becomes an economic investment no different from any

THE CRITIC'S VIEW: WEST END THEATRE

George Ebenezer Morrison, theatre critic of the *Morning Post* and chairman of the Critics Circle, describes West End audiences in 1918:

To millions who rarely or never visited the theatre before, the war had made it a solace almost as familiar as their newspaper or their pipe. In becoming a nation of warriors we may have become also a nation of theatre-goers.

other business — a financial speculation run from an armchair in London's clubland.

During the war, soldiers on leave from the front swelled audiences for light, undemanding entertainment. In general, London theatre in the mid-1920s remains conservative. 'The plays on view are,' says Roberts, 'stories about upper-class people often set in country houses', and he gestures as if to say, 'Like this one.' They are social comedies of manners set in drawing rooms where Bright Young Things might arrive onstage through French windows and announce in cut-glass voices, 'Anyone for tennis?' 'But there are some exceptions,' he says, getting up and taking a volume of the plays of George Bernard Shaw from one of the shelves. His late works, such as *Heartbreak House* and *Saint Joan*, which in 1924 stars a young Sibyl Thorndike, are notable successes. Otherwise, plays by William Somerset Maugham, Frederick Lonsdale, A A Milne and Noël Coward dominate the West End. Maugham's best work — satirical comedies such as *Home and Beauty* (1919) and *Our Betters* (1923); or more serious plays such as *The Letter* (1927), starring the glamorous Gladys Cooper, and his best play, *The Circle* (1921) — present a rather cynical view of marriage. 'But the public like them,' says Roberts.

Favourite genres are thrillers and murder mysteries, once again set in country houses: in 1927 Michael Morton's *Alibi*, an adaptation of Agatha Christie's *The Murder of Roger Ackroyd*, introduces West End audiences to her Belgian detective, Hercule

Poirot. Played by the awkward Charles Laughton with what Roberts, quoting *The Times*, calls a 'weird, sly smile', and directed by Gerald du Maurier, the play is a hit. In 1921, du Maurier adapts H C Sapper McNeile's *Bulldog Drummond*, for the Wyndhams Theatre and plays the title role in this thriller for more than 420 performances. Drummond is an upper-class English gent who finds life uneventful and hankers after the excitement he experienced during the war, so he becomes a private detective. Other plays also explore murder: one of the most popular is *Rope* by novelist Patrick Hamilton, staged at the Ambassadors Theatre in 1929. Set in Mayfair, but based on the Leopold and Loeb case in Chicago,

Gerald du Maurier

Rope is about two university students — Wyndham Brandon and Charles Granillo — who, to demonstrate their intellectual superiority, kill a fellow-student. 'Memorably, if viciously,' says Roberts, 'they invite the family of their victim to eat a cold supper off the chest in which the dead man's body is hidden.' In the end, the gruesome crime is uncovered by Rupert Cadell, their former schoolmaster and mentor in moral matters, and a jaundiced war hero. After this success, Hamilton goes on to write *Gaslight* (1938), a tribute to Victorian melodrama and with a plot in which a husband persecutes his wife until she turns the tables, and exposes him as a murderer. We know of these plays because they are now classic films.

The other notable genre is farce, and this is given a real boost when a series of twelve of them are staged at the Aldwych Theatre from 1923 to 1933. Most are written by Ben Travers, and they usually feature a group of instantly recognizable characters caught

Ben Travers

in an accelerating sequence of preposterous incidents involving misunderstandings, concealments, borrowed clothes and lost trousers. Under the watchful eye of the Lord Chamberlain, and motivated by a desire to please a respectable audience, there is no sex, no adultery and nothing but mild double meanings in the script. 'But the mere threat of sexual impropriety,' says Roberts with a raised eyebrow, 'is enough to titillate the audience.' Travers's work includes *A Cuckoo in the Nest* (1925), *Thark* (1927) and *Plunder* (1928). But his most celebrated is *Rookery Nook* (1926), where a country house is the setting in which a 'young and very pretty girl in pink silken pyjamas', who, having lost her clothes, plays havoc with the men in the house, whether married or not. Add an officious bullying wife, Gertrude, and the comedy escalates. Travers's plays feature the same company of actors, who play similar parts and acquire a loyal following. So Tom Walls is the young hero, Ralph Lynn his raffish friend, Robertson Hare the hen-pecked husband, Mary Brough the eccentric but domineering old lady, and Yvonne Arnaud or Winifred Shotter the young girls. 'The key to these plays,' says Roberts, who has evidently enjoyed them on more than one occasion, 'is to play them with aplomb and deadly seriousness.'

But, as we finish our tea, Roberts's expression turns grave. *Journey's End* by Robert Cedric Sherriff, the best play about the First World War, is making headlines at the moment. Having lost a brother in the conflict, Roberts clearly finds discussing it quite painful. But we help him by telling him that our generation still commemorates the conflict, and that a 2015 film version of the play features some of the best actors of our time. *Journey's End* is originally put on by a private theatre club in 1928, with a very young Laurence Olivier playing Captain Stanhope, and transfers to the Savoy Theatre, where it runs for almost 600 performances. Set in a dugout, in the Western Front trenches near St Quentin, on the eve of the great German offensive of March 1918, in the final year of the conflict, it shows how Captain Stanhope and his fellow upper-class officers endure the stark realities of war. They are all clearly doomed to die. When one of them, Hibbert, tries to report sick, Stanhope just points out: 'They all feel like you do in their hearts, and just go on sticking it because they know it's — it's the only thing a decent man can do.' Based on Sherriff's own experiences during the war, the play has a deeply authentic feel, steering clear of false heroics or exaggerated bravery.

Roberts says that *Journey's End* is not explicitly an anti-war tract, although the implication in the play is that the military top brass are incompetent at managing the fighting. At one point, Stanhope says sarcastically, 'How awfully nice if the brigadier's pleased.' Nor is there any personal animosity towards the German soldiers, who are in the same boat as the Brits. They are seen as 'really quite decent'. Sherriff evokes the war in an unsentimental and honest way, and by doing so breaks your heart. Roberts pauses, takes a deep breath, and continues. The play did not please everyone. The Irish playwright, Sean O'Casey, who wrote his own drama about the war in *The Silver Tassie* (1929), attacks Sherriff's play for turning 'all the mighty, bloodied vulgarity of war foreshortened into a pretty, pleasing picture'. The chat of the officers, according to O'Casey, is like a polite drawing-room comedy. When the officers have tea, it's all a bit too cosy for the Irishman.

'And actually,' Roberts says, 'however misguided this view might be, it is worth taking the Irish playwright seriously.' He was born in Dublin, and grew up a committed socialist. Roberts might not approve of his politics but he does appreciate his playwriting skills. In 1923, O'Casey's play, *The Shadow of a Gunman*, is accepted for performance by W B Yeats at the Abbey Theatre in Dublin. It is staged just after the Irish War of Independence (1919-21), during which Sinn Féin and the Irish Republican Army successfully fought the British Army, resulting in the creation of the Irish Free State in 1922. Set in a Dublin slum tenement, the play evokes the time when British Black and Tan auxiliary forces were terrorising the population. The drama shows how a young poet, Davoren, is mistaken for an IRA gunman on the run. His reputation attracts Minnie Powell, a young woman, who falls for him — with terrible consequences for her. In O'Casey's next play, *Juno and the Paycock* (1924), Johnny, an IRA quartermaster wounded in the war against the British, betrays the commander of his battalion to the Free State soldiers during the ugly civil war that follows independence. Set once again in a Dublin slum, the play shows what happens to Johnny's family when his father Jack, the paycock of the title, is told that he has inherited £2000, although the legacy never materialises. Memorable for his vivid characters — Jack's wife Juno and his crony Joxer — and its picture of poverty and death, the play is sharply critical of empty nationalist rhetoric.

The same is true of the last of the Dublin Trilogy, *The Plough and the Stars* (1926), one act of which is set in a pub where an offstage Republican makes a speech extolling bloodshed as 'a cleansing and a sanctifying thing' while onstage a prostitute complains that political meetings are bad for business.

> Sean O'Casey's *The Plough and the Stars* (1926)
> *Rosie the prostitute complains of the lack of business:*
> **BARMAN** *(Wiping counter.)* Nothin' much doin' in your line tonight, Rosie?
> **ROSIE** Curse o' God on th' haporth, hardly, Tom. There isn't much notice taken of a pretty petticoat of a night like this... They're all in a holy mood. Th' solemn-lookin' dials on th' whole o' them an' they marchin' to th' meetin'. You'd think they were th' glorious company of th' saints, an' th' noble army of martyrs thrampin' through th' sthreets of paradise. They're all thinkin' of higher things than a girl's garthers.

Then a brawl breaks out and the Irish tricolour, as well as the Plough and the Stars (flag of the Republican movement), are brought onstage. At its first performance, this scene precipitates riots, as Republicans in the audience protest against such a disrespectful view of their movement. Yeats has to come on stage and try to calm the rioters. In general, Roberts sums up, O'Casey is noted for his sympathetic and realistic treatment of ordinary people, especially his characterisation of strong women, and his ability to create a rounded picture of life.

When Yeats rejects *The Silver Tassie*, O'Casey's expressionistic play about the First World War, complaining that it is not based on experience, O'Casey gets it produced at the Apollo in London, designed by artist Augustus John and starring Charles Laughton. But such serious plays are rare in the West End. As James Agate, theatre critic of *The Sunday Times*, writes: 'A large part of the London theatre is given up to plays about dope fiends and jazz maniacs; other large tracts are abandoned to the inanities of musical comedy.' But now it's time to go and, as we leave this stately pile and head back to London, there's the sound of a gramophone coming from an upstairs room. We can hear the distinctive sound of Noël Coward singing 'The Stately Homes of England'.

Cowardy custard

The next day, during the afternoon, Roberts takes us to the finest hotel in London, the Ritz in Piccadilly. It's a French chateau-style building, created by the Swiss hotelier César Ritz, which opened in 1906. Along the front is a rusticated arcade, which is, our guide explains, modelled on the Rue de Rivoli in Paris. We sweep into the hotel, past the doormen in their elegant top hats, spotless uniforms and white braid. Then, horror of horrors, our trainers are spotted by the vigilant staff and the way is barred. Luckily, Roberts is ahead of the game. He opens his capacious bag, producing two pairs of perfect shoes in the right size. Phew, we can proceed! He's a star. We head for the Palm Court. Wow: it is a cream-coloured, opulent Louis XVI interior, with gilded mirrors, magnificent crystal chandeliers and acres of starched white table-cloths and silver. We will be taking tea here, while Roberts introduces us to the life and work of Noël Coward, a regular guest, a member of the glitterati and the West End's brightest and wittiest new star.

Noël Coward

Born into a background that can be described as one of genteel suburban poverty ('Much like my own,' says Roberts), Coward soon discovers that he has, in his own words, 'a talent to amuse'. He takes dancing lessons, he sings and, at the age of eleven, makes his professional debut in the role of Prince Mussel in *The Goldfish*, a children's play. Later, Coward's career gets a leg up from André Charlot, the Paris-born impresario and manager of the Alhambra music hall. But their relationship begins badly. Charlot auditions Coward in 1917, and then tells the person who introduced them: 'He plays the piano badly and sings worse. Kindly do not waste my time with people like that ever again.' But the following year he buys one of Coward's songs, 'Peter Pan', for *Tails Up!*, a revue at the Comedy Theatre in London. In 1921, Coward visits New York and drinks deep of the style and energy of Broadway shows. Once back home he injects this dynamism into the staid British drama to create a high-octane rush for the jazz-mad, dance-crazy 1920s. In 1923 Charlot sees the light and stages *London Calling!*, a musical revue at the Duke of York's Theatre. It is Coward's first musical and includes the song 'Parisian Pierrot', his first big hit. It is sung by Gertrude Lawrence, an all-round performer and his friend. His collaboration with Gertie, as she is known, will last until her death in 1952. By the early 1920s, Coward is a one-man theatre-machine, showing off shamelessly and frenetically writing dozens of songs, sketches and parodies.

His breakthrough play is *The Vortex*, which is first performed in 1924 at the small Everyman Theatre in north London, which today hosts the Everyman Cinema. Set in the apartment of Mrs Florence Lancaster, the play provocatively, if melodramatically,

NOËL COWARD

Born: 16 December 1899, Teddington, London.

Family: Father Arthur, piano salesman, and mother Violet, theatrical lady.

Education: Chapel Royal Choir Society.

Private life: Homosexual but discrete. After his relationship at the age of fourteen with bohemian artist Philip Streatfeild, Coward's most important relationship — with the South African actor Graham Payn — begins in the mid-1940s and lasts until his death. In 1948, Coward settles in Jamaica.

Career: Actor, singer, lyricist, composer, playwright. The controversy over *The Vortex* (1924) makes him an overnight sensation. Coward follows this with a series of light comedies, often with his stage partner Gertrude Lawrence. Total of some 140 shows. Plus operetta *Bitter Sweet* (1929) and pageant *Cavalcade* (1931). Also prolific writer of popular songs. Knighted in 1970.

Greatest hits: *The Vortex* (1924), *Hay Fever* (1925), *Private Lives* (1930), *Design for Living* (1932), *Blithe Spirit* (1941), *Present Laughter* (1942).

Scandal: Portrait of drug addict in *The Vortex*.

Death: 26 March 1973, Port Maria, Jamaica.

Epitaph: 'He died as he had lived: with no self-pity and a ruthless instinct for the quick curtain' (*Guardian*).

Afterlife: Wrote the greatest comedies of the twentieth century.

examines the themes of sexual compulsion and drug addiction. Florence is an ageing society beauty, who openly takes beautiful young lovers half her age. Her son Nicky returns from Paris with his fiancée Bunty, and an addiction to cocaine. When Bunty runs off with Florence's latest lover, mother and son hammer out their differences in a dark night of the soul, an episode which is a modern version of the closet scene in *Hamlet*. What begins as a frothy comedy turns into an anguished drama as Florence throws her son's cocaine box out of the window and Nicky sweeps her make-up jars, pots of rouge and hair-brushes off her dressing table.

He finally tells her: 'You're going to be my mother for once — it's about time I had one before I go over the edge altogether.' Both agree to mend their ways. The image of the wayward mother, Roberts notes, becomes something of a motif in Coward's work — and you don't have to be a follower of Sigmund Freud to appreciate that this reflects the playwright's own feelings about his mother.

Coward writes the role of Nicky for himself: Roberts says that he has heard gossip that his main motive for writing plays is to give himself 'good fat parts'. Lilian Braithwaite is Florence (she is drafted in during the last week of rehearsals when the original actress quits after Coward cuts some of her lines). The play is a sensation, shocking audiences with its frank portrayal of sexual desire and drug abuse. As he performs the role of Nicky in a nervy and hectic way, Coward also plays up to the image of decadence that the play suggests. In one publicity photograph, he is shown lying in bed — with the caption saying he is working! Despite the play's edginess, it has a rather conventional morality, summed up by the line: 'It's the fault of circumstance and civilization', followed by the bleak despair of 'How can we help ourselves? We swirl about in a vortex of beastliness.' 'As the play transfers to the West End, some of its catchphrases become common currency,' says Roberts, 'among his lordship's daughter's friends.' Annabel and her set spend half their time saying things such as 'Too thrilling for words!', 'How perfectly marvellous!', 'Divine!'

From now on, Coward dominates the West End stage, as actor, singer, lyricist, composer and playwright. He cultivates his image of chic sophistication, with a debonair appearance, well groomed and beautifully dressed, and frequently seen at all the best London venues. Gradually, he accumulates a following of fans, who imitate his dress, wearing the same scarves and repeating his witty Noëlisms. His songs become bestsellers on the new gramophone records: 'A Room with a View', 'I'll See You Again', 'Mad Dogs and Englishmen', 'Don't Put Your Daughter on the Stage, Mrs Worthington'. Idolized by the youth of high society, his public persona exemplifies the self-indulgent pursuit of hedonism of the 1920s. We get the impression that Roberts doesn't really approve of such blatant decadence.

Reeling from the scandal that *The Vortex* causes, and realising that its style is a bit too melodramatic, Coward turns to comedy. A prolific playwright, he works fast, dashing off *Hay Fever* over one weekend. Set in the hall of a country house, home of the Bliss family, the play is based on Coward's experience of being a guest of the highly strung and theatrical Manners family in New York. It features Judith Bliss, an ageing actress who — like Florence in *The Vortex* — is vain and has a penchant for young men. She, her writer husband David, son Simon and daughter Sorel each invite a guest to stay for the weekend. But when the guests arrive in the first act, the Blisses — who are selfish and self-absorbed — snub or insult each other's guests. In the second act the family plays a version of the game of charades, called 'adverbs', requiring the guests to act out various given words. Needless to say, the Blisses are good at role play while their guests get more and more humiliated. When the guests sneak away in the third act, set on the following morning, David, who is unaware of their hurt feelings, says, 'People really do behave in the most extraordinary manner these days.' The family is left quarreling over the Parisian street names in David's latest novel. Nothing can ruffle their blissful self-absorption.

The first production of *Hay Fever* opens at the Ambassadors Theatre in June 1925, with star actress Marie Tempest as Judith, and is an immediate hit. Although it has not much plot, points out Roberts, it is full of language games in which clichés are parodied and the emptiness of the characters exposed. Judith is first seen attempting to learn the names of flowers in her garden by heart as if words will make up for her ignorance of country life. From the banal — 'Spain is very beautiful' — to the baroque — 'I always longed to leave the brittle glamour of cities and find rest in some old-world nook' — the language of the play is its chief delight. And so is its humour. When Judith says, 'You can see as far as Marlow on a clear day', there's a pause before she adds, 'so they tell me.' As if she's never looked out of her own window. But the key line is Sorel's 'We none of us mean anything'.

As a chamber orchestra begins to play in the Palm Court corner, Roberts tells us about *Private Lives*, Coward's masterpiece, which he writes during one of his world tours. At the Imperial Hotel in Tokyo, during one sleepless night, he has a vision of actress

Gertrude Lawrence in a white Molyneux dress and by 4am he has constructed the play, title and all. A few weeks later, in Shanghai, recovering from flu, he writes it. At his bedside is a small golden Cartier book, which opens to reveal clock, calendar and a picture of Gertie, who has given him this present to remind him of his promise to write a play for her. With *Private Lives*, he delivers triumphantly on this promise. It is a beautifully symmetrical play with four characters, two couples, and three tight acts. Act One opens on a double balcony of a hotel in the South of France. Elyot and his new young wife Sibyl are on their honeymoon. It is his second marriage, and it soon emerges that his first wife, Amanda, is staying in the adjacent room, with her new husband Victor. Both Elyot and Amanda are appalled and want to leave immediately, although they don't tell their new spouses why. When Elyot and Amanda hear the orchestra play a tune they both once loved, Elyot says longingly, 'Strange how potent cheap music is', and it is clear that they are still passionately attracted to each other. So much so that they leave their new spouses and run off to Paris together. In Act Two, they are in Amanda's Parisian flat, clearly in love but also full of recriminations. As they start to fight physically, falling to the floor, Victor and Sibyl arrive. In Act Three, the following morning, the two couples are forced to speak to each other. More recriminations. But as Victor and Sibyl — who have grown closer in the absence of their spouses — begin to argue, Elyot and Amanda quietly leave. They can't live apart, but can't live together either.

First staged at the Phoenix Theatre in the West End in September 1930, with Coward both directing and playing Elyot, *Private Lives* also features Gertie as Amanda and the young Laurence Olivier as Victor. Coward's stage persona, with his silk polka-dot dressing gown, elegant cigarette holder and clipped voice, becomes iconic. Roberts shares a story about the opening night. When the *grande dame* of theatre Mrs Patrick Campbell goes backstage, she says, 'Don't you just love it when Noël does his little hummings at the piano?' Despite mixed reviews, the play is popular and goes to Broadway the following year. 'Its British staging,' says Roberts, 'attracts the attention of the Lord Chamberlain, who is not amused by some of the frank talk about sex in Act Two, and the play is daring for its time in its satirical attitudes to marriage, divorce and remarriage.' The show includes one of his most popular songs, 'Some Day I'll Find You'. The dialogue is fast and alternates between wit and seriousness, with the occasional paradox thrown in. At one point, Elyot tells Amanda that his enemies are 'All the futile moralists who try to make life unbearable'. He advises her to: 'Laugh at them. Be flippant. Laugh at everything, all their sacred shibboleths. Flippancy brings out the acid in their damned sweetness and light.' This praise of frivolity captures the spirit of the Bright Young Things even as the 1920s turn into the darker 1930s, with the clouds of war approaching. Yet it's not a play to be po-faced about — the best thing is to yield to its pleasures.

Noël Coward's *Private Lives* (1930)

Amanda and Elyot discuss their new spouses:

AMANDA Have you known her long?

ELYOT About four months, we met in a house party in Norfolk.

AMANDA Very flat, Norfolk.

ELYOT How old is dear Victor?

AMANDA Thirty-four, or five; and Sibyl?

ELYIT I blush to tell you, only twenty-three.

AMANDA You've gone a mucker alright.

ELYOT I shall reserve my opinion of your choice until I've met dear Victor.

AMANDA I wish you wouldn't go on calling him 'Dear Victor'. It's extremely irritating.

ELYOT That's how I see him. Dumpy, and fair, and very considerate, with glasses. Dear Victor.

AMANDA As I said before I would rather not discuss him. At least I have good taste enough to refrain from making cheap gibes at Sybil.

ELYOT You said Norfolk was flat.

AMANDA That is no reflection on her, unless she made it flatter.

ELYOT Your voice takes on an acid quality whenever you mention her name.

AMANDA I'll never mention it again.

ELYOT Good, and I'll keep off Victor.

Coward writes not only comedies, but also a handful of serious plays. Chief among them is *Cavalcade*, a patriotic pageant staged in 1931 at the Theatre Royal Drury Lane in London. This spectacular epic spans the first three decades of the twentieth century — including the Relief of Mafeking and the sinking of the *Titanic* — as seen through the eyes of one family. Its success confirms that Coward the boy wonder has become the Master, not only supremely talented, but also the highest earning author in Britain. Yet while Roberts admires this huge spectacle, and tells us that its strongly patriotic flavour helped Stanley Baldwin's Conservatives win the General Election of 1931, he is a bit more cautious about Coward's *Design for Living* (1933). This is a study of a *ménage a trois*: Gilda, Otto and Leo live and love together until Gilda marries Ernest. But this doesn't work, and she ends up living with Otto and Leo again. Conventional morality is scorned: what matters is honesty of feeling and real affection. The enemy is hypocrisy. Laughter dissolves human chains; moralism binds. 'His moral daring injects an energy into Coward's work which makes it fizz with ideas, even if one can't always agree with them,' says Roberts, raising an eyebrow. Coward has a good war, and his comedy *Blithe Spirit* (1941) makes a star of redoubtable Margaret Rutherford as the scatty medium Madam Arcarti. In *Present Laughter* (1942) the classic Coward character is Gary Essendine, a temperamental actor who is selfish, maddening but attractive because of his intelligence and lust for life. A pain to live with, but painful to live without. Other war hits include the song 'Don't Let's Be Beastly to the Germans' and the script of David Lean's classic film *Brief Encounter* (1945). 'If Coward slips out of fashion in the 1950s,' says Roberts, 'at least he had a jolly good run.'

The bard is back

The next day, we are crossing the concourse of Waterloo Station during the morning rush hour, and the hustle and bustle of the station feels familiar, as does the noise and smell of the diesel trains, the crush of the commuters. Despite the mass unemployment that follows the Great Crash of 1929, when stock markets all over the world collapse catastrophically, the civil servants, secretaries and office staff in London still hang onto their jobs, and the rush hour is as hectic as ever. Striding confidently through the crowds, and using his elbows to good effect, Roberts leads us across the station and the traffic-filled road to the Old Vic, one of the most important theatrical venues of 1930s London.

We are in the lobby now, and as we look at the Victorian interior with its faded decoration, Roberts outlines its recent history. Since the death of the philanthropist Emma Cons in 1912, the theatre has been run by Lilian Baylis. Born into a family of musical performers, she is a dynamic woman who wears

Lilian Baylis

large round glasses and has a reputation for being an eccentric. She is also a devout Anglican with a social conscience. But she is certainly not humourless. Roberts says that she is famous for her prayer: 'Dear God, send me good actors, but send them cheap.' When her staff ask for a pay rise, Baylis says that she has to ask God, and invariably comes back with the reply: 'Sorry, dear, God says no.' The conditions inside the Old Vic are poor: the seats are wooden benches, the floor is sprinkled with sawdust, there are no proper dressing rooms for the actors and the scenery and lighting are primitive. Until 1927, the front part of the theatre — where we are standing — was a temperance restaurant, called Pearce and Plenty, a large, high steamy room with a long counter holding a large tea urn.

Baylis's unique selling point is Shakespeare. In the decade ending in 1923, she manages to produce every single one of the bard's plays — a mammoth task. But sometimes audiences are tiny: Sibyl Thorndike recalls playing Lady Macbeth to barely a dozen spectators. Baylis's mission is to provide for 'the crying need of working men and women who want to see beyond the four walls of their offices, workshops and homes into a world of awe and wonder'. And so she keeps prices low (seats cost the same as a pint of beer) — she wants the local population of Southwark to enjoy the best of culture. Her audience is mainly ordinary lower-middle-class people — clerks, typists and shopworkers — and is an important part of the atmosphere of the Old Vic. Similarly characteristic are the school matinees, organised through the London City Council, when many kids get their first taste of Shakespeare. Their teachers are also regular patrons. But with the Depression and wage cuts, many teachers stop coming. What's so impressive about Baylis is her energy and ambition. In 1925, she leads a campaign to rebuild the then-derelict Sadler's Wells theatre. Three years later, she employs Ninette de Valois, who sets up a ballet group which will become the Royal Ballet in 1956. By 1931, the Vic-Wells companies use both venues. When, in that year, she is involved in a car accident and is lying seriously injured, some witnesses recognise her: 'It's Miss Baylis. Miss Baylis of the Old Vic.' Despite her injuries, the indomitable Baylis corrects them: 'And Sadler's Wells,' she shouts. Today we are grateful for her shrewd programming of ballet, dance and opera which laid the foundations for both the English National Opera and the National Theatre.

Laurence Olivier

Baylis's great gift to British theatre is her willingness to invite the best of a new generation of directors and actors to work with her. Director Harcourt Williams, for example, takes up the torch of Harley Granville Barker and Edward Gordon Craig by using simple and bold designs, breaking once and for all with the fussiness of Edwardian staging. What's more, his opening production of *Romeo and Juliet* in 1929 stars young actors John Gielgud and Peggy Ashcroft, and features fast verse speaking and quick scene changes. 'This,' says Roberts, 'is the most memorable Shakespeare performance of the age — lyrical, intense, passionate.' Gone are the ponderous declamations of old: in comes fleet-footed wordplay. Gielgud not only emerges as the most alluring verse speaker of his generation, the Voice Beautiful caressing words as if seducing them, but he also accepts wages of £10 a week, a fifth of what he could get in the West End. And he is not alone. Soon after his arrival, he is joined by Laurence Olivier, Vivien Leigh and Flora Robson. The names of others who cross Waterloo Bridge for a chance to play Shakespeare reads like a *Who's Who* of twentieth-century acting: Ralph Richardson, Edith Evans, Michael Redgrave, Alec Guinness and James Mason. Gradually the rivalry between Gielgud (cerebral, precise, mellifluous) and Olivier (physical, rougher, earthy) develops, especially when they alternate roles in the same play (Romeo and Mercutio in *Romeo and Juliet*). In 1932, Williams invites Gielgud to direct *The Merchant of Venice*, and his success establishes him as a major director. He teams up with Motley — an all-female design team — and they create a style of Shakespearean production which lasts well into the 1950s. Turning financial weakness into visual strength, Motley productions recycle rags, rope and hessian to make striking costumes and create an elegant, but inexpensive, *mise-en-scène* that is distinctly modern.

In 1933, Baylis invites Tyrone Guthrie — the great-grandson of the Irish actor Tyrone Power and cousin of the Hollywood actor of the same name — to direct at the Old Vic. Guthrie is a follower of Sigmund Freud and his Shakespeare productions are noted for their emotional realism. When he stages *Macbeth*, casting the deliberately unglamorous Charles Laughton and Flora Robson in the main roles, he cuts the witches from Scene One and concentrates on the psychology of the Macbeths. He then casts Olivier — an up-and-coming golden boy — as Romeo, the start of his long rivalry with Gielgud. Roberts clears his throat, before muttering that Guthrie introduces sexual motivation into Shakespeare. Our guide clearly doesn't approve; what's the point of it? In 1933, Guthrie's *Measure for Measure* stars Laughton as a creepy Angelo and emphasizes both Angelo's desire and Isabella's sexuality. At another point, the actor Emlyn Williams plays Richard III as a psychologically disturbed sovereign who almost swoons with ecstasy at each new murder. Soon after, Olivier's 1937 Hamlet is played with renewed attention to the Oedipus Complex and becomes the most famous Freudian performance of the century. By now, the Old Vic is the most important theatre in the land.

Back in the West End, with a couple of exceptions such as Gielgud's transfer of his *Romeo and Juliet* in 1935 from the Old Vic, Shakespeare's plays virtually disappear. The most significant commercial Shakespeare production is *Othello*, starring the black American actor Paul Robeson, at the Savoy in 1930. Son of a runaway slave, Robeson is an international star: lawyer, athlete, singer, actor and civil rights campaigner. He is the first black actor to play Othello in London since Ira Aldridge in 1825. A couple of years earlier, Robeson had captured London's heart with a sell-out performance singing 'Ol' Man River' in Jerome Kern's barnstorming musical *Show Boat*. But when he tries to tackle Shakespeare, the press reaction is hostile, if not downright racist. His Desdemona is Peggy Ashcroft, and she is asked if she minds being kissed by 'a coloured man'. Her reply: 'I look on it as a privilege to act with a great artist like Paul Robeson.'

Outside London, by contrast, the bard is thriving. When the Shakespeare Memorial Theatre in Stratford-upon-Avon burns down in 1926, it is replaced by a new modern building, designed by Elizabeth Scott, which is opened on Shakespeare's birthday (23 April) in 1932 by the Prince of Wales (the future King Edward VIII, who will abdicate four years later in order to marry the divorced American socialite Wallis Simpson) and former Prime Minister Stanley Baldwin. From the start, this new Shakespeare Memorial Theatre is 'a symbol of patriotism,' says Roberts with a hint of quiet pride in his voice. Despite the celebrations, which include a radio broadcast by the BBC of the Stratford *Richard II*, the new venue is not without its problems. It has a badly designed proscenium stage, with a large orchestra pit that hampers all contact between the actors and the audience. The circle and gallery look like a cinema and most of the cheaper seats are miles away from the action.

But Stratford does attract talent. Norman Wilkinson, a maverick director with a drink problem caused by shell-shock, comes out of retirement to produce *A Midsummer Night's Dream*. Having previously worked on the same play for Harley Granville Barker in 1914, he designs scenes that combine historical costumes with modernistic settings. By contrast, the migrant Russian director Theodore Komisarjevsky, one of the most colourful figures in European theatre, makes his actors move like clockwork toys in plays such as *The Merchant of Venice* and *The Taming of the Shrew*. Drained of all emotion, they seem like puppets in the hands of destiny. Other talents that are attracted to Stratford include the craggy faced Donald Wolfit, who plays Hamlet in 1936. He tries to persuade the governors to finance a tour of the play around Britain. When they say no, he cashes in his own savings and begins a life of Shakespearean peregrinations, becoming one of the last great touring actor-managers. Roberts says that he has heard that the actress Hermione Gingold made this comment: 'Olivier is a tour-de-force, and Wolfit is forced to tour.' Meanwhile, at the Birmingham Rep, Barry Jackson continues with his modern-dress Shakespeare, most famously his *Hamlet*, with the cast in plus-fours. At the same time, the wealthy Terence Gray runs the Cambridge Festival Theatre. Inspired by Gordon Craig, Gray mocks the reverence of most Shakespearean productions by introducing human touches: in his *Merchant of Venice* the nobles, instead of listening to Portia's great 'Quality of mercy' speech, yawn and play with a yo-yo. Yes, concludes our guide, director's Shakespeare has well and truly arrived.

Taking a stand

In the aftermath of the 1917 Russian Revolution, many idealistic young people in Britain begin to see the light. After the Crash of 1929, during the Depression of the 1930s, young militants join the Communist Party of Great Britain, believing that they can create a more just and equitable society, while others, more pragmatically inclined, swell the ranks of the Labour Party. This is the era that the poet Wystan Hugh Auden (who also writes plays, such as the Expressionist-style *Dance of Death* of 1934) calls 'a low dishonest decade', a time of mass unemployment and hunger marches, the struggle against fascism in Spain and the rise of Benito Mussolini in Italy, Adolf Hitler in Germany and Oswald Mosley's Blackshirts in Britain. Economic crisis and the appeasement of European dictators gives an urgency to the leftwing cause.

In the theatre, this agitation for social justice is exemplified, in the years 1926 to 1935, by the formation of the Workers Theatre Movement. The WTM attracts young Communist Party members, white-collar workers in the south of England and proletarians in the north, who take theatre to the streets, using an agitprop style of songs and short sketches akin to music hall. Other political companies include the Salford-based Red Megaphones and the Hackney People's Players. In 1932, the Group Theatre is set up, dedicated to socialist total theatre (their plays include Auden and Christopher Isherwood's co-written 1937 verse play, *The Ascent of F6*). All around the country, young people turn up with a flatbed truck at the factory gates and perform short agitprop plays for the workers. Sternly setting themselves against what they see as middle-class theatre, they want to create a more physical theatre that reflects workers' concerns in the machine age. Popular plays are German leftwing playwright Ernst Toller's *Masses and Men* and *The Machine Wreckers*, as well as Karel Capek's futuristic nightmare *RUR*, which shows how machines are used to replace the working class. The play gives the word robot to the English language.

Other theatres take a radical approach to staging challenging work. A handful of small club theatres, including London venues such as the Everyman, the Gate, the Arts and the Embassy, as well as independent producing companies such as the Stage Society, the Pioneer Players, the Three Hundred Club and the Venturers, put on work of high quality which is ignored by commercial managements because it is too difficult, or too foreign. They put on stage playwrights such as Henrik Ibsen and Anton Chekhov, and any writer banned by the Lord Chamberlain. Because of unrest at the time of the General Strike, the Lord Chamberlain is vigilant not only about sex, but also about class. He refuses a licence to Strindberg's *Miss Julie* in 1925 because he thinks that its theme of sex between a lady and her servant is unsuitable at a time of 'growing tensions between masters and servants'. But some radicals are popular: *Our Ostriches*, about the plight of working-class women whose lives are blighted by continuous pregnancies, is written by contraception campaigner Marie Stopes, and runs for 91 performances at the Court in 1923. Generally, this is a time of great ferment, and in 1929 the Actors' Union is renamed Actors' Equity and it improves its ability to get better pay and conditions for members of the profession. Even in the West End a handful of plays, such as Ronald Gow and Walter Greenwood's *Love on the Dole* in 1935, examine the effects of the Depression on ordinary people. At the same time, the economic downturn means that — apart from the flamboyant musicals of Ivor Novello, such as *Glamorous Night* (1935) at the Theatre Royal Drury Lane — the lavish stagings of yesteryear are gone for ever.

In London, the Unity Theatre is formed in February 1936. An offshoot of the Workers Theatre Movement, Unity is first based in St Jude's Hall in King's Cross and then moves to an old chapel in Goldington Street, where its members convert the building. Its aim is to 'to foster and further the art of drama in accordance with the principle that true art, by effectively presenting and truthfully interpreting life as experienced by the majority of people, can move the people to work for the betterment of society', and thus stages plays on social and political issues. It is so successful that more than a dozen other Unity theatres are set up in places like Bristol, Glasgow, Sheffield and Merseyside. London Unity's 1938 production of *Waiting for Lefty* by American writer Clifford Odets is a landmark in the history of leftwing theatre in Britain. In it, a group of New York cabbies meet to discuss taking strike action 'to get a living wage'. While the cabbies wait for their leader, Lefty Costello, they tell their stories in rapid, realistic scenes. The play ends with the news that Lefty has been shot, and this provokes full support for the strike. The actors speak directly to audience members as if they were at the meeting. This breaking down of the barrier between actors and audience is a feature of Unity's style. Sympathetic audiences join in with the thrilling chant of 'Strike, strike, strike'. Unity also pioneers new forms of documentary theatre, the Living Newspaper and satirical pantomimes, as well as introducing new writers. In 1938, it produces the first play by radical German director and theorist Bertolt Brecht in Britain: *Señora Carrar's Rifles*. And it premieres Sean O'Casey's *The Star*

Turns Red (1940), a four-act antifascist play in which the star of Bethlehem turns red.

Another red star makes an appearance during this time. John Boynton Priestley is a plump, pipe-smoking Yorkshireman who doesn't suffer fools gladly, and who is more than prepared to support the underdog. A novelist and journalist, he is a socialist who in the 1930s writes a series of stage plays which combine a firm moral stance, radical new ideas about time while simultaneously using traditional English settings. Priestley not only writes dramas full of radical ideas, but also acts independently to make his message heard. At one point, he leases a West End theatre, the newly built Duchess (one of the few new theatres built in London between the wars), and stages his own plays there.

Priestley is a great educator. He is not afraid of ideas, and is influenced by both the philosophical books of the mathematician John William Dunne, who argues that the past, present and future can co-exist on the same temporal plane, and of the Russian esoteric mystic Peter Demianovich Ouspensky, who speculates that there are an infinite number of possible alternative time sequences. Armed with these ideas, Priestley writes a handful of time plays, such as *Dangerous Corner* (1932), *Time and the Conways* (1937) and *I Have Been Here Before* (1937). *Dangerous Corner* is about three couples at a dinner party, listening to a radio play about the need to tell the truth — whatever the consequences. While they discuss this, their own secrets emerge. As a result one of them commits suicide; then events are replayed, but instead of the fatal discussion the three couples dance to radio music and tragedy is avoided. In *Time and the Conways*, the Conway family is shown in 1919, 1937 and then in 1919 again. The play illustrates how the postwar hopes of 1919 are disappointed by 1937; the third act is a re-run of the first, but 1919 is now viewed through the irony of knowing how things will turn out. In *I Have Been Here Before*, Priestley introduces the mysteriously foreign Dr Gortler, who performs experiments in which past, present and future are linked in a fourth dimension — and in so doing he manages to avert a tragedy. With his time plays, Priestley makes difficult concepts accessible to a wider public, while at the same time lecturing them about shared moral responsibility. This is evident also in his state-of-the-nation BBC radio series, *Postscripts*, which starting in 1940 builds up a huge wartime following. His concern with the condition of Britain is also apparent in the most popular of his time plays, *An Inspector Calls*.

An Inspector Calls opens in the home of the Birlings, a prosperous middle-class family who live in a northern industrial town, in 1912. They are celebrating their daughter Sheila's engagement to Gerald Croft, whose father — like her own — is a wealthy manufacturer, when a mysterious Inspector Goole arrives, with the news that Eva Smith, a young working-class woman, has committed suicide 'in great agony' after swallowing disinfectant. It is gradually revealed that she was connected in different ways to every member of the family. As events unfold, the Inspector proves that each of them was partly responsible for her death. Mr Birling sacked her for helping to organise a strike; Sheila got her fired from her next job as a store assistant; Croft found her in a bar and set her up as his mistress, then left her; Eric, Sheila's brother, picked her up and made her pregnant; and Mrs Birling rejected her application for help to the charitable society she runs. Near the play's end, Goole argues that 'It would do us all a bit of good if sometimes we tried to put ourselves in the place of these young women counting their pennies in their dingy back bedrooms', then delivers a speech about social responsibility, and leaves.

J B Priestley's *An Inspector Calls* (1945)

The Inspector takes his leave:

INSPECTOR But just remember this. One Eva Smith is gone — but there are millions and millions and millions of Eva Smiths and John Smiths still left with us, with their lives, their hopes and fears, their suffering, and chance of happiness, all intertwined with our lives, with what we think and say and do. We don't live alone. We are members of one body. We are responsible for each other. And I tell you that the time will soon come when, if men will not learn that lesson, then they will be taught it in fire and blood and anguish. Good night. *(He walks straight out.)*

When he's gone, the family discuss his visit and soon establish that there is no Goole working for the local police. It was all a hoax! While the older Mr and Mrs Birling carry on in their old complacent, hypocritical ways, the Inspector's visit provokes a crisis of conscience in Sheila and Eric, who embrace change. They have learnt that personal decisions have public consequences. Then the phone rings. A young woman has indeed committed suicide and a police inspector is on his way to interrogate the family. The curtain falls as they 'stare guiltily and dumbfounded'.

An Inspector Calls is first staged in Moscow in 1945, at a time when the Soviet Union is an ally of Britain's in the fight to defeat Nazi Germany, because there are no London theatres free at the time. A year later, its first London production at the New Theatre stars Alec Guinness and Ralph Richardson. It is then filmed by Guy Hamilton for British Lion in 1954. The play's plot combines Priestley's plea for justice and equality with his obsessive interest in theories about the circularity of time. It is also a fine example of how he uses the traditional model of the three-act play to draw people into the story. In Priestley's 'Introduction' to his collected plays, he explains that he sets his dramas in respectable sitting rooms as a way of persuading people that they are watching a real story — once they are hooked, he regales them with his moral message. By setting his play in 1912, he is able to make some satirical points about Edwardian complacency: two years before the outbreak of the First World War, old man Birling declares that: 'There will be no war. Scientific progress makes it impossible. Why, look at the new liner, the *Titanic* — unsinkable, absolutely unsinkable!' In the future, he blusters, there will be neither wars nor strikes. Audiences listening to this tirade, just after the end of the Second World War, must have condemned him utterly.

War and peace

It's a dark February afternoon during the Blitz in 1941 and as we walk behind Roberts through London's West End, we can see the signs of war — piles of rubble, sandbagged shops and 'Business as usual' signs. All in all, over a period of 270 days the capital is attacked some seventy-one times, with about 22,000 civilian deaths. All over the West End, theatres have been hit by bombs — the Old Vic, Duke of York's, Queen's and the Royal Court (formerly the Court). There's a smell of smoke, charred timbers, gas leaks and chemicals from high explosives. 'Yet,' says Roberts, pausing on one corner in Shaftesbury Avenue, 'despite all this the Blitz spirit is alive in theatreland.' Several venues remain open, and Noël Coward's hit *Blithe Spirit* remains immensely popular, notching up 1700 performances by July 1945. Roberts points out that this is a comedy, with a dark side, dealing as it does with death, which is on the mind of every member of the audience. Then, as we come around the corner to Leicester Square station we see an orderly queue of people standing in a line outside. At 4pm, our guide explains, they will be allowed to come in and use the tube station as a bomb shelter. Ever since the previous September, when the Blitz began, some 100,000 people every night have used stations across London for this purpose. He takes us down, and we end up in the corner of a platform. After we manage to settle in, with some blankets and a flask of tea, Roberts outlines the effects of war on the theatre.

War leads to a big surge of interest in the arts. In the years 1939–45 the arts in general and theatre in particular are used to help boost morale. The government sets up the military Entertainments National Service Association (ENSA) and the civilian Council for the Encouragement of Music and Arts (CEMA) to provide both education and entertainment. Funded by the state, these bodies put on theatre, opera and ballet performances in both army camps and civilian venues all over the country. Likewise, the Army Bureau of Current Affairs (founded in 1941 to help educate the troops) sets up a Play Unit in 1943. In its first six months it produces fifty-eight shows, seen by 20,000 troops. Plays tend to be patriotic agitprop documentaries with titles such as *United We Stand*, as well as work such as J B Priestley's *Desert Highway*, a celebration of the country's hopes and fears for the future.

CEMA organizes no fewer than sixteen touring productions, reaching towns and villages that have never before seen a Shakespeare play or an opera. Sybil Thorndike and her husband Lewis Casson tour the mining villages of Wales performing Shakespeare and Greek tragedies, and the Sadler's Wells Ballet, Sadler's Wells Opera and symphony orchestras perform in military camps across the country. CEMA helps set up the Citizens'

Theatre in Glasgow in 1943. Meanwhile, ENSA — an acronym, chuckles Roberts, which cheeky soldiers say stands for Every Night Something Awful — takes over the Theatre Royal Drury Lane as its HQ, and produces shows in every theatre of war around the world. Performers live and work in harsh conditions: often acting in sandstorms in North Africa, snowstorms in Italy, rainstorms in the Pacific, and sometimes close to the front line. There are performances in submarines, on the decks of ships, in aircraft hangers, in halls or on portable stages in the open air.

In London, after the Old Vic is damaged, CEMA helps the venue to create an alternative home at the New Theatre (today the Noël Coward Theatre) in 1944. Here, under the leadership of Laurence Olivier, the company continues its good work, with his Richard III and Ralph Richardson's Falstaff both highpoints. Olivier's film of *Henry V*, released in 1944, proves to be one of the most patriotic and successful films of Shakespeare's work ever made. On a lighter note, the one theatre to stay open every night despite the Blitz is the Windmill in Soho, which boasts: 'We never closed.' Its nightly fare — variety plus nude tableaux — encourages wags to say: 'We never clothed.' We are surprised to see that Roberts allows himself a naughty smile. Elsewhere in the West End serious plays are performed to full houses, and at the Arts Theatre there are four ballet performances a day: Lunch Ballet, After-Lunch Ballet, Tea Ballet and Sherry Ballet, when audiences can eat during the show and then return to work, or their shelters. During the worst of the bombing, theatres prefer to put on matinees rather than evening performances, and when evening shows resume they start at 6pm, rather than the normal 8.30pm of pre-war years, to avoid audiences having to stumble home in the middle of the blackout. Other changes include patrons in the dress circle and stalls abandoning the habit of wearing evening dress, suggesting a 'We are all in it together' attitude. But Roberts does miss the old habits. He spends part of the war as a fire-watcher and has a lot of stories about near-misses. As we suspected, he's a bit of a Tory, so he's not very pleased that the people of Britain reject Winston Churchill, the great war leader, in favour of Clement Attlee's Labour Party, which is elected in a landslide victory in the 1945 General Election. 'To think,' says our guide, 'that back in

May 1945, Churchill's approval rating was 83 per cent. The mind boggles!'

Postwar playwrights

To cheer us up after the dark days of the war, our guide proposes a trip to Royal Ascot one sunny summer afternoon. Ascot is one of Europe's premiere race meetings, and dates back to 1711 when it was founded by Queen Anne. Now in the early 1950s, the Royal Enclosure is full of classy men in top hats and morning suits, and women dressed in the flamboyant fashions of the day: huge hats, elaborate full skirts. Roberts says that the Gold Cup is the big race of the third day, traditionally the busiest and known as Ladies' Day. He also reminds us that the racecourse is the setting for a scene in the Alan Jay Lerner and Frederick Loewe musical *My Fair Lady*, with its 'Ascot Gavotte' that includes the line: 'Everyone who should be here is here.' Roberts hums the tune for us. As we mingle with the fashionable crowd, he points out some stars of postwar theatre. The one that most grabs our attention is an elegantly slim and attractive man with a tight smile and lively eyes, suave in his immaculate grey Savile Row suit. So who is he?

'That's Binkie Beaumont,' says Roberts, '*the* prime mover and shaker of postwar West End theatre.' He heads H M Tennent, one of the companies that have a virtual monopoly of theatre production. Due to numerous buy-outs, the number of managements has shrunk to a small elite group. This cartel is called The Group and is made up of big players such as Emile Littler, Stuart Cruickshank, and of course Binkie. It runs fifteen out of twenty-four of the largest London venues and more than fifty per cent of theatre seats in the country. However, playwrights such as J B Priestley are not happy with this set-up. He complains: 'Theatre at present is not controlled by dramatists, actors, producers or managers, but chiefly by theatre owners, men of property who may or may not have a taste for the drama.' In London, Binkie is king of the West End and his taste rules. His mission is to present the brightest stars in the most alluringly designed classics. So he revives Oscar Wilde's *Lady Windermere's Fan*, with sumptuous sets by fashion photographer Cecil Beaton, and imports American musicals such as Richard Rodgers and Oscar Hammerstein's *Oklahoma!*, staged at the Theatre Royal Drury Lane, which cheer up audiences and dispel postwar gloom. Only occasionally, his productions are controversial. For example, he stages American playwright Tennessee Williams's *A Streetcar Named Desire* at the Aldwych Theatre in 1949, directed by Laurence Olivier and starring his wife Vivien Leigh. The play's emotional rawness scandalizes prim and proper audiences. Roberts quotes one Baroness Ravensdale of the Public Morality Council who says that it's all 'thoroughly indecent and we should be ashamed that children and servants are allowed to sit in the theatre and see it'. But, with Leigh's fragile and yet almost indecently alluring Blanche Dubois, it's a big hit and runs for more than 300 performances.

After pausing to watch his favourite horse running a race, Roberts resumes his account. In the first postwar season of the Old Vic, still at the New Theatre, the athletic Olivier plays the title role in Sophocles's *Oedipus Rex*. Here, his cries of anguish are particularly memorable. The young critic Kenneth Tynan reports, 'The two cries were torn from beyond tears or shame or guilt: they came from the stomach, with all the ecstatic grief and fright of a newborn baby's wail.' One year later, Olivier performs a legendary *King Lear*, whose highpoints are described by Harold Hobson, theatre critic of *The Sunday Times*, as: 'The cries and lamentations, the curses and the threats that are torn out of his breast are like the crash of thunder and the stab of lightning.' When the company returns to the repaired Old Vic building in the 1950s it is with a new generation of actors such as Claire Bloom and Judi Dench.

It's time for refreshment at the Jockey's Club, and while sipping a glass of Pimm's we discuss the merits of a new development in postwar theatre. Championed by John Maynard Keynes, who is an arts lover as well as a world-class economist, the Arts Council — the first body for state funding the arts — takes over from CEMA. Outside London, Arts Council grants help set up the Bristol Old Vic, and aid the creation of new theatres in Guildford, Ipswich, Canterbury and Derby. North of the border, things also look up. In the late 1940s, Glasgow Unity Theatre stages Ena Lamont Stewart's *Men Should Weep* — a story about that city's tenement life in the Depression — and Robert McLeish's *The Gorbals Story*.

The Edinburgh Festival is set up in 1947 and gradually becomes the biggest theatre festival in the world. Meanwhile, at the Shakespeare Memorial Theatre (SMT) in Stratford-upon-Avon, first Barry Jackson and then actor Anthony Quayle lead the institution into the 1950s. Jackson invites the twenty-year-old director Peter Brook and his 1946 version of Shakespeare's *Love's Labours Lost* is playful yet ravishingly beautiful. Stratford adopts the Binkie Beaumont formula, employing the best stars and the most exquisite costumes on the most attractive

Terence Rattigan

sets. Quayle invites Binkie onto the SMT board, and this means that the theatre can employ some of Binkie's stars: Brook's 1949 *Measure for Measure* features John Gielgud as Angelo. Rising actors such as Paul Scofield and Richard Burton also help to reinvigorate Shakespeare.

But by far the finest playwright to emerge from Binkie's stable is Terence Rattigan. Known as Terry to his friends, he is handsome, tall, elegant, always immaculately dressed in a Savile Row suit and often pictured with a cigarette holder. His image is that of a charming, cool Englishman. Yes, a toff. Roberts simply adores him, and says that rumour has it that his Eaton Square flat is furnished with Aubusson rugs, heavy brocade curtains and paintings by Toulouse-Lautrec. Yes, he's successful, and rich with it. After his prewar hit, *French Without Tears* — an elegant light comedy about a group of young people in a language school — runs for more than 1000 performances, Rattigan turns to more serious themes. His *Flare Path* (1942) is based on his wartime experiences in the Royal Air Force, and along with *While the Sun Shines* (1943) and *Love in Idleness* (1944), he has three plays running simultaneously in the West End — a record! After the war,

The Winslow Boy (1946), set during the Edwardian era, examines the real-life case of a naval schoolboy who is wrongly accused of stealing a postal order, while his short play *The Browning Version* (1948) is an immensely sympathetic account of a repressed public-school classics master who finds some inspiration to stand up for himself in a schoolboy's gift of a translation of Aeschylus's *Agamemnon*. His double bill, *Separate Tables* in 1954, looks at the denizens of a small Bournemouth hotel, and one of them features the story of a bogus major who is arrested for molesting women in cinemas. His best work typically involves lonely individuals who repress their emotions, while experiencing obsessive passions.

This is the case with *The Deep Blue Sea*, Rattigan's greatest play. When the curtain comes up on a shabby flat, the audience sees a woman lying next to a gas fire. She has tried to kill herself, but she's saved by the fact that the gas meter has run out of money.

TERENCE RATTIGAN

Born: 10 June 1911, Kensington, London.

Family: Distinguished line of lawyers, diplomats and imperial administrators. His father, Frank Rattigan, is a diplomat; his mother Vera comes from a family of top Irish lawyers.

Education: Harrow and then Oxford, which he leaves without finishing his degree.

Private life: Homosexual but discrete. Relationships with the Tory MP Sir Henry Chips Channon; actor Kenneth Morgan, who then gases himself; long-term with Michael Franklin, almost twenty years younger. In 1966, Rattigan settles in Bermuda.

Career: From an early age decides to be a playwright. Writes twenty-five stage plays, plus numerous one-act plays, radio, television and film scripts. Best film: *The Prince and the Showgirl* (starring Laurence Olivier and Marilyn Monroe). Knighted in 1971.

Greatest hits: *French Without Tears* (1936), *The Winslow Boy* (1946), *The Browning Version* (1948), *The Deep Blue Sea* (1952), *Separate Tables* (1954).

Death: 30 November 1977, Hamilton, Bermuda.

Epitaph: 'A novelist may lose his readers for a few pages; a playwright never dares lose his audience for a minute.' (Rattigan)

Afterlife: His centenary in 2011 prompts Rattigan fever, with many revivals including *Flare Path* (Theatre Royal Haymarket), *Cause Célèbre* (Old Vic) and *After the Dance* (National Theatre), which wins four Olivier awards.

CRITIC'S VIEW: TYNAN ON SEPARATE TABLES

Kenneth Tynan on *Separate Tables, Observer*, 26 September 1954:

Aunt Edna Yet you sound a trifle peaky. Is something biting you?

Young Perfectionist Since you ask, I regretted that the major's crime was not something more cathartic than mere cinema flirtation. Yet I suppose the play is as good a handling of sexual abnormality as English playgoers will tolerate.

A E For my part, I am glad it is no better.

Y P I guessed you would be; and so did Mr Rattigan. Will you accompany me on a second visit tomorrow?

A E With great pleasure. Clearly, there is something here for both of us.

Y P Yes. But not enough for either of us.

She is revived by Mrs Elton, the building's caretaker, along with other residents such as the German refugee ex-doctor Miller. Her name is Hester and she's a posh clergyman's daughter. Some months before, she left her upper-class barrister husband, Sir William Collyer, and is living with her lover, Freddie, a veteran of the Battle of Britain who is now an unemployed test pilot with a drink problem. In despair because Freddie's love for her seems lukewarm (he's forgotten her birthday), while her passion instead feels overwhelming, Hester has attempted suicide. As she says to Mrs Elton, 'When you're between any kind of devil and the deep blue sea, the deep blue sea sometimes looks very inviting.' After one of the other residents phones Collyer, Hester has to explain that she lost control because of her 'illogical emotions' of 'anger, hatred and shame'. But although Collyer wants her back, Hester is determined to stay with Freddie. He, however, finds being with her too emotionally exhausting — he 'can't be a ruddy Romeo all the time' — and finally leaves her in order to take up a job as a test pilot in Brazil. He realises that: 'We're death to each other, you and I.' At first, it seems as if Hester will try and kill herself again, but finally — after a frank confrontation with Miller — she decides not to. But neither will she return to her husband. She finds the courage to go on living alone.

The play is rooted in Rattigan's own experience: in 1949 he falls in love with Kenneth Morgan, a young actor, who starts seeing another man, then commits suicide when that relationship fails. But, in a period when homosexual relationships are still illegal, Rattigan can't write a play with overtly gay characters — it would never get a licence from the Lord Chamberlain.

Terence Rattigan's Deep Blue Sea (1952)

Hester explains her feelings:

COLLYER Hester, what's happened to you?

HESTER Love, Bill, that's all — you know — that thing you read about in your beloved Jane Austen and Anthony Trollope. Love. 'It droppeth as the gentle dew from heaven.' No. That's wrong, isn't it? I know. 'It comforteth like sunshine after rain —'

COLLYER Rather an unfortunate quotation. Go on with it.

HESTER I can't. I've forgotten.

COLLYER 'Love comforteth like sunshine after rain and Lust's effect is tempest after sun.'

HESTER Tempest after sun? That would be very apt, wouldn't it, if that were all I felt for Freddie.

COLLYER In sober truth, Hester, isn't it?

HESTER *(Angrily.)* Oh, God, Bill, do you really think I can tell you the sober truth about what I feel for Freddie? I've got quite a clear mind — too clear, I've just been told — and if it were only my *mind* that were involved... But in sober truth, Bill — in sober truth neither you nor I nor anyone else can explain what I feel for Freddie. It's all far too big and confusing to be tied up in such a neat little parcel and labelled lust. Lust isn't the whole of life — and Freddie is, you see, to me. The whole of life — and of death, too, it seems. Put a label on that, if you can —

Instead, Rattigan describes the play as 'a study of obsession and of the shame that a sensitive, clear-minded and strong-willed woman must feel when she discovers she has inside her a compulsion that seems too strong for her to resist.' Critic Kenneth Tynan, although unconvinced by Hester's final decision to live rather than die, hails it as 'the most absorbing new English play for many seasons'. The drama, directed by Frith Banbury at the Duchess Theatre, stars Peggy Ashcroft and Kenneth More (who fails his first audition, and gets the part only after Rattigan gives him a couple of stiff whiskies to overcome his nerves). It runs for over 500 performances in London, but does less well in New York. Later on, it is made into a film starring Vivien Leigh as well as More.

Rattigan's best plays are about destructive emotions such as shame, sexual desire and one-sided passions. His own emotional restraint, which our guide puts down to his hidden homosexuality, chimes in with the expectations of his audience, which prefers subtle hints to overt displays of feeling. 'British reticence at its best,' says Roberts. In the preface to his published plays Rattigan creates the fictional character of Aunt Edna, a 'respectable, middle-class, middle-aged, maiden lady' who 'must never be made mock of, or bored, or befuddled'. Rattigan creates well-made plays that put characters through believable conflicts, avoiding melodrama while emphasising psychology. He believes in the traditional craft of good playwriting and his plays are elegant and effective. Among his achievements as a playwright is to bring up-to-date the Problem Play, as pioneered by Arthur Wing Pinero. In March 1950 he writes a piece, 'Concerning the Play of Ideas', for the *New Statesman* defending his method, and arguing that in any good drama ideas should be second in importance to character.

As we finish our Pimm's, and head back to the car, Roberts rounds off his brief account of a very active time in British theatre. 'In contrast to Rattigan's plays,' he says, 'there is also a vogue for poetic drama.' But the most notable thing about the West End in the early 1950s is how completely indifferent it is to contemporary events. There are no plays about the nuclear bomb, the problems of Empire or the scourge of poverty; no serious plays about workers, or Northerners. Tynan, now critic of the *Observer*, writes scathing articles complaining about the domination of upper-class social comedies set in country houses, a genre he calls the Loamshire Play, and defines as 'a glibly codified fairy-tale world' detached from the everyday reality of most British people. He concludes: 'There is nothing in the London theatre that one dares discuss with an intelligent man for more than five minutes.' While

POETIC DRAMA

As a reaction against the ordinary well-made play, with its rather literal and naturalistic representation of reality, there is a postwar vogue for poetic drama, modern plays written in blank, and occasionally rhyming, verse. Examples include Christopher Fry's *The Lady's Not for Burning* in 1948 or his adaptation of French playwright Jean Anouilh's *Ring Round the Moon* in 1950, both presented in the West End. Other examples include the modernist poet T S Eliot's *The Cocktail Party* (1949), following up his prewar blank verse plays *Murder in the Cathedral* (1935) and *The Family Reunion* (1939). Other precursors include W B Yeats in Ireland, W B Auden and Christopher Isherwood's work with the Group Theatre. Another practitioner is Ronald Duncan. This revival of blank verse plays, after centuries of prose dialogue, signals a moment of imaginative vision, which is however short-lived. While it lasts, directors such as Peter Brook and Laurence Olivier, and actors such as John Gielgud, Claire Bloom, Richard Burton and Paul Scofield, are swept up in the excitement.

Roberts thinks that Tynan is being a little unfair, he acknowledges that he may have a point. In 1952, for example, Agatha Christie's *The Mousetrap* opens, and Roberts is amazed to learn that the play is still running today, at the St Martin's Theatre, and flabbergasted by the fact that it is the longest-running play in history. After all, it is just a run-of-the-mill country house murder mystery.

Hello new Britain

But something new is afoot. The 1951 Festival of Britain allows the nation to display inventions with pride and provides a showcase for novelty. For our final visit, Roberts heads to his lordship's town house in Eaton Square, where in the elegantly furnished drawing room, he points out one of the first postwar television sets. It has a small screen and a polished veneer cabinet, which stands proudly among the furnishings of the room. As Roberts switches on the black-and-white set and as we settle back in battered armchairs, the screen comes alive. The quality of the picture is not great and we can barely make out the familiar figure of Queen Elizabeth II as she is handed the four symbols of authority — the orb, the sceptre, the rod of mercy and the royal ring of sapphire and rubies — while the Archbishop of Canterbury places St Edward's Crown on her head. Respectful commentary is provided by the veteran BBC broadcaster Richard Dimbleby. It's 2 June 1953, and we are not alone in watching this historic event live: more than twenty million people witness it, nearly double the radio audience. Since there are only about 2.7 million television sets, this means that some seven or eight people gather around every

Queen Elizabeth II

set. But this is no discomfort compared to the past. To think that our first guide, Walter, went to all that trouble, braving crowds, smells and noise, to show us the triumphal progress of Queen Elizabeth I four hundred years ago. If only he could be here now!

Book list

Jonathan Bate and Russell Jackson (eds), *Shakespeare: An Illustrated Stage History*, Oxford University Press, 1996.

Jean Benedetti, *David Garrick and the Birth of Modern Theatre*, Methuen, 2001.

Michael R Booth, *Theatre in the Victorian Age*, Cambridge University Press, 1991.

John Brewer, *The Pleasures of the Imagination: English Culture in the Eighteenth Century*, Harper Collins, 1997.

Bill Bryson, *Shakespeare: The World as a Stage*, Harper, 2009.

Ian Clarke, *Edwardian Drama: A Critical Study*, Faber, 1989.

Joseph Donohue (ed), *The Cambridge History of British Theatre: Vol. 2, 1660-1895*, Cambridge University Press, 2004.

Andrew Gurr, *Playgoing in Shakespeare's London*, Third Edn, Cambridge University Press, 2004.

Andrew Gurr, *The Shakespearean Stage 1574-1642*, Fourth Edn, Cambridge University Press, 2009.

Michael Holroyd, *Bernard Shaw*, Vintage, 1997.

Philip Hoare, *Noël Coward: A Biography*, Sinclair-Stevenson, 1995.

Elizabeth Howe, *The First English Actresses: Women and Drama 1660-1700*, Cambridge University Press, 1992.

Baz Kershaw (ed), *The Cambridge History of British Theatre: Vol. 3, Since 1895*, Cambridge University Press, 2004.

Ian McIntyre, *Garrick*, Penguin, 2000.

Jane Milling and Peter Thomson (eds), *The Cambridge History of British Theatre: Vol. 1, Origins to 1660*, Cambridge University Press, 2004.

Jane Moody and Daniel O'Quinn (eds), *The Cambridge Companion to British Theatre 1730-1830*, Cambridge University Press, 2007.

Christopher Morash, *A History of Irish Theatre 1601-2000*, Cambridge University Press, 2002.

Benedict Nightingale, *Great Moments in the Theatre*, Oberon Books, 2012.

Deborah Payne Fisk (ed), *The Cambridge Companion to English Restoration Theatre*, Cambridge University Press, 2000.

Kerry Powell (ed), *The Cambridge Companion to Victorian and Edwardian Theatre*, Cambridge University Press, 2004.

Gamini Salgado, *English Drama: A Critical Introduction*, Edward Arnold, 1980.

Samuel Schoenbaum, *William Shakespeare: A Compact Documentary Life*, Rev Edn, Oxford University Press, 1987.

James Shapiro, *1599: A Year in the Life of William Shakespeare*, Faber, 2005.

Dominic Shellard, *British Theatre Since the War*, Yale University Press, 1999.

Peter Thomson, *Shakespeare's Theatre*, Second Edn, Routledge, 1992.

Peter Thomson, *The Cambridge Introduction to English Theatre, 1660-1900*, Cambridge University Press, 2006.

Simon Trussler, *The Cambridge Illustrated History of British Theatre*, Cambridge University Press, 1994.

Stanley Wells, *Shakespeare: The Poet and His Plays*, Methuen, 1997.

Stanley Wells, *Shakespeare and Co: Christopher Marlowe, Thomas Dekker, Ben Jonson, Thomas Middleton, John Fletcher and Other Players in His Story*, Penguin, 2007.

Website

V&A Museum Theatre and Performance website, http://www.vam.ac.uk/page/t/theatre-and-performance/

Acknowledgements

Parts of this book were written while Aleks Sierz was Senior Research Fellow at Rose Bruford College of Theatre and Performance, and he would like to acknowledge the help of Principal Michael Earley and Professor Nesta Jones for their sustained encouragement during the long process of researching and writing the book. Together, we owe Andrew Walby, and his team at Oberon Books — James Illman, Lewis Morgan and Tia Begum — a debt of gratitude. Thanks also to Michael Billington, Christopher Frayling, Quentin Letts and Benedict Nightingale for their encouragement. We would also like to acknowledge the help of all our friends, who listened to us talking about this project for longer than we are prepared to admit, and whose patience and enthusiasm helped us on our way: you know who you are — so many thanks.

Aleks Sierz and Lia Ghilardi

Index

Abbey Theatre 251, 265
Abington, Frances 148
Addison, Joseph;
 Cato 106, 137
Adelphi Theatre 185, 203
Admiral's Men 19, 21, 22, 23, 41
Agate, James 267
Allen, Giles 25
Alleyn, Edward 15, 16, 19, 21, 22, 31
Ambassadors Theatre 263, 271
Archer, William 221, 229, 231, 233, 234, 235
Arne, Thomas 114, 121, 125
Astley's Amphitheatre 145, 155, 160
Auden, Wystan Hugh;
 Dance of Death 279
and Christopher Isherwood;
 The Ascent of F6 280
Austen, Jane 150, 157
Avenue Theatre 251

Bancroft, Squire 178
Barker, Harley Granville; 228, 229, 233, 250, 276, 278
 The Marrying of Ann Leete 230
Barrie, James Matthew;
 Peter Pan 248
 The Admirable Crichton 248
Barry, Elizabeth 81, 88, 91, 92, 96
Barrymore, William;
 The Dog of Montargis 160
Bate, Henry;
 The Blackamoor Washed White 127
Beaumont, Binkie 287, 289
Beaumont, Francis 56, 69
and Thomas Fletcher;
 The Knight of the Burning Pestle 56
Bedford Theatre 197
Beeston, Christopher 52
Behn, Aphra;
 The Rover 87, 88
Benson, Frank 249
Betterton, Thomas 73, 74, 77, 78, 82, 90, 91, 92, 94, 95, 96, 98
Bickerstaffe, Isaac;
 The Padlock 152
Birmingham Repertory Theatre 254
Blackfriars Theatre 49, 50, 52, 61, 68
Booth, Barton 105, 107, 118

Boucicault, Dion;
 The Colleen Bawn 184, 185
 The Corsican Brothers 175, 184
 Jessie Brown 184
 London Assurance 183
 The Octoroon 184
 The Shaughraun 186
Boutell, Elizabeth 72, 85
Bowdler, Thomas 169
Bracegirdle, Anne 91, 92, 94, 96
Brayne, John 10, 11, 12, 14
Bristol Old Vic 118, 288
Brighouse, Harold;
 Hobson's Choice 253
Brome, Richard;
 A Jovial Crew 61
Bulwer-Lytton, Edward;
 Money 189
Burbage, James 9, 10, 24
Burbage, Richard 22, 27
Byron, George Lord 157, 167
Byron, Henry James;
 Our Boys 189

Calvert, Charles 182
Capek, Karel;
 RUR 280
Cedric, Robert 264
Centlivre, Susannah;
 A Bold Stroke for a Wife 95
 The Busy Body 95
 The Wonder 95
Chamberlain's Men 22, 24, 26, 27, 35, 41
Chapman, George;
 Conspiracy and Tragedy of Charles, Duke of Byron 51
with Ben Jonson and John Marston;
 Eastward Ho 45
Christie, Agatha 262, 294
Cibber, Colley;
 The Non-Juror 108
 The Provoked Husband 113
Coburg Theatre 165, 166, 174
Cockpit Theatre 52, 58, 70
Coliseum 197, 248
Collier, Jeremy 93
Collins, Wilkie 175, 204
with Charles Dickens;
 The Frozen Deep 175
Colman, George;
 Bluebeard 160
Condell, Henry 28

Congreve, William;
 The Way of the World 95, 96, 112
Court Theatre 226, 227
Coward, Noël;
 Blithe Spirit 267, 274, 285
 Cavalcade 269, 274
 Design for Living 269, 274
 Hay Fever 269, 270, 271
 Present Laughter 269, 274
 Private Lives 269, 271, 272, 273
 The Vortex 269, 270, 271
Cowell, Sam 196
Cowley, Hannah;
 The Belle's Stratagem 150
 The Runaway 151
Craig, Gordon 279
Craig, Edith 246
Cross Keys Tavern Theatre 8
Cruickshank, Stuart 287
Curtain Theatre 47

Davenant, William;
 The Cruel Brother 68
 The Temple of Love 60
Dekker, Thomas;
 The Shoemaker's Holiday 46
with William Rowley and John Ford;
 The Witch of Edmonton 56
with Thomas Middleton;
 The Roaring Girl 57
Dickens, Charles 159, 170, 176, 179, 187, 191
Dock Street Theatre 100
Dorset Garden Theatre 77, 78, 82, 87, 88, 91
Dryden, John;
 The Indian Emperor 73, 98
Dudley, Robert, Earl of Leicester 9
Duffet, Thomas 75
Dumas père, Alexandre;
 Kean 168

Elizabeth I 3, 5, 7, 10, 47
Elizabeth II 295
Ellis, Walter W;
 A Little Bit of Fluff 255
English National Opera 276
Etherege, George;
 The Comical Revenge 81
 Man of Mode 82, 83
Everyman Theatre 268

Farquhar, George;
    The Beaux' Stratagem 100, 150
    The Constant Couple 98
    Love and a Bottle 98
    The Recruiting Officer 99,
    100, 117, 121, 131
Fawcett, John;
    Obi 152
Fenton, Lavinia 118
Field, Nathan 50
Fielding, Henry;
    *The Historical Register for
    the Year 1736* 115
    Pasquin 115
    Tom Thumb 50, 167
    The Welsh Opera 115
First Folio 28
Fletcher, John 26, 56, 57, 69
Foote, Samuel;
    The Minor 128
Ford, John;
    'Tis Pity She's a Whore 58
with William Rowley and
Thomas Dekker;
    The Witch of Edmonton 56
Fortune Theatre 46, 47, 48, 57

Galsworthy, John;
    Strife 245
Garrick, David;
    Lethe 121
    Miss in Her Teens 122, 146
with George Colman;
    *The Clandestine
    Marriage* 121
Gay, John;
    The Beggar's Opera 109,
    110, 111, 112, 113, 118, 165
    Three Hours after Marriage
    110
    What D'Ye Call It? 110
Giffard, Henry 113, 119

Gilbert, William Schwenck,
with Arthur Sullivan;
    HMS Pinafore 205
    Iolanthe 205
    Patience 205
    The Pirates of Penzance 205
    Trial by Jury 205
Gillette, William 192
Globe Theatre 25, 62
Goldsmith, Oliver;
    She Stoops To Conquer 129,
    130
Goodman's Fields Theatre 113
Ronald Gow, and
Walter Greenwood;
    Love on the Dole 281

Griffin, Gerald;
    The Collegians 184
Grimaldi, Joseph 169
Guthrie, Tyrone 227
Gwyn, Nell 72, 73, 76, 80

Hackney Empire, 248
Haines, Joe 70, 85
Hamilton, Patrick;
    Gaslight 163, 263
    Rope 263
Handel, George Frederick 105,
    112, 114, 175
Hart, Charles 69, 76, 85, 91
Hazelwood, Colin Henry;
    Lady Audley's Secret 193
Heminges, John 15, 28
Henslowe, Philip 21, 22, 53
Heywood, Thomas 56
Hoadley, Benjamin;
    The Suspicious Husband 121
Holcroft, Thomas;
    A Tale of Mystery 158, 159
    The Road to Ruin 158
Home, John;
    Douglas 168
Houghton, Stanley;
    Hindle Wakes 253
Hughes, Margaret 71

Ibsen, Henrik 219, 220, 221,
    222, 225, 228, 234, 235,
    236, 238, 280
Inchbald, Elizabeth;
    Every One Has His Fault 150
    I'll Tell You What 149
    Such Things Are 149
Irving, Henry 198, 199, 200,
    206, 223
Ivory, Thomas 117

Jackson, Henry 44
Jermyn, Henry 68

Jerrold, Douglas William;
    Black-Eyed Susan 166
Jones, Henry Arthur;
    The Case of Rebellious Susan
    225
and Henry Herman;
    Breaking a Butterfly 221
    The Silver King 181
Jones, Inigo 59, 60, 61, 66, 70
Jonson, Ben;
    The Alchemist 42, 43, 44, 121
    Bartholomew Fair 41, 42
    The Masque of Oberon 61
    Volpone 42, 44, 45
Jonson, with George Chapman

and John Marston;
    Eastward Ho 21, 45

Kemble, John Philip, 147, 148,
    149, 155, 156, 157
Kemp, Will 22
Killigrew, Thomas;
    The Parson's Wedding 67, 77
Knell, William 15
Knipp, Elizabeth 72, 85
Kyd, Thomas;
    The Spanish Tragedy 16, 17,
    18, 60, 76
Kynaston, Edward 71, 85, 90

Langley, Francis 24
Lawrence, Gertrude 74, 264,
    268, 269, 271
Lessingham, Jane 146
Lewis, Matthew Gregory;
    The Castle Spectre 160
    Timour the Tartar 160
Lillo, George;
    The London Merchant 108,
    192
Linley, Thomas 132
Little Theatre Haymarket 113,
    115, 128, 148, 152, 155,
    164
Littler, Emile 287
Lloyd, Marie 195, 244
Lonsdale, Frederick 262
Lord Leicester's Men 9
Louthbourg, Philippe Jacques
    de 122

Macklin, Charles 119, 120, 128
Macready, William Charles 168,
    169, 177, 178
Marlowe, Christopher;
    Doctor Faustus 18, 19, 20, 21
    Edward II 18, 58
    Tamburlaine 18, 19, 147
Marshall, Rebecca 72
Marston, John;
    The Malcontent 54
with Ben Jonson and
George Chapman;
    Eastward Ho 45
Massinger, Philip;
    *A New Way To Pay Old
    Debts* 167
Mathews, Charles 176
Mathews, Charles James 175, 183
Maturin, Charles;
    Bertram 160
Maugham, William Somerset;
    The Circle 262
    Home and Beauty 262

The Letter 262
Our Betters 262
McLeish, Robert;
  The Gorbals Story 288
McLaren, Archibald;
  The Negro Slaves 152
Metropolitan Theatre 197
Middleton, Thomas;
  A Game at Chess 58
  The Revenger's Tragedy 54, 58
with Thomas Dekker;
  The Roaring Girl 57
with William Rowley;
  The Changeling 58
Mohun, Charles 92
Mohun, Michael 69, 85,
Moncrieff, William Thomas;
  The Cataract of the Ganges 160
  Tom and Jerry; or, Life in London 165
Morton, Michael;
  Alibi 262
Morton, Thomas;
  Speed the Plough 156
Mountford, William 92

National Theatre 230, 231, 251, 276, 290
New Street Theatre 117
New Theatre 286, 288
Norton, Thomas and Thomas Sackville;
  Gorboduc 6, 8, 17, 48
Novello, Ivor;
  Glamorous Night 281
Novelty Theatre 221
Noverre, Jean-Georges 126

O'Casey, Sean;
  The Silver Tassie 265, 267
  The Shadow of a Gunman 265
  Juno and the Paycock 266
  The Plough and the Stars 266
Odets, Clifford;
  Waiting for Lefty 281
Ogilby, John 77
Oldfield, Anne 99
Olivier, Laurence 265, 272, 276, 277, 278, 279
Olympic Theatre 175
Otway, Thomas;
  Venice Preserved 89, 91
Oxford Music Hall 195

Palace Theatre 247
Palladium, The 248
Palmer, John 145
Pavilion Theatre 142
Penkethman, William 113

Pepys, Samuel 72, 76, 79
Phoenix Theatre 272
Pinero, Arthur Wing;
  The Magistrate 223
  Sweet Lavender 223
  The Profligate 223
  The Second Mrs Tanqueray 222, 223, 224
  The Notorious Mrs Ebbsmith 225
  Trelawney of the Wells 228
Pitt, George Dibdin;
  The String of Pearls 192
Pix, Mary 95
Planché, James Robinson;
  Charles XII 175
  The Vampire 160
Poel, William 229, 249, 250
Priestley, John Boynton;
  An Inspector Calls 282, 283, 284
  Dangerous Corner 282
  Desert Highway 285
  I Have Been Here Before 282
  Time and the Conways 282
Princess's Theatre 178, 181
Prynne, William 57

Queen's Men 14, 15, 22, 41
Quin, James 120, 121, 126

Rattigan, Terence 289, 290, 291, 292, 293
  The Browning Version 290
  The Deep Blue Sea 290, 291
  Flare Path 289, 290
  French Without Tears 289
  Love in Idleness 289
  Separate Tables 290, 291
  While the Sun Shines 289
  The Winslow Boy 289
Red Bull Theatre 48, 52, 54, 61, 67
Red Lion Theatre 10
Reynolds, Frederick;
  The Caravan 160
Rich, Christopher 92, 108
Rich, John 108, 112, 169,
Robertson, Thomas William;
  Caste 187, 188
  Ours 187
  School 187
  Society 187
Robeson, Paul 278
Robey, George 195
Robins, Elizabeth;
  Votes for Women 226, 227
Rochester, Earl of 72, 73, 76, 80, 81, 82, 91

Rodgers, Richard, and Oscar Hammerstein;
  Oklahoma! 288
Rose Theatre 46, 53
Rotunda 125, 161
Rowe, Nicholas;
  Jane Shore 107
  Lady Jane Grey 107
  The Fair Penitent 121
Rowley, William;
with William Thomas Dekker and John Ford;
  The Witch of Edmonton 56
with Thomas Middleton;
  The Changeling 58
Royal Academy of the Dramatic Arts (RADA) 201
Royal Albert Hall 203
Royal Amphitheatre 128
Royal Ballet 276
Royal Circus 145
Royal Opera House 112
Rymer, Thomas 75

Sackville, Thomas, and Thomas Norton;
  Gorboduc 6, 8, 17, 48
Sadler, Richard 128
Sadler's Wells Theatre 128, 145, 154, 164, 276, 285
Sans Souci Theatre 164
Saunderson, Mary 74
Savoy Theatre 205, 206, 232, 265
Sawyer, Elizabeth 56
Shadwell, Thomas 88
Shakespeare Memorial Theatre 249, 278, 288
Shakespeare, William;
  As You Like It 26, 27, 30, 146
  Coriolanus 24, 26, 149
  Hamlet 26, 27, 28, 29, 30, 31, 33, 49, 51, 74, 120, 126, 148, 176, 177
  Henry IV Part One 27, 32, 33
  Henry IV Part Two 27, 32, 33
  Henry VI 24, 32
  Henry VIII 5, 26, 34, 40, 48
  Julius Caesar 26, 30, 107
  King Lear 26, 31, 76, 121, 124, 176, 177, 200, 288
  Richard II 26, 31, 32, 35, 56, 89
  Richard III 26, 32, 33, 120, 277, 286
  Romeo and Juliet 26, 30, 276, 277, 278
  Macbeth 26, 27, 31, 41, 70, 119, 121, 124, 147, 148, 149, 157, 177, 200,

203, 275, 277
The Merchant of Venice 26, 30, 182, 277, 279
The Merry Wives of Windsor 31
A Midsummer Night's Dream 26, 30, 182, 201, 250, 279
Othello 26, 27, 28, 31, 72, 119, 153, 168, 278
Sir Thomas More 33
The Tempest 26, 30, 52, 60, 163, 201
Titus Andronicus 26, 58
Twelfth Night 26, 27, 60, 201, 250, 254
The Winter's Tale 26, 31, 250
Shaw, George Bernard;
  Arms and the Man 236, 240, 251
  The Devil's Disciple 138, 240
  Heartbreak House 236, 242, 262
  John Bull's Other Island 236, 240
  Major Barbara 263, 240
  Mrs Warren's Profession 228, 236, 238, 239
  Pygmalion 236, 240, 242
  Saint Joan 236, 242, 262
  You Never Can Tell 240
  Widowers' Houses 237
Shelley, Percy Bysshe;
  The Cenci 157
Shepherd's Bush Empire 248
Sheridan, Richard Brinsley;
  The Critic 137
  The Rivals 132, 133
  The School for Scandal 133, 135, 136, 137, 146, 155
  with Thomas Linley;
  The Duenna 132
Sheridan, Thomas 117, 128, 133
Sherriff, Robert Cedric;
  Journey's End 264, 265
Shirley, James 52, 61
Siddons, Henry 162
Siddons, Sarah 146, 147
Smock Alley Theatre 117, 128, 132
Southerne, Thomas;
  The Wives' Excuse 94
  The Fatal Marriage 94, 147
  Oroonoko 87, 94, 152, 165
  Isabella 147
Sowerby, Githa;
  Rutherford and Son 245, 246
Spencer, Gabriel 42
St James Theatre 175, 209, 223
Steele, Richard;
  The Conscious Lovers 105,

106, 130
Stewart, Ena Lamont;
  Men Should Weep 288
Stoker, Bram 200
Strand Theatre 89, 154
Strindberg, August 220, 280
Swan Theatre 24
Synge, John Millington;
  The Playboy of the Western World 251, 252

Tarlton, Richard 15, 22
Taylor, Tom;
  The Ticket-of-Leave Man 189
  Our American Cousin 189
Terry, Ellen 200, 246
The Theatre 12
Theatre Royal Drury Lane 71, 78, 86, 91, 92, 105, 143, 161, 204, 273, 281, 286, 288
Theatre Royal Haymarket 189, 204, 290
Thomas, Brandon;
  Charley's Aunt 206
Tilney, Edmund 14, 33
Toller, Ernst 33, 280
Tourneur, Cyril 58
Travers, Ben;
  A Cuckoo in the Nest 264
  Thark 264
  Plunder 264
  Rookery Nook 264
Tree, Herbert Beerbohm 201, 241, 247, 249
Trotter, Catherine 95
Tynan, Kenneth 288, 292, 293

Unity Theatre 281, 288

Van Amburgh, Isaac 175
Vanbrugh, John 93, 113;
  The Relapse 94
  The Provoked Wife 94, 121
Vaudeville Theatre 189, 202, 246
Vauxhall Pleasure Gardens 114
Veigel, Eva Maria 123
Verbruggen, John 96
Vestris, Eliza 165, 175, 183

Walker, John;
  The Factory Lad 165
Webster, John;
  The White Devil 52, 53, 54
  The Duchess of Malfi 25, 53, 54, 76
Wilde, Oscar;
  Lady Windermere's Fan 209, 210, 287
  A Woman of No Importance 209

An Ideal Husband 209
  The Importance of Being Earnest 209, 210, 211, 212
Wilkinson, Tate 117, 149
Wilks, Robert 98, 99, 100, 105
Williams, Harcourt 276, 277
Wilton, Marie Effie 178, 194
Woffington, Peg 121, 129
Wycherley, William;
  The Country Wife 83, 84, 85
  The Plain Dealer 84, 86
Wyndham, Charles 202, 226, 247, 263

Yeats, William Butler;
  The Land of Heart's Desire 251